D1080482

STRATFORD-UPON-AVON STUDIES 8

General Editors
JOHN RUSSELL BROWN
& BERNARD HARRIS

Already published in this series:

LATER SHAKESPEARE

EDWARD ARNOLD

© EDWARD ARNOLD (PUBLISHERS) LTD. 1966

First published 1966
by Edward Arnold (Publishers) Ltd
25 Hill Street, London W1X 8LL

Paperback edition first published 1973

Cloth edition ISBN: 0 7131 5029 7
Paper edition ISBN: 0 7131 5527 2

Printed in Great Britain by
Butler & Tanner Ltd, Frome and London

Contents

List of Plates

Coriolanus

Preface

THIS volume of *Stratford-upon-Avon Studies* is devoted to the range of Shakespeare's late dramatic activity. The plays studied are not the customary 'Last Plays', nor is an analysis of relationships between the romances a main purpose of this book, which seeks rather to observe the nature of specific, individual achievements within the fuller record of Shakespeare's late work. And though the ten contributions have been arranged in a sequence determined by certain principles, the order of treatment depends less upon the supposed chronology of the plays, or upon considerations of the progressive development of Shakespeare's art, but more upon the natural grouping of interests pursued by the contributors.

George Hunter's opening chapter moves through the plays from *Timon* to *The Tempest* tracing the themes of exile, deprivation, and diminution in the worlds of the last tragic heroes, and relating their condition to the context of *King Lear*. Robert Ornstein concentrates upon the ironies and ecstasies of *Antony and Cleopatra* and their resolution in the art of that play. Stanley Wells explores afresh Greek, Elizabethan, and Shakespearian romance, attending to analogues and also to connections with Shakespearian comedy and romance. Francis Berry considers pictorial composition, grammatical inflexion and relationships of 'narrative' and 'drama' in the same group of plays.

Three central chapters deal further with aspects of Shakespeare's theatre-craft. John Brown places the comic elements of the romances within Elizabethan, Jacobean, and perennial conventions, using the evidence of texts, production, and theatre history. Daniel Seltzer analyses the staging techniques of the Jacobean playhouse explicitly required by stage-directions, or warranted by dramatic necessity. Glynne Wickham recounts the particular problems experienced in the staging and performance of *Coriolanus*.

The last three chapters touch upon matters of source, occasion and environment. Philip Brockbank provides a reading of *The Tempest* in close comparison with the suggestive and thematic emphases of its source material. Bernard Harris reviews *Cymbeline* and *Henry VIII* from the aspect of their place in Jacobean court entertainment, and

Richard Proudfoot surveys the theatrical influences and conditions prevailing in the last years of Shakespeare's career, and completes the volume with a critical study of *The Two Noble Kinsmen*.

In accordance with the practice in *Stratford-upon-Avon Studies* each chapter is prefaced by a note, specifying editions used and indicating works of criticism and reference relevant to the subsequent discussion. Unless specified, quotations are taken from the Globe edition of Shakespeare's works, and line references refer to that text.

Acknowledgement is here made that Chapter IV has appeared in different form in Francis Berry's *The Shakespeare Inset* (1964).

The next volumes in the series of *Stratford-upon-Avon Studies* will be *Elizabethan Theatre*, *American Theatre*, and *Victorian Poetry*.

JOHN RUSSELL BROWN
BERNARD HARRIS

Note

The Chronology of Shakespeare's Plays: Henry VI, Parts I, II, and III, 1589–91; *Richard III*, 1592–3; *The Comedy of Errors*, 1592–3; *Titus Andronicus*, 1593–4; *The Taming of the Shrew*, 1593–4; *The Two Gentlemen of Verona*, 1594–5; *Love's Labour's Lost*, 1594–5; *Romeo and Juliet*, 1595–6; *Richard II*, 1595–6; *A Midsummer Night's Dream*, 1595–6; *King John*, 1596–7; *The Merchant of Venice*, 1596–7; *Henry IV*, Parts I and II, 1597–8; *Much Ado About Nothing*, 1598–9; *Henry V*, 1598–9; *Julius Caesar*, 1599–1600; *The Merry Wives of Windsor*, 1597–1601; *As You Like It*, 1599–1600; *Twelfth Night*, 1599–1602; *Hamlet*, 1600–1; *Troilus and Cressida*, 1601–2; *All's Well That Ends Well*, 1602–4; *Measure for Measure*, 1603–4; *Othello*, 1603–4; *King Lear*, 1605–6; *Macbeth*, 1605–6; *Timon of Athens*, 1605–8; *Antony and Cleopatra*, 1606–7; *Coriolanus*, 1607–8; *Pericles*, 1608–9; *Cymbeline*, 1609–10; *The Winter's Tale*, 1610–11; *The Tempest*, 1611–12; *Henry VIII*, 1612–13.

The dates given must be regarded as approximate.

I

The Last Tragic Heroes

G. K. HUNTER

★

THE modern outlook which sees *King Lear* as the central Shakes-pearian statement, and the modern interest in the Last Plays as reposi-tories of symbolic wisdom—these are not entirely separate aspects of modernity. For *Lear* is treasured as the play which, more than any other, tested and proved the 'positive values' of the Last Plays; it is this view, I suppose, that causes Traversi to speak of '*Lear* and the plays which follow: *Pericles, The Winter's Tale, The Tempest*, and even *Cymbeline*'—as if the subjects of this essay, *Timon, Macbeth, Coriolanus, Antony and Cleopatra*, had sunk without trace from the Shakespearian horizon.[1] It is one of my principal purposes here to complicate the relationship of *Lear* to the Last Plays by suggesting ways in which the group of 'Last Tragedies' acts as intermediary, charting the direction of Shakespeare's mind between the 'Great Tragedies' and the Romances.

The word which most clearly leads the modern eye straight from *Lear* to the Last Plays is the word 'reconciliation'.[2] *Lear* is seen as the greatest of the tragedies because it not only strips and reduces and assaults human dignity, but because it also shows with the greatest

---

[1] Derek Traversi, *An Approach to Shakespeare* (1938), p. 102. Cf. his p. 112.
[2] Bradley thought that *Coriolanus* and *Antony* were too concerned with reconciliation to be real tragedies (*Shakespearean Tragedy*, p. 84). Tillyard (*Shakespeare's Last Plays*, pp. 20 f.) quotes this and denies its truth. He is fairly representative of the modern position in finding the last tragedies to be a blind alley, from which Shakespeare escaped only when he came to *Cymbeline*: 'the hints of a regeneration in the mind of Othello count for more than all the dying ecstasies of Antony and Cleopatra or Coriolanus's yielding to his mother' (p. 21). In this view the Last Plays pick up the genuine reconciliations of the Great Tragedies, and thus 'develop the final phase of the tragic pattern' (p. 20); for 'in the last three plays [*Cymbeline, Winter's Tale* and *Tempest*] the old order is destroyed as thoroughly as in the main group of tragedies' [Bradley's four, I suppose].

force and detail the process of restoration by which humanity can recover from this degradation. Lear is exiled from his throne, his friends, his dependants, his family, even from his own reason and his own identity:

> Doth any here know me? This is not Lear:
> Doth Lear walk thus? speak thus? Where are his eyes?
>
> . . . .
> Who is it that can tell me who I am?   (I. iv. 246)[3]

But what is lost on one side of madness and exile is seen to become unimportant when set against what is discoverable on the further shore:

> We two alone will sing like birds i' th' cage
>
> . . . .
> And take upon's the mystery of things
> As if we were God's spies.

When Lear leaves the warmth, the society, the 'civilization' of Gloucester's castle he might seem to be leaving behind him all of the little that is left to make life bearable. But the retreat into the isolated darkness of his own mind is also a descent into the seed-bed of a new life; for the individual mind is seen here as the place from which a man's most important qualities and relationships draw the whole of their potential. Lear continues to assert his innermost perceptions (that justice is a word with meaning, that there is an order in nature, broken by ingratitude and immorality), and continues to do so even when it is only through madness that he can pursue the tenor of his own significance, when it is only in this context that he can set at naught the palpable success of opposite views. But by preserving these 'mad' assumptions the hero is, in fact, preserving the substance of a moral life, of which comfort, dignity and society are only the shadows.

Lear stands on the edge of his exile and states his vision of what he sees to be involved:

> . . . But for true need—
> You heavens, give me that patience, patience I need.
> You see me here, you gods, a poor old man,
> As full of grief as age; wretched in both.
> If it be you that stirs these daughters' hearts
> Against their father, fool me not so much
> To bear it tamely; touch me with noble anger,

[3] All quotations in this chapter are of Peter Alexander's text, with line references to the Globe edition.

> And let not women's weapons, water-drops,
> Stain my man's cheeks! (II. iv. 267)

The hero here sees himself as an inextricable part of a universal order. What has happened to him is no less involved in the divine dispensation than are his own feelings. The speech is one of a convulsive series of efforts to *understand* what has happened, in terms that relate to his assumptions, an effort that drives him through madness to the strange hushed acceptance that has been thought to reappear only in the Last Plays.

The same emphasis on his own complicity appears in the first scene on the heath:

> Let the great gods
> That keep this dreadful pudder o'er our heads,
> Find out their enemies now. Tremble, thou wretch
> That hast within thee undivulgèd crimes
> Unwhipp'd of justice. Hide thee, thou bloody hand;
> Thou perjur'd and thou simular man of virtue
> That art incestuous; caitiff, to pieces shake,
> That under covert and convenient seeming
> Hast practis'd on man's life. Close pent-up guilts,
> Rive your concealing continents, and cry
> These dreadful summoners grace. I am a man
> More sinn'd against than sinning. (III. ii. 49)

The last two lines of this great plea for justice allow that Lear is himself a man of sin; what they cry for is not revenge so much, but a fairer distribution of punishment, so that Lear's condition on the heath may find its echo in the punishment of the hypocrites, and so be recognized as an inevitable part of the condition of man. Lear in exile absorbs humanity, and assimilates it to his own condition, rather than (as one might expect) rejecting it.

With this in mind one may look at another exile speech, from a play that has been called 'the still-born twin of *Lear*'—*Timon of Athens*:

> Piety and fear,
> Religion to the gods, peace, justice, truth,
> Domestic awe, night-rest and neighbourhood,
> Instruction, manners, mysteries, and trades,
> Degrees, observances, customs and laws,
> Decline to your confounding contraries
> And let confusion live. Plagues incident to men,

Your potent and infectious fevers heap
On Athens, ripe for stroke. . . . Breath infect breath,
That their society, as their friendship, may
Be merely poison! Nothing I'll bear from thee
But nakedness, thou detestable town.   (IV. i. 15)

Timon outside Athens' walls fixes his gaze not on his own condition, seen as a part of a universal evil, but on the evil society of Athens, seen as radically distinct from the self who is leaving it. Lear's speeches show anger and self-pity of course, but his self-regard does not explain all the sentiments that appear in them; they are not merely documents of a desperate mind; there is also a genuine insight into an objective reality. Timon's sentiments, on the other hand, do not tell us anything very penetrating about Athens. Lear's effort to understand makes his vision more complex; Timon's hatred merely simplifies. His mind remains so monomaniacally fixed in hatred of society that it is obviously as dependent on Athens now as it was in the old days of acceptance. The mind in exile is not here a point of refuge and new growth; Timon remains the creature of his society, only maimed by his inability to accept it.

This difference between the exile speeches of Lear and Timon is symptomatic of a difference between the two plays; *Timon* does not explore the condition of the outcast as symbolic of basic humanity, but only shows the outcast *set against* his society; the change is even characteristic of a difference between the tragedies which lead up to *Lear* and those which lead down on the other side of the watershed. The tragedies normally thought of as following *Lear—Timon, Macbeth, Coriolanus, Antony and Cleopatra*—are all in some sense plays of exile; there is an obvious physical exile in *Timon* and *Coriolanus*, and a more complex psychological exile from social normality in *Macbeth* and *Antony*. And all of them are plays of exile in the *Timon* rather than the *Lear* sense, for in none does the individual hero succeed in creating a new world of value inside himself, finding the point of growth which will absorb and transmute the world as it is. The temporizing and compromising society is rejected, but the rejection leaves the hero maimed and incomplete.[4] There is no sense in which Lear (or Hamlet

[4] To this extent the thesis presented here is similar to that of Willard Farnham, whose *Shakespeare's Tragic Frontier* (1950) presents the heroes of the last tragedies as 'deeply flawed': 'each of these heroes has faulty substance reaching to the very center of his character'. Farnham's treatment is mainly concerned

or Othello, for that matter) is diminished by his failure to accept integration into society; but there is a real sense in which this is true of the later heroes.

The whole behaviour of Timon shows the curious paradox of the man, superlatively endowed and favoured by Fortune, who thinks that it is his privilege to move through society like an earthly god:

> He moved among us, as a muttering king,
> Magnificent, would move among his hinds.

He dispenses largesse with an open, undiscriminating hand; he refuses reward; he never counts the cost. It is certainly magnificent; but it is also inhuman. The word *inhumanity* is no doubt only appropriate to a god, and can be seen as a proper part of his praise; but when used of Timon, a man, the word can only be pejorative:

> For bounty, that makes gods, does still mar men.
>   (IV. ii. 41)

And this paradox applies equally in both halves of the play. For Timon the indiscriminate hater of men has the same hunger for the absolute as Timon the indiscriminate lover. If we recoil from the inhumanity of the former we must also recoil from the latter.

The censure that I see aimed at Timon's indiscriminateness seems to be paralleled by a similar censure aimed at the Senate. The Senate refuses to see any mitigating circumstances in the crime of Alcibiades's anonymous friend. With Angelo-like incapacity to discriminate law from justice, they rest on the assertion, 'We are for law', and banish Alcibiades for questioning this. But at the end of the play, when they themselves are the victims, they take an opposite view:

> We were not all unkind, nor all deserve
> The common stroke of war. . . .

> . . . All have not offended;
> For those that were, it is not square to take
> On those that are, revenges: crimes, like lands,
> Are not inherited . . . Like a shepherd
> Approach the fold and cull th' infected forth,
> But kill not all together.   (V. iv. 21)

with this kind of judgement of individual character; he does not deal with the social aspects of the plays, which I take (in what follows) to be central to their meaning.

Alcibiades, and the play as a whole, accepts the plea; he makes his victory an occasion for compromise;

> I will use the olive with my sword;
> Make war breed peace, make peace stint war, make each
> Prescribe to other as each other's leech.   (V. iv. 82)

But in the very same speech we have his appreciation of the magnificence of Timon who never learned to compromise. The paradox of an absoluteness which simultaneously exalts and maims the hero remains unresolved at the end of the play.

The life of Alcibiades, who fled and conspired against his country, provides a natural bridge between Timon, who forecast his career (as Plutarch tells us), and Coriolanus, who formed his Roman 'parallel'. Certainly Shakespeare's *Coriolanus* provides the obvious instance of exile and hatred to be compared with that in *Timon*. And, again, the speech spoken at the point of exile serves to focus the attitude of the hero:

> You common cry of curs, whose breath I hate
> As reek o' th' rotten fens, whose loves I prize
> As the dead carcasses of unburied men
> That do corrupt my air—I banish you.
>   . . . Despising
> For you the city, thus I turn my back;
> There is a world elsewhere.   (III. iii. 120)

The gesture is magnificent, but the same reservation still applies: it is inhuman, or rather anti-human. The 'world elsewhere' of Coriolanus does not turn out to be in the least like Lear's world of introspective anguish and revaluation; it is only the same Roman political world, at a certain geographical remove, and equally resistant to the monomaniac individual. And however proud that individual, he continues to need a populace, a city, that accepts his dominance. *Coriolanus* makes quite clear what is only implicit in *Timon*: the political nature of the scrutiny to which these later heroes are subjected. The aspirations of Hamlet, Othello, and Lear relate centrally to their families; their principal effort is to comprehend and adjust the strains and tensions arising in that context; the wider sphere of politics is present only as a background.[5] But the difficulties of the later heroes involve

[5] Brutus might seem to be an exception to the division being attempted here: he is an 'early' hero, whose dramatic life is concerned with politics and hardly

organized society in a much more direct way: Macbeth, Coriolanus, Antony all feel the pressure to pursue a political course which runs against their natural individualities. Moreover the 'family life' of Coriolanus, as of Macbeth or Antony, is only a particular aspect of this general social pressure. Volumnia, the type of the Roman matron, sees home as a parade-ground for training in leadership; the pressure of her love is always exercised for a political end. Indeed the play shows a paucity of relationships which are entirely private in intention. One might indeed allow Virgilia to be unswayed by public interests; but it is notorious that Virgilia is the most ineffectual character in the play. There is no evidence that her love is any more listened to than that of Flavius the steward in *Timon*, who is dismissed as statistically meaningless, too exceptional to count; in the political or social contexts of these plays the humble and disinterested love of the private individual can exercise little power, for the minds of their heroes are too little attuned to such cadences.

A unique feature of these late plays is of relevance here. *Macbeth*, *Coriolanus*, *Antony and Cleopatra* has each as its deuteragonist a woman of mature years and of amply developed political instincts.[6] Each of these exercises on the protagonist a dominating influence which is eventually destructive of his life. In the homes dominated by these

---

at all with family. But Brutus cannot justly be assimilated into the later group of heroes: his real life remains locked inside his self-consciousness; the political scene does not ever come to seem the whole of his life. His relationship with Portia remains set apart from his political life, and closer to his heart.

[6] It may seem strange that just before giving the world his picture-gallery of fresh and even extravagantly innocent heroines—Marina, Imogen, Perdita, Miranda—Shakespeare should have been lavishing his attention on ladies whose innocence is their least obvious characteristic. But I think that there is a fairly straightforward connection between the two sets of characters. The archetype of Snow-White, evident behind Imogen, requires the complementary archetype of the wicked queen; both the Queen in *Cymbeline* and Dionyza in *Pericles* carry on an already established line of plotting females. The change from Tragedies to Romances involves a general change in atmosphere, a recession of historical reality, so that character becomes caricature (or line drawing); as this change reduces the complexity of the ageing female figure, using her charms to impose a selfish will on the commonwealth, so it gives new prominence to the innocent girl who is the natural victim of sophisticated guile, whose goodness owes much of its appeal to the situation of danger in which it lives, and who survives less through her own skill than by the good fortune that we suppose to have a natural attachment to innocence.

women the domestic emotions, love, loyalty, mutual comfort, thus become the prey of political ambition; and the mind of the hero is left with no counters to stake against the devouring claims of the political world.

The loss of a domestic scene whose values of trust and repose are believed by the hero to be distinct from those of the jostling political world, providing him therefore with an alternative vision of life—this loss is to be associated with a decline in the sense of an immanent sustaining metaphysical order, also characteristic of the last tragedies. In this respect, as in some others, *Macbeth* is obviously a transitional play. In the earlier tragedies—*Hamlet*, *Othello*, *Lear*—the political world is peripheral; the real conflict occurs inside the protagonist, whose struggle it is to absorb the assumptions of the world he lives in and transmute them into something metaphysically meaningful; the effect of Brutus, Hamlet, Othello and Lear is to spiritualize by their sufferings the self-interested assumptions of those who live around them and have power over them. But Coriolanus and Antony do not try to make this effect; they make gestures of opposition to the world they live in, gestures towards apparent alternatives, but their opposition is more apparent than real; neither Corioli nor Egypt really exists on a different plane from Rome, nor does Timon's cave offer a really alternative life to that of Athens. These exiles make claims which have a metaphysical resonance, but the real effects in the play are determined on the lower plane of *Realpolitik*. In *Macbeth*, on the other hand, the two worlds of politics and metaphysics exist side by side in a state of almost perfect balance, where personal ambition is seen as a breach of both orders simultaneously, where Scotland and 'th' estate o' th' world' are almost interchangeable terms. Macbeth has an agonized knowledge of what a true domestic relationship ought to provide:

Honour, love, obedience, troops of friends,

but, of course, he tries to act as if he did not know, as if the stuff of ambition were the stuff of life.

In these terms it is probable that *Timon* also should count as a transitional play, though in a less obvious or satisfactory way; and one cannot avoid the suspicion that 'transitional' here may be a mere synonym for 'unfinished'.[7] The possibility of political action in *Timon*

[7] See U. Ellis-Fermor, '*Timon of Athens*: an unfinished play', *R.E.S.*, XVIII (1942), reprinted in *Shakespeare the Dramatist* (1961).

is limited and complicated all the time by metaphysical assumptions about human nature. Timon sees man as an accursed creature, and this effectively prevents him from seeking to affect human life by leadership or any other political activity.

Lear's curses when he goes into exile ask the gods to intervene or at least to observe; Timon's only ask that the *human* observances of religion (seen as symptoms of order) should cease to exist. Coriolanus manages to curse his banishers without mentioning the gods at all. The gods are invoked constantly, of course, even in this markedly secular play. There is a notable example in Coriolanus's speech after his capitulation in Act V:

> Behold, the heavens do ope,
> The gods look down, and this unnatural scene
> They laugh at. (V. iii. 183)

But the gods who appear out of Coriolanus's heaven are quite different from those who, in *Lear*, 'keep this dreadful pudder o'er our heads'. Coriolanus's gods only reflect back the human scene; most often, indeed, they appear to be the mere conveniences of Roman political faction;[8] certainly a gulf of irony separates them from involvement in the tragedy of any one individual.

Their withdrawal from possible involvement further isolates the hero, leaves him alone with his own standards and the political urge to fulfil the sense of individual greatness in terms of distinction from and dominion over his fellows. Unfortunately for Coriolanus's fulfilment, the *distinction* and *dominion* are not entirely compatible. He desires to be a nonpareil, to behave

> As if a man were author of himself
> And knew no other kin.

He speaks of the people

> As if you were a god, to punish; not
> A man of their infirmity. (III. i. 81)

Like Timon, he denies reciprocity. 'He pays himself by being proud', his wounds 'smart to hear themselves remembered'. His condescensions are general, hardly at all concerned with individuals. An episode,

[8] e.g. I. i. 191; I. viii. 6; I. ix. 8; II. iii. 142; III. i. 290; III. iii. 33; IV. vi. 36; V. iii. 104.

which seems to mirror Shakespeare's desire to make this point obvious, is that in which we see Coriolanus pleading for the exemption of a Volsci who had once sheltered him—but he cannot remember his name. As the bastard Faulconbridge tells us:

> . . . new made honour doth forget men's names:
> 'Tis too respective and too sociable.
>
> (*John*, I. i. 187)

Coriolanus's pretension to be a god takes him rather further into action than does Timon's, and this undoubtedly reflects his greater involvement in politics, his interest in leadership:

> He is their god; he leads them like a thing
> Made by some other deity than Nature,
> That shapes men better.   (IV. vi. 90).

But his involvement is also his destruction. To fulfil his distinction above other men he has to seek dominion over them; but he is bound to fail in this because the distinction is too great; he is too inhuman. Indeed the more godlike he seeks to be, the more *inhuman* he becomes. The play has very usefully been seen in relation to Aristotle's celebrated dictum: 'He that is incapable of living in a society is a god or a beast'; or (as the Elizabethan translation expanded it): 'He that cannot abide to live in company, or through sufficiency hath need of nothing, is not esteemed a part or member of a Cittie, but is either a beast or a God.' [9] The ambiguity of Aristotle's remark is nicely adjusted to the ambiguity that I find in these last tragedies, the moral ambiguity of heroes who are both godlike and *inhuman*. The inhumanity of Coriolanus is conveyed to us in terms both of a beast and of a machine. Sometimes the two are combined as in the following:

> he no more remembers his mother now than an eight-year-old horse. The tartness of his face sours ripe grapes; when he walks, he moves like an engine and the ground shrinks before his treading. He is able to pierce a corslet with his eye, talks like a knell, and his hum is a battery. He sits in his state as a thing made for Alexander. What he bids be done is finished with his bidding. He wants nothing of a god but eternity, and a heaven to throne in.   (V. iv. 16)

Coriolanus, like Timon, and like Macbeth, searches for an *absolute* mode of behaviour, and like them he finds it; but the finding it is the

[9] F. N. Lees, 'Coriolanus, Aristotle and Bacon', *R.E.S.*, I (1950), 114-25.

destruction of humanity in him, as it was in them. And as far as it concerns personality, the process is as irreversible for Coriolanus as for Timon or Macbeth; he can, however, avoid that final stage, where the absoluteness of the individual is only to be guaranteed by the destruction of his society. He is unable to sustain the absoluteness of 'Wife, mother, child, I know not'; but I do not think we should see the collapse before Volumnia as a great triumph of human love.[10] The play's judgement on the beast-machine nature of 'absolute' man stands unchanged. Only death can chillingly enough satisfy the hunger for absoluteness; and the final scene in Corioli, with its ironic repetition of the political and personal pattern already set in Rome, makes it clear that nothing in Coriolanus has altered or can alter. Greatness is seen as a doubtful and destructive blessing; love is powerless to change it.

Antony and Cleopatra is, of all the tragedies after *Lear*, the one which has least obvious connection with the line of thought pursued here. But the connections are there, I think, and to pursue them is to remove some of the difficulties of this 'most quintessential of Shakespeare's "Problem Plays"' (as it has recently been called).[11] Is Antony an exile? I suggest that he is, though only in a different sense from Timon and Coriolanus. He is an exile from a world that we never see in the play, which existed splendidly in the past and will never be recovered again, a world in which

> his goodly eyes
> . . . o'er the files and musters of the war
> Have glow'd like plated Mars   (I. i. 2)

and where

> his captain's heart
> . . . in the scuffles of great fights hath burst
> The buckles on his breast   (I. i. 6)

The play is remarkable in the sense it gives of living in a second age; it is full of references to the heroes of the recent past; Julius Caesar and Pompey the Great still overshadow the world of the present, whose major characters were then being formed. In the past it had seemed possible to be both glamorous and efficient, heroic and political. But Antony's 'heroic' gestures—challenging Caesar to single combat,

---

[10] It has been so represented by Bradley and (more ecstatically) by G. Wilson Knight.

[11] E. Schanzer, *The Problem Plays of Shakespeare* (1963).

seeking to fight again at Pharsalia—are seen to be quite inappropriate to the present in which he lives. The minor characters display this obviously enough: Ventidius, who knows how to avoid seeming to be a hero, is the real man of the time; Enobarbus tries to be, but fails miserably. Pompey indeed has the choice set before him more clearly than anyone else in the play, when Menas offers to cut the throats of the triumvirs; but Pompey feels he cannot stoop to success:

> Thou must know
> 'Tis not my profit that does lead mine honour:
> Mine honour it.   (II. vii. 81)

He 'will not take when once 'tis offer'd', and thus (as Menas sees) he becomes (at that very moment) a man of the past.

It is in the contrast between Antony and Octavius, of course, that this split in the world of the play is developed most fully. Octavius suffers from none of the scruples which affect Pompey; his treatment of Lepidus may serve to characterize his whole mode of proceeding:

> ... having made use of [Lepidus] in the wars 'gainst Pompey, presently denied him rivality, would not let him partake in the glory of the action; and not resting here, accuses him of letters he had formerly wrote to Pompey; upon his own appeal, seizes him.
> (III. v. 7)

He is everywhere marked by the celerity and decisiveness of his moves. ''Tis done already' and 'most certain' are his typical locutions; when he fights, 'this speed of Caesar's | Carries beyond belief'. There is no sense in which Caesar, like the other major characters, is still living in the past. Time is not for him a destroyer, but a whirlwind he rides to command the future.

Antony, on the other hand, is, as I have said, an exile from a glorious past that cannot be recovered. As an 'ebb'd man', time is not his to command. In Egypt he is becalmed in the dramatic equivalent of Spenser's Lake of Idleness; Cleopatra has the role of Phaedria:

> But that your royalty
> Holds idleness your subject, I should take you
> For idleness itself.   (I. iii. 91)

In this fertile and stagnant atmosphere of Nilus' mud, of

> The dull billows thick as troubled mire,

> Whom neither wind out of their seat could force,
> Nor timely tides did drive out of their sluggish source,

time has a function other than that of developing the future out of the present:

> Now for the love of Love and her soft hours,
> Let's not confound the time with conference harsh;
> There's not a minute of our lives should stretch
> Without some pleasure now. What sport tonight?
> (I. i. 44)

The deviousness of Cleopatra, the sense of time stopping when Antony leaves her, the impossibility of forecasting her actions, her capacity to say and unsay—all these are means to bend the time of action into a hoop of enjoyment, the time of thinking into the time of the heart:[12]

> And now like am'rous birds of prey
> Rather at once our Time devour
> Than languish in his slow-chapt pow'r.

In this atmosphere it is easy enough for Antony to be 'heroic' (in the old, Herculean, sense of 'generous', 'large-scale'); but if heroism is to be more than sentimental self-indulgence, then it must allow also that every action, taken or avoided, is the moulding of the future. And this the play never allows us to forget, with its repeated reference to 'our slippery people' who constantly shift their allegiance to the new-comer, to the primal law by which

> This common body,
> Like to a vagabond flag upon the stream,
> Goes to and back, lackeying the varying tide.
> (I. iv. 44)

Antony himself knows that

> The present pleasure,
> By revolution low'ring, does become
> The opposite of itself.   (I. ii. 128)

[12] In these respects the relationship of Cleopatra and Antony is very close to that of Falstaff and Hal. The characters of the queen and the knight are very similar in their power to tease the literal-minded critic; each is the im-presario of his own performance, which he arranges to affect others rather than to establish any inner consistency. See my 'Shakespeare's politics and the rejection of Falstaff', *C.Q.*, I (1959), p. 235.

But even Antony's capacity to break out of this Idle Lake where 'we bring forth weeds | When our quick minds lie still', and to return to the Roman world of action, cannot heal the schism in the world of the present. Critics often write as if it was open to Antony to choose a complete and satisfactory life as a Roman, married to Octavia and sharing rule with Caesar. But Caesar himself knows better:

> I must perforce
> Have shown to thee such a declining day
> Or look on thine; we could not stall together
> In the whole world. But yet let me lament
>   . . . that our stars,
> Unreconcilable, should divide
> Our equalness to this.   (V. i. 37)

In the present of the play the partial life lived by Octavius, and the other partial life, lived to the full by Antony, are as incapable of fusion as time present and time past. Octavius and Antony are affected equally by this; but Octavius can hardly be called an exile from the completer world of the past, for he never belonged to it; his speeches move in the present and the future. But Antony is an exile and is aware that he is an exile, living on borrowed time in an inevitably hostile world. The idea is particularly well conveyed by the continuous play on the word *Antony* as representing not only the name of the man we see before us, but also the *Idea* of the man as he was once, and as he ought to be:

>   Since my lord
>   Is Antony again, I will be Cleopatra
>   (III. xiii. 186)

> He comes too short in that great property
> Which still should go with Antony   (I. i. 58)

> O my oblivion is a very Antony   (I. iii. 90)

> I dream'd there was an Emperor Antony
> . . . Think you there was or might be such a man?
>   (V. ii. 76)

>   yet t'imagine
>   An Antony were nature's piece 'gainst fancy,
>   Condemning shadows quite   (V. ii. 98)

>   she looks like sleep,
>   As she would catch another Antony
>   In her strong toil of grace   (V. ii. 349)

The magic of an image of *Antony* has the power to hold the heroic past alive for the moment of the present; but the magic is a kind of confidence-trick. Nothing in the present really supports the idea; and as soon as the charm of immediate power weakens (at Actium) the empire shatters like quicksilver. The most telling of these *Antony* references comes in his death-speech:

> Here I am Antony;
> Yet cannot hold this visible shape my knave
> (IV. xiv. 13)

The effort to be *Antony*, to identify the actions of the present with this heroic figure, is fully revealed in the necessity to die for it, and so, by this means, to deny and defeat the reductive currents of time and policy. Antony's choice here is as much a choice of the absolute as is that of Coriolanus or Timon; but the absolute is of the opposite kind. They choose detachment, hardness, inhumanity; he prefers the grand illusion of an absolute magnetism, loyalty, love:

> The nobleness of life
> Is to do thus [*Embracing*] when such a mutual pair
> And such a twain can do it.

This is magnificent, but it is undercut by self-indulgent sentimentality as surely as are the 'victories' of Act IV. The will to be godlike must have set against it the fact that 'the god Hercules whom Antony lov'd' leaves him when his fortunes decline.

The later tragedies offer the alternative heroisms of stone or water, of petrifaction or deliquescence; death can be shown to seal the opposite magnificences of Timon and Antony, but in neither case can it conceal the price that has been paid—the abandonment of the good ordinariness of a life lived among compromises, or the loss of a sense of reverence for the unknown in destiny, a sense of submission to the immanence of higher powers.

* * *

The theme of exile, which bulks so large in these later tragedies, does not wither away when Shakespeare turns to the writing of the 'Romances'. Pericles, very obviously, lives his life around his exile; Belarius and Posthumus are exiled from the British Court; Perdita and Camillo live in banishment (though she does not know it); Prospero's exile provides the whole subject of *The Tempest*. The societies which exile these characters are all corrupt ones; but, as in the later tragedies, the corruption is viewed as something basic in human nature so that it has to be dealt with by compromise and acceptance rather than by extirpation. It is as if the figure of Timon were to be removed from the play that bears his name and the attitude of Alcibiades developed as the basis of the plot. The hero, whose quest for absoluteness has been scrutinized in these last tragedies and whose mode of life has been seen as inhuman, now ceases to be the magnetic centre of interest. *The Tempest* is rather exceptional in this respect and will be dealt with separately. Certainly *Cymbeline* and *The Winter's Tale* lack dominating central figures, whose developing feelings carry us along the main channel of the play's movement. In these plays (and in *The Tempest* and even *Pericles* as well) it is in terms of the social embodiment of virtue that the play develops, rather than towards the achievement of virtue in the individual conscience. We are less interested in the 'redemption' of Leontes or Posthumus than in the complex of interests and attitudes inside which their redeemed lives will have to be accommodated. The state of exile is not here (as in *Lear*) an opportunity to discover the true quality of humanity; it is rather that the structure of society is seen as coming to recognize its need for the elements it has rejected. This is true of *Timon* and *Coriolanus* as well; but there our point of view remains closely attached to the exile himself; we see society's repeated offers of compromise from his viewpoint and we recognize that he owes it to his absoluteness to refuse them. In the Last Plays the individual is seen much more as an inextricable part of the social group, and his actions are followed from that standpoint. Alonso's need for Prospero's comfort, Leontes' for the friends and family he dispersed, and (most clearly of all) Britain's need for soldiers like Belarius and Posthumus, finds a natural answer in a restoration of the original social alignments. This does not occur because the individual has changed in his exile; it is not even that society has changed in any basic way. The mixture of good and evil is much as it was; it is only that time has brought the unchanged elements into a new arrangement. Clearly we are meant to rejoice at this; but (the mode of vicissitude so obvious in the construction of these plays serves to insist) time will change all things again. Time himself tells us so when he appears before us in *The Winter's Tale*:

> I, that please some, try all, both joy and terror
> Of good and bad, that makes and unfolds error

> ... so shall I do
> To' th' freshest things now reigning, and make stale
> The glistering of this present. (IV. i. 1)

Mutability is not an important theme in *Lear*; but the heroes of the last tragedies all live within its scope, though they try to outface it; the Last Plays accept it as basic and inevitable, and the natural result is a diminution in the scope of the individuals who initiate action. The exiles of *Cymbeline* and *The Winter's Tale* return, not to take any 'absolute' revenges, but rather to accept again the society in which we first saw them—the place to which they belong.

It is only thematically that the situations of these plays are similar to those of the last tragedies. But in *The Tempest* Shakespeare returns also to a plot-line which is parallel. Prospero is exiled from political office, and exiled for an absoluteness of temperament which made him too much like a god and too little like a man. And the 'god' image is now more than a metaphor; Prospero's magic gives him the power to enact what the curses of Lear, Coriolanus and Timon only imagined:

> I will do such things—
> What they are yet I know not; but they shall be
> The terrors of the earth. (*King Lear*, II. iv. 283)

But here again (as, most notably, in *Coriolanus*) the power to execute such threats can only be bought at the price of inhumanity; Ariel's sense of what is proper to a man reveals the quality of the danger:

> Hast thou, which art but air, a touch, a feeling
> Of their afflictions, and shall not myself,
> One of their kind, that relish all as sharply,
> Passion as they, be kindlier mov'd than thou art?
> (*The Tempest*, V. i. 21)

Prospero's acceptance of *kindness*—the feeling of necessary fellowship between one member of the human *kind* and the rest of the species—implies the rejection of his earlier notion that he could isolate himself:

> being transported
> And rapt in secret studies.
> (*The Tempest*, I. ii. 76)

It also implies the rejection of his later delusion that he could change mankind, or execute justice upon it. The recognition here of the isolated individual's ultimate powerlessness picks up what I take to be the central theme of the later tragedies. The splendid self-will of the last tragic heroes existed in defiance of this recognition; and, given their celerity in dying, they may even be said to *defeat* it. For in death (and only in death) they are able to fix the image of greatness they lived by, and free it from the necessary decay of still-living things. The last tragedies explore that *splendour*; the Last Plays describe the quality of the *living*; both groups of plays accept that the two concepts will appear on opposite sides of the dramatic conflict; and it is this that gives their worlds their common and unique quality.

From the views advanced in this essay it follows that the Last Plays have to be greatly simplified before we can see them just as fables of reconciliation. Their relation to the last tragedies suggests a different point of view; the capacity to accept the world-as-it-is has had to be bought by a sacrifice of heroic pretensions, by a loss of confidence in the heroic individual. In reading the Last Plays we should feel the sense of this loss even as we rejoice in the sweetness of their reconciliations.

Note

First edition. Antony and Cleopatra was first entered in the Stationers' Register on 20 May, 1608 (together with *Pericles*), and re-entered in 1623, when it was first published in the *First Folio* of that year.

Modern editions. The play has been edited by M. R. Ridley in the New Arden edition (1954), and by J. Dover Wilson in the Cambridge New Shakespeare edition.

Scholarship and criticism. Among collections of the source material are the edition of North's translation of Plutarch's *Lives* in the Tudor Translations Library (6 vols., 1895); selections necessary for the study of Shakespeare include W. W. Skeat's *Shakespeare's Plutarch* (1895), and those contained in G. Bullough's *Narrative and Dramatic Sources of Shakespeare*, Vol. VI (1964): the material is most conveniently presented in T. J. B. Spencer's *Shakespeare's Plutarch* (Penguin Books, 1964), which has an informative introduction.

Among the many critical discussions of *Antony and Cleopatra* may be indicated those in A. C. Bradley's Oxford Lectures (1909), G. Wilson Knight's *The Imperial Theme* (1931), T. R. Henn's *The Harvest of Tragedy* (1956), and L. C. Knights' *Some Shakespearean Themes* (1959). J. I. M. Stewart inspects 'The Fatal Cleopatra' in *Character and Motive in Shakespeare* (1949); Michael Lloyd writes on 'Cleopatra as Isis' in *Shakespeare Survey*, 12 (1959), and on 'The Roman Tongue' in *Shakespeare Quarterly*, X (1959); L. J. Mills analyses 'Cleopatra's Tragedy' in *Shakespeare Quarterly*, XI (1960).

Two works which provide full relationships for this play are Maurice Charney's *Shakespeare's Roman Plays: The Function of Imagery in the Drama* (1961), and Ernest Schanzer's *The Problem Plays of Shakespeare* (1963).

II

The Ethic of the Imagination :
Love and Art in 'Antony and Cleopatra'

ROBERT ORNSTEIN

★

THE last scene of *Antony and Cleopatra* would be less difficult if it were more obviously solemn and serious. There is no lack of grandeur in the dying Cleopatra, but the comic note struck in her conversation with the Clown persists and mingles with the ceremonial mystery of her death. She is amused as well as ecstatic; when she thinks of Octavius, her visionary glances turn into a comic wink. She jests with Iras and Charmian, and she plays a children's game with the asps at her breast. It is difficult, of course, to complain about a scene that comes so very near the sublime. But now and then we may wish that Cleopatra had a more sober view of her own catastrophe, which she treats as a marriage feast (not where she eats, but where she is eaten), a tender domestic scene, an apotheosis, and a practical joke on the universal landlord.

Those who see no majesty in the earlier Cleopatra argue that the glitter of the Monument scene is not gold or complain that the Cleopatra of the last act is a new and exalted creature fashioned for the sake of a resplendent artistic conclusion. But for most of us the problem of the last scene is not focused in Cleopatra's character as such. Here at least her emotions are translucent: she has no thought but of Antony and no desire except to join him in death. What vexes us is Cleopatra's immortal longings. For even as we cannot resist the spell of her rapturous lyricism, neither can we assent to her vision of eternal love, which is embarrassingly physical, and worse still, smacks of a literary conventionality—of the Petrarchan 'forever'. We expect Cleopatra to dream of a long love's day since she is a creature of illusion. But we are not ready to equate her dream with Shakespeare's vision of love, which, in the sonnets at least, belongs very much to this world. Unlike

naissance poets, Shakespeare does not deny the brief hours and
of human love; it is enough for him that love triumphs *to* the
f doom.

There would be no problem in the final scene if there were an
Enobarbus to comment on Cleopatra's immortal longings as he comments on Antony's attempts to outstare the lightning; or if there were
a Charmian, immune to her mistress's self-intoxication, to mock
Cleopatra's last imaginings. Octavius disappoints us by speaking am-
biguously of Cleopatra's 'strong toil of grace'; and before him there is
only the Clown, who speaks paradoxically of 'a very honest woman,
but something given to the lie, as a woman should not do, but in the
way of honesty'. Are we to assume that Cleopatra is at her death a
very honest woman but something given to the lie? The question of
honesty is very important in the play: Enobarbus and his honesty
begin to square; Antony's misfortunes corrupt honest men; and Octavius' words to Cleopatra bear little relation to his thoughts. We have
heard Cleopatra lie many times before, even as we have seen Antony
again and again turn his back on reality. An honest thought would
almost seem out of place among the illusions, charms, and enchantments
of Egypt. It is a land of dreaming, playing, and acting, where deaths
are not quite deaths (or not quite believable); where illnesses, like
tears, are profuse but only momentary; and where spectacles like that
at Cydnus and the Monument are contrived to seduce the senses and
the imagination. We have to admit that Cleopatra's barge, which
Enobarbus describes as the purest mythic fancy, is a glorious and very
honest illusion. But her death scene, which is a second Cydnus, is more
difficult to judge because it envisions a reality that is past the size of
dreaming and it seems to demand from us an impossible act of poetic
faith. Shall we say that some jesting about the worm alters the fact of
Cleopatra's death, or that her queenly robes make Octavius' victory
illusory? She speaks of the babes milking her breast, but the drowsiness
she feels is of death, not of maternal fulfilment.

We lose the profounder meanings of *Antony and Cleopatra* if we
insist that questions of truth and honesty are irrelevant to Cleopatra or
that her splendid poetic vision is beyond reason itself. For nothing less
is at stake in the final scene than the honesty of the imagination and the
superiority of its truths to the facts of imperial conquest. What we
share with Cleopatra is not a visionary experience but the delight of
her conspiracy with the Clown that unpolicies Octavius. She is used to

playing jokes on these Romans, and her skill as a comedian shines brightly in the farce of the Seleucus episode, and in the irony of her grave submission to the sole sir of the world. Even as she earlier tormented Antony with references to the immortal Fulvia ('Can Fulvia die?'), in the last Act her thoughts dwell humorously on Octavia, the Roman matron, who is demurely sharpening her fingernails in anticipation of Cleopatra's arrival in Rome. There is so much laughter earlier in the play that the comedy of the last Act does not surprise us. It does bother us, however, because we think that the story of Antony and Cleopatra should have been as tragic to Shakespeare as it was to the illustrators of De Casibus tales and to Shakespeare's French and English contemporaries. Or if we do not insist that it is tragic despite its final mood of joyous triumph and release, then we would have it an ironic comedy like *Troilus and Cressida*, in which ageing sensual love is shadowed by deceptions, jealousies, and fears. Ignoring the contrary evidence of the poetry, we imagine a relatively detached Shakespeare, who could delight in the paradoxical qualities of his lovers, but who would not have us take their professions at face value.

Most of the ironies in *Antony and Cleopatra* are not present in Plutarch's account, because they arise from the extravagant declarations and sublime aspirations which Shakespeare gives to his lovers. Antony would die a bridegroom, but his longing is prompted by the lie of Cleopatra's death, and he fails to imitate the noble Roman suicide of Eros. Cleopatra melts into lyric grief but she will not open the Monument, and so Antony must be hauled aloft to die in her arms. Then she speaks bravely of dying in the high Roman fashion but equivocates with life, charms Dolabella, and trifles with Seleucus before she shackles up all accidents. Even as we list these ironic episodes, however, we wonder if irony is the primary effect which these scenes have upon an audience. And when we take a larger view of plot we see that again and again irony is transformed into paradox by a felicitous turn of events that offers to the lovers something like the second chance given to the characters of the late romances. Though only for a dying moment, Antony and Cleopatra have the opportunity to call back yesterday, and to rediscover the love which they had thought was lost forever. Indeed, if Antony's death in Cleopatra's arms is a mocking irony, then it is an irony devoutly to be wished for.

Though some critics dwell on Antony's disillusionment, his rages more often approach the melodramatic hyperbole of Leontes' speeches

c

than the torments of Troilus'; in fact Antony is most comic when he takes a high moral tone with his Egyptian dish and laments his Roman pillow left unpressed. We are urbane enough, of course, to admit some joking about adultery in *The Winter's Tale*. We smile at the thought of Sir Smiles fishing in his neighbour's pond because we know that Hermione is chaste. But we would have a more serious view of sexuality in *Antony and Cleopatra* because Cleopatra's innocence is only a pose and her fidelity is open to question. Why should her promiscuous past be cheerfully dismissed as 'salad days'? And why should the lack of honesty in women, which is so bitter a theme in *Hamlet* and *Troilus and Cressida*, be reduced at last to the Clown's silly joke? If we assume that a personal disillusion lies behind the view of sex in the great tragedies, then we can infer from *Antony and Cleopatra* (as from the late romances) that in time Shakespeare recovered from the sexual nausea and sickness of generation expressed in *Hamlet* and *King Lear*. But biographical interpretations are at best dubious; what we find in *Antony and Cleopatra* is not a changed attitude towards sexual love, but rather a new perspective on the relations between the sexes. In his great tragedies and in the problem comedies, Shakespeare is concerned with the masculine view of sex. Hamlet's lines, for example, express a typically masculine contempt for woman's frailty and a masculine horror at the sexuality that breeds generations of sinners. Similarly Troilus and Othello are haunted by the masculine desire for sexual possession, a desire that is accompanied by the fear of loss and of the general mock. The darker side of romantic (i.e. masculine) ideals of fidelity is revealed in the anguish of the corrupted Moor, who would not keep a corner in the thing he loved for others' uses.

Where the masculine hunger is for sexual possession and domination, Cleopatra's womanly desire is to be possessed, and to triumph in surrendering. She would be taken; she would yield and feel again the weight of Antony. In his moments of rage, Antony is tormented by the thought that other men have enjoyed Cleopatra. Her womanly jealousies are of another kind: she envies in Fulvia and Octavia the title and place of a 'married woman'. Only superficially does the imagery of feeding in *Antony and Cleopatra* recall that of *Troilus and Cressida*, for Cleopatra's lines do not express the pang of unsatisfied appetite or of frustrate longing; her thoughts linger over the delicious memory of a fulfilment that is maternal as well as sexual. She has borne the weight of Antony in her womb as on her body; she has fed the lover and the babes at her breast. It is striking, moreover, how often Cleopatra's sexuality is an emotion recollected, not an immediate desire. Her scenes with Antony are filled with talk of war, with wranglings, and reconciliations. Only when Antony is absent is Cleopatra's thought 'erotic', and then her longing is not of the flesh but of the total being, one that is rapturously satisfied by news of Antony. In an ageing Falstaff passion is merely ludicrous; but the love which survives the wrinkles and grey hairs that Shakespeare adds to Plutarch's portrait of the lovers is not quite Time's fool. The injurious gods cannot cheat Cleopatra as the stars cheat Juliet, because she has known years of love and revelry with Antony. Even the sorrow she feels in bearing his dying weight is transmuted by the memory of their earlier dyings. And if her last dream of Antony is an illusion, it is an illusion born out of the deepest reality of her experience—she is again for Cydnus.

Vaster than orgiastic memory, the past touches every character and every scene of *Antony and Cleopatra*. We hear of Antony's former greatness as a soldier, of Caesar and Pompey, Brutus and Cassius. The historical events depicted in *Julius Caesar* are recalled, and the past seems to live again in the present as Antony takes Brutus' place as Octavius' antagonist, and as once again love is opposed to imperial ambition. The ruthless impersonalism of the Triumvirate depicted in *Julius Caesar* lives on in the cold efficiency of Octavius, and the fidelity which the defeated Brutus inspired is reflected again in the deaths of Antony and Cleopatra and of those who loved them. To look back at *Julius Caesar* is to realize that Shakespeare did not expediently darken his portrayal of Rome in *Antony and Cleopatra* in order to soften our judgement of Egypt. He saw Caesar's ambition as a symptom of the decay of the Roman state, and he saw the decline of Roman political idealism as a process which had begun even before the assassination of Caesar unloosed the spirit of empire in Antony and Octavius. The end of an era of nobility was marked in *Julius Caesar* by the execution of a hundred Senators and by the suicides of Portia, Cassius, Titinius, and Brutus. In *Antony and Cleopatra* the decay of Roman idealism is so advanced that it is difficult to say whether a Roman thought is of duty or of disloyalty. Yet the decay of the Roman state is paradoxical, because it is not a melting into Egyptian softness but a hardening into the marble-like ruthlessness of the universal landlord. No trace of Brutus' stoicism remains in Octavius' Rome; the prevailing philosophy is the cynical prudence of the Fool's songs in *Lear*. Weakness is merely despised, misfortune corrupts honest soldiers, and loyalty belongs only to the rising man. The pattern of Roman history unfolds for us on Pompey's galley. At present Rome is led by men who (with the exception of Octavius) would rather feast than rule and who make treaties of convenience they do not intend to keep. The Rome that was is recalled by Pompey, who is kept from treachery, not by a personal sense of honour, but by a memory of the honour once sacred to Rome —by a nostalgia for the ethic of his father. Unable to play falsely, Pompey loses the future, which belongs to a Menas who will desert the half-corrupted Pompey, and to an Octavius, whose honour demands only the justification of unscrupulousness. Far more than in the days of Brutus, Rome is bent on empire and ruled by the sword; yet compared to the past, the present is not a time of great soldiery. The continual talk of war only emphasizes that the great military exploits live in memory. All the leaders, including Antony, deal in lieutenantry, and their lieutenants fear to win great victories. Except for the moment when Antony and Scarus beat back Octavius' legions, the battlefield is not a place where honour is won. It is a place where great men defeat themselves; it is the scene of shameful weakness or of the shameless policy that places revolted legions in the van.

The echoes of a nobler past are important because they remind us that the Rome which Octavius rules is not the eternal reality of political life. Only here and now must men like Enobarbus choose between the ways of soldiery and of personal loyalty, that were before a single path. But even as Shakespeare bounds his present scene by placing it in a larger historical framework, his use of archetypal imagery suggests that the worlds of Rome and Egypt are eternal aspects of human experience and form a dichotomy as elemental as that of male and female. The hard masculine world of Rome is imaged in sword, armour, and terms of war, in geometry and stone, and in the engineering that builds or destroys. The soft yielding feminine world of Egypt is poetically imaged as uniting the artifices of sexual temptation to the naturalness of fecundity and to the processes of growth and decay which depend on sun, wind, and water. But the absolute distinctions between Rome and Egypt which the imagery enforces are qualified by the dramatic action, that reveals the extent to which these worlds are mirror images of one another and divergent expressions of the same fundamental human impulses. Although by Roman standards, Antony is unmanned, the Roman standard of masculinity is itself examined by the dramatic action and found deficient. Moreover, although Antony's decline in Egypt is from the Roman measure, his decline also measures the decay of the Roman ideal of soldiery.

The tension between image and plot in *Antony and Cleopatra* leads again and again to paradox. The patterns of imagery insist that Egypt is a Circean land of mandragora and lotus-eaters, where sensuality breeds forgetfulness of Rome and duty. But the action shows us that it is Cleopatra, the Serpent of Old Nile, not Antony, who would hear the Roman messengers; and it is Cleopatra, not Octavia, who demands her place in the war by Antony's side. Thus it may not be completely ironic that the finest Roman words of the play are spoken by Cleopatra to Antony in Act I, Scene iii:

> Your honour calls you hence,
> Therefore be deaf to my unpitied folly,
> And all the gods go with you! Upon your sword
> Sit laurel victory, and smooth success
> Be strew'd before your feet!

The imagery contrasts the enduring monumental quality of Rome to the melting evanescence of Egypt. But the Roman leaders know that the marble-constancy of Rome is founded precariously on the shifting loyalties of a disaffected populace and is forever subject to the battering ram of ambition. The violent spasms of destruction common to Rome are alien to Egypt, where there is permanence in the recurring cycle of growth and decay that dungs the earth, and where the bounty of the Nile requires that nothing be cultivated except the human sensibility. While the imagery insists upon the oversophisticated appetites of Egypt, the Roman leaders tell of wars that make men drink the stale of horses and eat flesh that men die to look upon. Recurrent allusions to snare, serpent, toil, and charm depict Cleopatra as archetypal temptress and seducer. And yet there is no Egyptian snare or temptation as degrading as that which Menas offers Pompey or that which Octavius twice offers Cleopatra. How, indeed, shall we compare Cleopatra's toils with the politic duplicities of Octavius, who tries to patch a quarrel with Antony, engineers the cynical proposal of the marriage to Octavia, and breaks his treaty with Pompey and his bond with Lepidus? The lies of Egypt are amateurish compared with those of Octavius and of the trustworthy Proculeius; not one Roman speaks the

truth to Cleopatra at the end except Dolabella, and he must be seduced
into telling the truth.

I do not mean that we are supposed to shudder at Rome. Though
its political principles have decayed, it is in other respects a healthy and
capable world, led by an Octavius who is cold not inhuman, un-
principled yet eminently respectable. His ambition is not seen as an
anarchic force in an ordered world; it is rather the normal bent of a
society shaped by masculine ideals of politics and power. Morally there
is not much to choose between Rome and Egypt; in matters of the heart
and of the imagination, however, they are polar opposites. Where
Antony and Cleopatra's thoughts have a cosmic poetic amplitude, the
Roman measure of bigness is earthbound and philistine; its imagination
stirs at thoughts of triumphal spectacle and arch. (Octavius would have
the trees bear men and the dust ascend to heaven when his sister enters
Rome.) Untouched by art, and unsoftened by feminine influence, the
Romans pride themselves on their masculine hardness and reticence.
Cold, and to temptation slow, they scorn tears and womanish emotion.
Despite the protective attitude they adopt, they are crass and patronizing in their relations with women, whom they value as sexual objects
and political pawns. Cleopatra rightly fears Antony's callousness because she knows that by Roman standards she is a diversion that
should not be missed or overprized. The coarseness of the Roman view
of sex is apparent throughout the play—in the lines of Octavius as well
as Enobarbus, in Pompey's smutty jests, and in the salacious eagerness
of Caesar's lieutenants to hear tales of Cleopatra. Although Enobarbus
describes her lightness, her artfulness, her wit, and her infinite variety,
the other Romans (like so many modern critics) can picture her only in
the conventional posture of a whore, drugging Antony with cloying
lascivious wassails.

In most respects the priggish Octavius is the very opposite of
Antony. In his treatment of women, however, he is Antony's Roman
brother. Antony adopts the pose of Cleopatra's general when he flees
his Egyptian 'dotage'. Octavius sends Thyreus to Cleopatra with
solemn assurances that her honour is unsullied. Antony babbles to
Octavia about his honour when he deserts her; Octavius marries his
sister to a man he despises and then wars to erase her dishonour.
Octavius, like Antony, hungers for Cleopatra but his desire to possess
her is more shameless and more contemptible. Indifferent to Antony's
fate (he would be content if Cleopatra murders her lover), he lies to

Cleopatra, cajoles her, and threatens her children in order to keep her alive so that she may be displayed as his trophy in Rome. He has no doubt that a woman like Cleopatra will be seduced into ignobleness when

> want will perjure
> The ne'er-touched vestal.

Warm and generous as well as callous, Antony is able to respond to the arts of Egypt, and he is so deeply altered by his response that it is difficult to say what is Antony or when he is less than Antony or when he is himself again. A legend in his lifetime, he is the hero of fantastic exploits and the stuff of soldierly brags and mythic imaginings. Contemning his Egyptian dotage, Philo, Demetrius, and Octavius recall a plated Mars and contrast Antony's earlier feats of battle to his present wassails. But Cleopatra and Enobarbus remember another, more sensual, Antony—Plutarch's gamester and reveller, the lover of plays in *Julius Caesar*, who did not learn the arts of dissipation in Egypt or desert them when he returns to Rome. When plagued by his Roman conscience, Antony sees his salvation in a flight from Egypt; in Rome he momentarily recovers his ability to command, which allows him to look over Octavius' head. But Antony is not reinspired by Roman ideals; on the contrary, his superiority is a personal honesty that contrasts with Octavius' devious and politic attempts to provoke a quarrel. No salvation awaits Antony in Rome because there is no honourable purpose to engage him; the Triumvirate feasts and gambles and despises the populace. The only Roman dedication is Octavius' desire to be the sole sir of the world. Moreover, if Antony's faults are Egyptian, he does not lose them in Rome, where he displays the very weaknesses that are later to destroy him: a desire to put off issues and to escape unpleasantness. In Egypt he is led by Cleopatra; in Rome he is led by Octavius' lieutenants into the foolish expediency of the marriage to Octavia. There is no point in the play, therefore, at which we can say, here Antony falls. His decline is a process that began in years past and which seems the inevitable destiny of a sensualist and opportunist who never shared Octavius' ambition to possess the entire world, but who wanted empires to play with and superfluous kings to feast and do his bidding. If we must have a reason for Antony's decline, we can say that he lost the desire before he lost the ability to command. He is never defeated in battle during the play. After the disaster at Actium, his fleet is intact and his army powerful though kings and legions desert. A doting braggart might have brushed aside the reality of his cowardice at sea; but Antony is shattered by the very trait which ennobled him in his dealings with Octavius, by an honourable shame at his failings as a leader.

It is characteristic of the handling of events in *Antony and Cleopatra* that we do not see Antony's failure of nerve at Actium; we see Canidius', Scarus', and Enobarbus' response to it, and, following that, we see Antony's reaction. Much use is made of messengers bearing tidings of conflict, disaster, and death, because this is a play of reaction rather than of action. We know Octavius, Cleopatra, Enobarbus, Pompey, and Lepidus by the way that they respond to news of Antony. And we know Antony by his response to Cleopatra and to his fading powers, by his alternating moods of depression and elation, by his moments of impotent rage or of bluster, when he will outstare the lightning, and by his reconciliations with Cleopatra. This vacillation of mood in Antony reminds us of Richard II, except that Richard's journey is towards the nihilism of endlessly circling thoughts, while Antony becomes a fuller man in his decline, more bounteous in his love and in his generosity. When he tries to express, after the second disaster at sea, his loss of soldierly identity, he convinces us that he has changed, not lost, his identity. The soldier has become a lover, the spendthrift a mine of bounty, and the callous opportunist a meditative poet.

The growth of poetic sensitivity in Antony was apparent to earlier generations of critics. It is less apparent to us, ironically, because our desire to read Shakespeare 'poetically' blurs our awareness of the poetic attributes of the characters in the plays. And to avoid critical naïveté, we make artificial distinctions between the form and substance of Shakespeare's dramatic verse. When Antony compares his state to the evanescent shapelessness of clouds in a dying afternoon, we grant to him the sense of weariness and loss which the lines convey; but the heavenly imagery and the poetic sensibility revealed in this passage we reserve for Shakespeare, who, we say, merely lends Antony his poetic faculty for artistic purposes. But it is only a step from this 'sophisticated' approach to Antony's speeches to the notion that the morbidity of Hamlet's soliloquies is 'saved' by the nobility of Shakespeare's poetry. If we grant Hamlet the nobility of his utterances, how shall we deny Antony his poetry? Not all the characters who speak in verse are poetic. Although Octavius' lines are at times richly metaphorical, he seems to us thoroughly prosaic, because the impression of poetic sensibility in Shakespeare's characters depends upon the nature of their response to life, not on the mere presence of figurative language in their speeches. Who but a poet would see the clouds as Antony does, and who but a poet would remember this heavenly image at the point of death? Antony's leave-taking of the world is an imaginative reverie untouched by the grandiosity that marks so many of his early 'poetic' declarations.

At the beginning of the play it is obvious that Antony does not know Cleopatra because he does not yet know what is evident to the audience, that his only desire is to be with this woman. We feel that the hyperbole of his early speeches is strained, because his extravagant professions of love are undercut by his harsh, grating response to news from Rome and by his sensitivity to the Roman view of Cleopatra. Though he says here is my space, he is unable to conceive of a world limited by love; and he is unaware that he uses Cleopatra to excuse his indifference to political issues. We smile at Cleopatra's role of betrayed innocence, but not at her keen perception of the emotional dishonesty of Antony's gestures of devotion and of the callousness that underlies them. She knows how easily an Antony who shrugs off Fulvia's death may desert her in turn. The first scenes show us an Antony who is caught between what he tells Cleopatra, and in part believes, and what he tells himself about her, and in part believes. In Rome he is irritated by every reference to her; he never speaks her name though his is always on her lips, and he never regards her as an equal or as having any claim upon him. When he decides to return to Egypt, he speaks of her as his pleasure.

As Antony's world shrinks, his hyperbole becomes, paradoxically, more convincing. When he is confronted by Octavius' legions, his chivalric pose becomes more than a pose, because at last he does fight for Cleopatra; and thus his arming before battle with Cleopatra's aid is more than one last parody of medieval romance. Now when Antony acts, he is aware of his pretendings; tutored by Cleopatra, he imitates after Actium her celerity in dying and, like her, he plays on the feelings of those who love him, making Enobarbus onion-eyed. His talk of death and his shaking of hands is an artful appeal to his followers' emotion and yet an honest piece of acting, because it expresses a true warmth and generosity of spirit. There are times, of course, when Antony's gestures are less honest, when he abuses Cleopatra for her treachery. But his Herculean rages are short-lived and his self-pity is untouched by genuine suffering. His despondency is always more painful to those who love him than it is to Antony, who is never deeply in conflict with himself, and who is more a spectator to, than a participant in, the final disaster at sea. His catastrophes are strangely beautiful: his gods desert to music, his loss of empire is signalled by shouts of joy in the fleets. Even at his nadir he shakes hands with Fortune as with an old familiar friend.

Whatever ironies attach to the manner of Antony's death, he is raised visually, and poetically, above the earth on which the melancholy Enobarbus sinks. The moralizing critic interprets Antony's fate as a warning to adhere to the path of reason; he forgets that Enobarbus follows reason to a fate more wretched than Antony's. Enobarbus chooses Rome lest he lose himself in Antony's dotage and like Antony be made a woman. In itself this choice is not shameful; Enobarbus' act has a hundred Roman precedents, and he has no reason—or, at least, no Roman reason—to follow a leader who can no longer command. What is shameful is Enobarbus' betrayal of himself, because he allows his reason and his honesty to square. Worse still, he goes over to Octavius knowing that to have stayed with Antony was to have 'won a place in the story'. Yet the place which Enobarbus wins is not as ignoble as he thinks, for we sense that his desertion of Antony is, like his death, an act of love. He leaves Antony when he can no longer bear to watch Antony's failure as a general, and he is redeemed by his response to Antony's generosity even though he has no chance to express to his master the full measure of his devotion. The lie of Cleopatra's death saves Antony from Enobarbus' fate because it ends the lie of his rage while Cleopatra is still alive. And Antony's failure to die in the high Roman fashion makes possible the final expression of his bounteous love, his dying wish that she save herself by making terms with Octavius.

Between the disaster at Actium and his final reunion with Cleopatra, Antony is the centre of the dramatic action. At the Monument, however, the dramatic focus shifts: the dying Antony plays the chorus to Cleopatra's impassioned grief, and she is from that moment on the supreme figure of the play. At Antony's death, we are told, a new Cleopatra is born—the wanton temptress rises to regal majesty. But what is really new in the Cleopatra who mourns over Antony? Her royalty, her poetic sensibility, and her capacity for profound emotion were evident before; her grief is hardly surprising when, from the beginning, her every thought is of Antony, and she is haunted by the fear of losing him. Is it the new Cleopatra who says, 'Husband, I come'? Or is she the same Egyptian who in the first scene of the play reveals her envy of Fulvia, the *married woman*, and her longing to be more to Antony than his pleasure?

Only Shakespeare could have imagined that the greatest courtesan of all time hungered to be Antony's wife—to be made 'an honest woman'. Only he could have dreamed of a Cleopatra who is, despite her lies and pretendings, always emotionally honest. When the messenger brings news of Antony's remarriage, she is furious, but her fury is directed at the messenger, not at Antony. If she pretends to die when Antony leaves her, it is because their partings are a form of death which leaves only the desire to sleep and dream of Antony. Those who read her thoughts announce that she intends to betray him when she listens to Thyreus. The text indicates only the elaborate irony of her submission and her comic surprise at Octavius' concern for her honour. It is quite explicit, moreover, that Enobarbus is able to uncover Cleopatra's intended treachery only because she insists that he be present at the interview with Thyreus. How foolish of this cunning woman to plan a betrayal of Antony in the presence of Enobarbus! What we witness is not Cleopatra's duplicity but Enobarbus' jealous revenge and the confusion of rage in Antony, who has Thyreus whipped for kissing the 'kingly' hand of that 'boggler' Cleopatra.

According to Plutarch, Cleopatra demanded a role in the war against Octavius because she feared that in her absence Antony and Octavius might be reconciled. Shakespeare fails to give Cleopatra a similar explicit motive. Against Enobarbus' warning and against her own nature, she insists upon bearing a charge in the war; she will have Antony fight by sea so that she may command her fleet at Actium. If Cleopatra were nothing more than the seductress whom critics describe, her desire to fight by Antony's side would seem to us incredible. It does not astonish us, however, because we see from the beginning her desire to be worthy of this Herculean Roman, and to imitate the noble Roman fashion of words and deeds. She bids a Roman farewell to Antony in the first Act even as she seeks a Roman death in the last act. Her desire to be a Roman wife, which becomes explicit at her death, leads Cleopatra to attempt at Actium the role of Fulvia, the only part she plays falsely before Antony.

Like Antony, Cleopatra does not die in the high Roman fashion; and though she earns the title of Antony's wife she remains more Egyptian than Roman, more various than marble-constant. Timidity,

vanity, and womanly fears plague her Roman resolution; she dies a
sensual creature of the Nile, artful, theatrical, jealous to the end of
Antony. Part of the mystery of her death is the fullness with which it
expresses the multiplicity of her nature. She is Antony's mistress and
his wife, the graceful courtesan and the tender mother, the great queen
and the simple lass. Her drowsiness is at once sensual, maternal, and
child-like, for though she nurses her imaginary babes, she is, as so
many times before, very like a child, who plays now at being mother,
and who is dressed in a royal costume to surprise Octavius. Her crown
slips, but Charmian mends it before she too plays.

More than a triumph over Octavius, Cleopatra's death is a triumph
over her own fears and over a deeply rooted instinct for life. She is not,
however, in love with death though she allows it to commit a loving
act upon her; she dreams of life and of Antony. And though she makes
a fellow-conspirator of the worm which will eat her, she knows it is
not worth the feeding; she knows too the horror of physical decay,
which she has envisioned before in striking images of fly-blown
bodies. Her death will not be a melting into eternal natural change; it
will be a change into changelessness that robs Octavius of his victory
and that mocks his immortal longings. He thinks that Cleopatra's 'life
in Rome | Would be eternal in our triumph' and he meditates in his
last speech on the glory he has won by the deaths of the lovers. But it is
paltry to be Caesar, whose quest of fame earns an ignominious place
in the story.

Cleopatra's sense of the comedy of imperial ambition is not a new
intuition that reaches 'beyond the tragic'. The paltriness of Caesar was
evident to the youthful Shakespeare, whose sonnets contrast the vital
power of art to the lifeless marble and gilded monuments of princes.
There are echoes of the sonnets, I think, in the antithesis of Egypt and
Rome, and in the depiction of a love which finally admits not even the
impediment of death. The themes of the sonnets are also relevant to
the echoes in the final scene of Capulet's Monument, where another
pair of lovers found in death the marriage union which life denied.
As *Romeo and Juliet* draws to a close, we sense that the true memorial to
the lovers is not the gilded statues which Montague and Capulet promise to raise, but Shakespeare's play. And we know that Cleopatra will
live in art because she fashions her own incomparable memorial, the
scene in the Monument, which overshadows the mythic wonder of
Cydnus. It is the artist in Cleopatra who stirs Shakespeare's deepest

imaginative sympathies and who receives the immeasurable bounty of his artistic love, which is immortality itself.

We need not turn *Antony and Cleopatra* into an allegory of art to see that its final paradox is the final paradox of Donne's 'Canonization': though deserted by those who observe Octavius' face, the lovers die and rise the same, and prove mysterious by their love. The defect of their passion becomes perfection because ultimately theirs is not a sublunary love: their 'faults' shine like the unchanging stars. Donne's lover is a poet who builds in sonnets' pretty rooms, and who fashions the legend of his love in immortal verse. Cleopatra is an artist who fashions out of her life a legend that is unfit for hearse or for Octavius' half-acre tombs. Her 'place in the story' is beside the legendary figures who live in ancient myth. She is another Thetis, an Isis, a Venus, a Dido; Cupids and Nereides attend her, the winds are enamoured of her, and she is wooed by Phoebus and, at last, by Death himself. She teaches a plated Mars an artful way of loving; and she turns this demi-Atlas after death into a very god who spreads the masculine seed of his inexhaustible bounty over the earth. In her mythopeic imagination Antony bestrides the ocean, making cities on the waves, and creating empires through a divinely prodigal carelessness—he drops realms and islands out of his pockets.

The foolish Clown is right after all. The biting of Cleopatra's worms is immortal, because it brings a death that lives in the artistic imagination. She dies in the last scene of Shakespeare's play as she has died so many times before in Plutarch, in medieval 'tragedy', and in Renaissance plays and poems. And because Shakespeare has written, she will die many times again and be staged over and over to the show—so long as men can breathe or eyes can see, Cleopatra is again for Cydnus. The terms *act*, *play*, and *show* are not metaphorical when applied to her, because she is in her essential being an actress. Her poses are too extravagant to deceive; they are meant to bewitch and captivate by their infinite variety. She will not allow herself to be carted through the streets of Rome in the posture of a whore or to be staged to the show in vulgar Roman fashion. But as if she knows that her destiny is art, she dons her robes and prepares one last dazzling scene that draws a gasp of admiration from Octavius. We have seen her metamorphoses before—her sudden changes from tears to laughter, from pettiness to regality, and from sickness to health. None of them is comparable, however, to the metamorphosis of her death, which turns life into art.

As early as the sonnets, Shakespeare knew that the enemy of love is not time or death; these can only refine its worth. Love's adversary is the unfeeling heart—those who are 'as stone | Unmoved, cold and to temptation slow'. He can accept a world of mutability in *Antony and Cleopatra*, as in the tragedies and the late romances, because it offers the possibility of renewing change, in later generations, and in the heart of a Lear, an Antony, or a Leontes. Shakespeare does not retreat in his later plays from the exalted humanism of his tragedies, which stresses the irreplaceableness of a Cordelia; he does not find comfort in a naturalistic faith in the continuance of life. The security of *Antony and Cleopatra* and of the late romances is founded on the paradox of tragic art, which depicts immeasurable loss and yet preserves forever that which the artist supremely values. Although great creating Nature may reincarnate some of the rareness of Hermione in Perdita, the true miracle of *The Winter's Tale* is Paulina's art, which preserves and enriches the wonder of Hermione herself.

In Shakespeare's great tragedies illusion and seeming are opposed to moral reality. But in Cleopatra's artful spectacles as in the masques of Prospero and Paulina, illusion and reality intermingle. Sober realists may agree with Dolabella that the Antony whom Cleopatra ecstatically recalls is only a dream of her imagination; they forget, however, that Dolabella, like Cleopatra, is only a dream of Shakespeare's imagination. The triumph of love and art in *Antony and Cleopatra* will not allow us to believe that Shakespeare, who celebrated in the sonnets the miracle of poetry, expressed in Prospero's lines a disillusioned awareness of the vanity of his dramatic art. After a lifetime spent in creating the magic of the stage, Shakespeare must have known that the 'idle' dreamlike play of an artist's imagination is the deepest reality of his experience, if not a clue to the fundamental reality of all experience:

> We are such stuff
> As dreams are made on, and our little life
> Is rounded with a sleep.

Note

Sources: Among Elizabethan texts Underdowne's important version of Helio-
dorus was reprinted in the Tudor Translations, *An Aethiopian History*, ed.
Charles Whibley and W. E. Henley (1895), and quotations in the following
chapter are modernized from this edition. Angel Day's version of *Daphnis and
Chloe* was edited by J. Jacobs (1890). William Burton's translation of Achilles
Tatius' *The most delectable history of Clitophon and Leucippe*, was edited by
Stephen Gaselee and H. F. B. Brett-Smith (Oxford, 1923). Modern translations
easily available include Sir Walter Lamb's *Ethiopian Story* of Heliodorus
(Everyman Library, 1961), Paul Turner's *Daphnis and Chloe* (Penguin Books,
1956), and S. Gaselee's edition of Achilles Tatius' *Clitophon and Leucippe* (Loeb
Classical Library, 1917).

Scholarship and criticism. S. L. Wolff's *The Greek Romances in Elizabethan Prose
Fiction* (New York, 1912; reprinted 1961) is standard and still relevant. E. C.
Pettet's *Shakespeare and the Romance Tradition* (1949) has more to say on the
earlier than the later plays. The possible influence of Longus on *The Tempest*
and Heliodorus on *Cymbeline* is discussed by Carol Gesner in '*The Tempest* as
Pastoral Romance', *Shakespeare Quarterly*, X (1959), and '*Cymbeline* and the
Greek Romance', *Studies in English Renaissance Literature*, ed. Waldo F. McNeir
(Louisiana, 1962). The present contributor's 'The Failure of *The Two Gentle-
men of Verona*' is in *Shakespeare Jahrbuch* (1963).

Recent work on *The Comedy of Errors* includes Harold Brooks's 'Themes and
Structure in *The Comedy of Errors*' (*Early Shakespeare*, *Stratford-upon-Avon
Studies* 3, 1961) and R. A. Foakes's New Arden edition (1962). John Lawlor
writes on '*Pandosto* and the Nature of Dramatic Romance' in *Philological
Quarterly*, XLI (1962); see also Inga-Stina Ewbank's 'The Triumph of Time in
The Winter's Tale', *Review of English Literature* (1964).

The Introductions to the New Arden editions of the last plays all contain
relevant material, as do S. L. Bethell's *Shakespeare and the Popular Dramatic
Tradition* (1944) and *The Winter's Tale: A Study* (1947).

III

Shakespeare and Romance

STANLEY WELLS

★

THOUGH in Shakespeare's day the word 'romance' had been in the language for two centuries,[1] it occurs in none of his writings. The Elizabethans generally found little use for it, and so far as I know it was never used to describe a play. To the editors of the First Folio, *The Winter's Tale* and *The Tempest* were comedies, *Cymbeline* was a tragedy, and *Pericles* was—for reasons that we can only surmise—beyond the pale. Modern critics, discerning common characteristics in these plays, have grouped them together, sometimes non-committally as 'last plays', sometimes as 'romances'—and the term is genuinely descriptive. But it has been increasingly recognized that the final romances are in many ways directly descended from Shakespeare's earlier comedies. These are often called 'romantic' comedies; are they not, then, also romances? It depends, of course, what you mean by a romance. The very word is shadowy, having associations with literature of various kinds, forms, and periods; with modes of sensibility; with languages; and with love. It can be spoken with an auspicious or a dropping eye; with a sob, a sigh, or a sneer; with the aspiration to define or with a defiance of definition. It means so much that often it means nothing at all.

If the literary genre of romance can be defined—or described—it is not by formal characteristics. Rather perhaps is it a matter of certain recurrent motifs, and also of a recognizable attitude towards the subject-matter. Romancers delight in the marvellous; quite often this involves the supernatural; generally the characters are larger than life size. All is unrealistic; the logic of cause and effect is ignored, and chance or fortune governs all. Characteristic features vary somewhat from one sort of romance to another; and attempts at definition are bound to be circular—we can only decide what makes a romance by

---

[1] The adjective, however, is not recorded before 1659.

looking at works to which the label has been attached and seeing what they have in common. But it is fair to say that Shakespearian romance frequently includes the separation and disruption of families, followed by their eventual reunion and reconciliation; scenes of apparent resurrection; the love of a virtuous young hero and heroine; and the recovery of lost royal children. In this chapter it will be my purpose first to sketch the background of material such as this, then to say something of Shakespeare's use of it in certain of his earlier comedies, and finally to discuss the romantic characteristics of *The Winter's Tale* and *The Tempest*.

Elements of romance can be traced far back in the history of the world's literature. *The Odyssey* itself is (like *Pericles*) the story of a voyage and its hero's reunion with his wife. Oedipus, like Perdita, was cast away in infancy; and Euripides' *Alcestis* is often cited as an analogue of *The Winter's Tale*—both tell of a wife restored to her husband from apparent death. Romance elements are found in greater concentration in classical comedy—a form we are apt to think of as the antithesis of romantic. The common features of Greek New Comedy, we are told, are 'loss of children, far wanderings over many years, fortunate recognition at a moment of imminent peril, and final happy reunion of parents and children'.[2] Menander's *The Girl with Shorn Hair* tells—as do Plautus' *Menacchmi* and its derivative, *The Comedy of Errors*—of the reunion with each other and with their father of twins separated in infancy. That the plays of Plautus and Terence include this sort of material is the more interesting since, of course, they were standard text-books in Elizabethan schools. But it would not do to exaggerate their romantic characteristics, which in most of these plays are rather treated as plot-mechanism than elaborated for their own sake.

Far more important are the Greek romances, prose tales whose influence on later literature has been incalculable. They date from the post-classical period—most of them from the second and third centuries A.D. Perhaps the three most important are *Daphnis and Chloe*, by Longus; Heliodorus' *Aethiopica*; and *Clitophon and Leucippe*, by Achilles Tatius. Here the familiar motifs abound. *Daphnis and Chloe* tells of a pair of abandoned infants who are brought up together, tend flocks, and in adolescence fall in love with each other. Daphnis is captured by pirates, but escapes in circumstances of wild improbability. Chloe too

[2] M. Doran, *Endeavors of Art* (Madison, 1954), p. 172.

is carried off, but is restored to Daphnis as a result of Pan's direct intervention. Finally their true identity is revealed, they are reunited with their families, and they marry. This is the most pastoral, and the least eventful, of the Greek romances.

Perhaps the most influential was the *Aethiopica*. Again the story centres on a pair of lovers—Theagenes and Chariclea. Many episodes could be paralleled at least in outline from Shakespeare's last plays. There is a wicked stepmother on the same pattern as the Queen in *Cymbeline*; there is more than one shipwreck; there are oracular dreams; insistence is placed on the heroine's virginity; the lovers are several times parted; and there is a scene of grief over a dead body mistakenly believed to be the beloved's—it is difficult not to think of Imogen with Cloten's body when we read how 'Theagenes, as though by violence one had thrust him down, fell on the dead body and held the same in his arms a great while without moving'.[3] Our memories of the same play must be still stronger when we read of the lovers' reunion; Chariclea

> ran to him like a mad woman, and, hanging by her arms about his neck, said nothing, but saluted him with certain pitiful lamentations. He, seeing her foul face (belike of purpose beblacked) and her apparel vile and all torn, supposing her to be one of the makeshifts of the city, and a vagabond, cast her off and put her away, and at length gave her a blow on the ear for that she troubled him in seeing Calasiris. Then she spake to him softly: 'Pithius, have you quite forgotten this taper?' Theagenes was stricken with that word as if he had been pierced with a dart, and by tokens agreed on between them knew the taper and, looking steadfastly upon her, espied her beauty shining like the sun appearing through the clouds, cast his arms about her neck.[4]

In the final book there is a protracted reunion scene, as well as an episode in which the hero, under sentence of death, performs deeds of great valour—again one is reminded of the last act of *Cymbeline*.

Some of Heliodorus' comments, too, are interesting in relation to Shakespeare. Towards the end of the last book he describes the rejoicing at the satisfactory conclusion of events in terms that could be paralleled from a number of Shakespeare's plays, and that might indeed almost serve as an epigraph to the last plays:

The people in another place rejoiced and almost danced for joy,

[3] .47.   [4] pp. 181–2.

and with one consent were all glad of that which was done; marry, all they understood not, but gathered the most part of Chariclea. Perhaps also they were stirred to understand the truth by inspiration of the gods, whose will it was that this should fall out wonderfully, as in a comedy. Surely they made very contrary things agree, and joined sorrow and mirth, tears and laughter, together, and turned fearful and terrible things into a joyful banquet in the end; many that wept began to laugh, and such as were sorrowful to rejoice, when they found that they sought not for, and lost that they hoped to find; and to be short, the cruel slaughters which were looked for every moment were turned into holy sacrifice.[5]

The third Greek romance to have some importance in the Elizabethan period is *Clitophon and Leucippe*. Achilles Tatius, imitating Heliodorus, tells of a pair of lovers who pass through many dangers and narrow escapes from death to final reunion. Again the story includes features reminiscent of Shakespearian romance, such as oracular dreams, shipwreck, mourning over the wrong body, and scenes of apparent resurrection; and again the heroine's virginity is heavily emphasized.

The Greek romances were written well over a thousand years before Shakespeare's time. In the interim, many subspecies of romance developed and flourished—it is noticeable how often we need to qualify the noun. We hear of chivalric and heroic romance; epic and pastoral romance; courtly love romance; and even religious romance.[6] Malory's translation of French Arthurian cycles into the English *Morte D'Arthur* was known in late-Elizabethan England; so were chivalric romances such as those of the Palmerin cycle (written in Spanish in the sixteenth century) and the slightly earlier tales of Amadis de Gaule (also written in Spanish but probably based on lost French originals). And there was *Huon of Bordeaux*, the French *chanson de geste* of the thirteenth century which, translated by Lord Berners, suggested to Shakespeare at least the name of Oberon.

To compile a list of romances written up to Shakespeare's time would not of course take us far; but merely the widespread currency of romance in the period has significance. It is true that stories, especially plays, using this material were often scorned. Gosson attacked the

[5] p. 288.
[6] In 1600 Robert Chambers, a Roman Catholic priest, published a most curious book called *Palestina*, which adapts the events of the Gospels to the conventions of romance.

artifices of recognition. Sir Philip Sidney (in a well-known passage of the *Apology for Poetry*) and Ben Jonson (in the Prologue to *Every Man in his Humour*) mocked at the violation of the neo-classical unities often necessitated by the adaptation of romance material. Nashe scorned those 'from whose idle pens proceeded those worn-out impressions of the feigned nowhere acts of Sir Arthur of the Round Table, Arthur of Little Britain, Sir Tristram, Huon of Bordeaux, the Squire of Low Degree, the Four Sons of Aymon, with infinite others'.[7] But the irritated utterances of literary and moral reformers should not suggest that romance was ever less than popular. Certain specimens went out of fashion, but others came in. It was during the later part of the sixteenth century that the Greek romances first began to be translated, and they immediately exercised a profound influence especially on the development of prose fiction. First came Heliodorus: a brief extract in 1567, and the full translation by Thomas Underdowne in 1569, with reprints in 1577, 1587, 1605, and 1622. Underdowne worked from the French of the invaluable Amyot, from whose version of *Daphnis and Chloe* Angel Day made the first English translation in 1587. Achilles Tatius was translated by William Burton in 1597.

We cannot prove that Shakespeare used these works directly; but the related tale of Apollonius of Tyre, on which *Pericles* is based, was of great importance to him. Though the earliest known version is a Latin manuscript of the tenth century, the original appears to have been another Greek romance. The story had a wide and long-lasting circulation—over a hundred medieval Latin manuscripts, in both prose and verse, are known—and was popular in many languages; it was translated, imitated, adapted, versified, and dramatized. (In Greece, we are told, it is still passed on by word of mouth.) Shakespeare of course can have known only a few of the versions extant in his time. He certainly knew Gower's (in *Confessio Amantis*), and also Lawrence Twine's (*The Pattern of Painful Adventures*). For the student of Shakespeare these obviously are the important versions; but it is helpful to be aware of the others—to know that Shakespeare was telling a story of great antiquity, familiar to many of his audience. The 'mouldy tale', as Jonson described it, must have seemed to his less censorious contemporaries rather to be part of their folklore; a tale they would no more consider rationally than we should question the motives of Cinderella or examine the psychology of the three bears.

[7] *The Anatomy of Absurdity*; ed. McKerrow, I, 11.

Of Shakespeare's romances, only *Pericles* is wholly based on a traditional tale; but all the others employ equally conventional motifs. Obviously Shakespeare, in employing the material of romance, must have been well aware that many other writers of the time used similar conventions. Some (such as Greene and Lodge) we remember mainly for their connections with Shakespeare; others (such as Emanuel Forde and Henry Roberts—both very popular in their day) we remember hardly at all. And a few survive with the status of 'classics': Spenser's *The Faerie Queene* (much influenced by Italian romantic epic) and Sidney's *Arcadia* (on which Heliodorus was an important influence) have been declared 'outstanding epitomes of all that was most vital at the time in the romance tradition'.[8]

These two works no longer enjoy the popularity that was once their lot. 'The *Arcadia*', T. S. Eliot has said, 'is a monument of dulness'; [9] and S. L. Wolff wrote 'one who reads for pleasure simply cannot understand the *Arcadia*'.[10] Scholars and critics have tried to help the modern reader to understand them, partly by assuring us how serious they are. The *Arcadia*, we are told, 'is as sage and serious as Spenser, or as anything Milton himself could have wished'. It is 'a study in Christian patience'—like *King Lear*.[11] This attitude can be overstressed. Undoubtedly many romances raise, or touch on, serious intellectual issues; at the same time they tend to resist intellectual schematization. The Elizabethans themselves, nervous lest their fictions be considered corrupting, tended to make exaggerated claims for their moral and ethical value. Defending romance, Sidney wrote: 'Truly I have known men that even with reading *Amadis de Gaule* (which God knoweth wanteth much of a perfect poesy) have found their hearts moved to the exercise of courtesy, liberality, and especially courage.' Clearly he expected moral benefits to come as a result of enjoyment and admiration rather than of any intellectual process induced by the work. No doubt he expected to confer similar benefits upon *Arcadia*'s readers. But no doubt either that he expected people (or at least his sister) to *read* his book, and to do so with enjoyment. And this happened: 'for a century and a half', writes John Buxton, it 'remained the best-loved book in the English language.' [12] Indeed, most prose romances, including some very poor specimens, were read much more widely than

[8] Pettet, p. 12.

[9] *The Use of Poetry and the Use of Criticism* (1933), p. 51.   [10] p. 352.

[11] Danby, pp. 71 and 72.   [12] *Elizabethan Taste* (1963), p. 246.

works for which the modern reader tends to have a higher regard. 'Today', we are told,[13] 'the most widely read work of Elizabethan fiction is *The Unfortunate Traveller*' of Thomas Nashe; a book which, though reprinted in the year of its publication (1594), had to wait till 1883 for its next edition. Of the far longer *Arcadia* on the other hand there were seventeen issues between 1590 and 1638. Clearly people read it—largely, we must assume, for pleasure, undeterred either by its great length or by the fact that parts of it are unfinished. Romances have a habit of being left unfinished; it is a symptom of their inclusive nature. Most of the motifs common in romance encourage copiousness, a virtue more admired perhaps in the Renaissance than at present. As Dr. Johnson put it, 'In romance, when the wide field of possibility lies open to invention, the incidents may easily be made more numerous.' There is no real reason why romances should not go on for ever. This is not to say that romance material cannot be combined with a classical respect for form and economy, as certain of Shakespeare's plays clearly show. But the inclusive quality of the genre may warn us that to seek in examples of it for a single dominant purpose or theme is to risk denying its very nature. Spenser, in his letter to Raleigh printed with *The Faerie Queene*, says that most men 'delight to read . . . an historical fiction . . . rather for variety of matter than for profit of the example'. Readers expected variety as one of their rightful pleasures.

It is important, then, that the romances were written, not to be studied, but to be read primarily for enjoyment — or 'entertainment', if the word may be allowed. I quoted the remark that 'one who reads for pleasure simply cannot understand the *Arcadia*'. It would be truer to say that *until* we can read it for pleasure we cannot understand it. Sidney, Spenser, and Shakespeare all had serious purposes; but this does not necessarily imply that they were consciously didactic in any way. It is serious to create images of the joys of reunion after long parting, of the loneliness of the parted, of the fears that assail men to whom, as to Marina, the world is 'like a lasting storm, whirring me from my friends'. To construct a verbal or dramatic structure that can stimulate our imaginations to a keener apprehension of these matters requires no further justification. The full response to the works of the romancers comes only when we find ourselves reading for pure pleasure, caught up in the swirl of the story, rapt in wonder and tense with anticipation —reading in fact as children read. Sidney, Spenser, and Shakespeare

[13] W. H. Allen, *The English Novel* (1954), p. 25.

appeal primarily to our imaginations, not our brains; and the standard motifs and conventions of romance were invaluable raw material to them.

Conventions can of course be both an advantage and a disadvantage. They enable an artist to establish a basis of communication; but they can all too easily harden into clichés, in which the intention of communication is mistaken for the act. Some situations can be relied on to produce an automatic response without much help from the author. This is particularly true of the theatre, where something can always be left to the performers. The romantic situation of recognition and reconciliation found in the last Acts of many of Shakespeare's plays recurs at other stages of our drama; but not always so well handled. An instance is the last page of *Lovers' Vows*, that play translated by Mrs. Inchbald from the German of Kotzebue, and rehearsed with such dire consequences at Mansfield Park. The once wicked but now reformed Baron is reunited with the mistress he has wronged, and their bastard. The tender scene is presented with remarkable verbal economy. Indeed the stage-directions are more eloquent than the dialogue.

> *Anhalt leads on Agatha—The Baron runs and clasps her in his arms —Supported by him, she sinks on a chair which Amelia places in the middle of the stage—The Baron kneels by her side, holding her hand.*

BARON: Agatha, Agatha, do you know this voice?
AGATHA: Wildenhaim.
BARON: Can you forgive me?
AGATHA: I forgive you (*embracing him*)

> [*Enter Frederick (their son)*]

FREDERICK: I hear the voice of my mother!—Ha! mother! father!

> *Frederick throws himself on his knees by the other side of his mother— She clasps him in her arms.—Amelia is placed on the side of her father attentively viewing Agatha—Anhalt stands on the side of Frederick with his hands gratefully raised to Heaven.—The curtain slowly drops.*

In its day this was a perfectly successful piece of dramatic writing, even though the convention behind it had already been burlesqued by Sheridan in *The Critic*. The convention will stand up to burlesque. In the once popular farce *Box and Cox* (1847), the conventional mark of recognition is similarly parodied:

BOX: Cox! You'll excuse the apparent insanity of the remark, but the more I gaze on your features, the more I'm convinced that you're my long-lost brother.

COX: The very remark I was going to make to you.

BOX: Ah—tell me—in mercy tell me—have you such a thing as a strawberry mark on your left arm?

COX: No.

BOX: Then 'tis he!

They rush into each other's arms.

We recognize the absurdity of the bare husk of the convention, but this need not prevent us from responding with genuine emotion to a properly devised use of it. The great writer can invest a stock situation with the weight of reality, illumining the commonplace. He can even call upon our awareness of the convention to produce a complex reaction in which the literary trick is transmuted into a symbol of the archetypal quality of a situation. In *Twelfth Night* there is a version of the 'strawberry mark' convention. 'My father had a mole upon his brow' says Viola, reunited with Sebastian. 'And so had mine' he replies. The exchange is sometimes cut in the theatre, presumably lest it arouse the wrong kind of laughter. Yet it can be spoken in such a way as to expand the stage situation until it becomes an image of a timelessly recurrent experience. At the same time, and paradoxically, our subconscious awareness of the weight of convention behind the situation may awaken just enough disbelief to arouse a sense of pathos that men should so often have needed to create such an image.

Shakespeare employed the conventions of romance to different effect at different stages of his career, and it is my purpose in what follows to explore some aspects of his use of romance material. In the romantic comedies, comedy is more to the fore than in the last plays. That the conventions of romance are not incompatible with comedy he could have learned from many sources: from, for instance, his reading of *Daphnis and Chloe*, *Arcadia*, or Greene's *Menaphon*. And the presence of comic elements in works such as these may well have been an encouragement to him in view of the dramatic convention of the comic underplot. In *The Two Gentlemen of Verona* he added comedy to a serious romance story; the result, in my view, is not altogether satisfactory. In *The Comedy of Errors*—perhaps the most interesting of the early comedies in relation to the late plays—he romanticized a mainly comic source, Plautus' *Menaechmi*. This he complicated in a number of ways. Some of his alterations, especially the addition of twin servants—the Dromios—increase the possibilities of comic confusion. Others are clearly designed to redress the balance by giving greater emotional weight. These latter are derived from seeds found in Plautus with the addition of material probably taken from the story of *Apollonius of Tyre*. The twins' father, merely mentioned in *Menaechmi*, appears before us in *The Comedy of Errors*, and in a peculiarly poignant situation—he is about to have his head chopped off. The tale he tells is pure romance, involving the birth of two pairs of twins 'in the self-same inn' (Egeon admits by implication that it is surprising) and a ship-wreck much out of the ordinary. To be shipwrecked once might have been regarded as a normal enough misfortune in Elizabethan times; but that a family, having escaped together from shipwreck, should then be separated when the mast to which they were tied was 'splitted in the midst' by 'a mighty rock' might well have been regarded by a con-temporary Lady Bracknell as carelessness. Certainly it lifts this story out of sordid reality into the realms of romance. Opening in this way, Shakespeare prepares us for improbabilities such as the fact that two pairs of identical twins who share not only the same name but even, it seems, identical clothes should be chasing each other around Ephesus. He prepares us too for some of the other variations he is going to play on the Plautine farce, especially for the multiple reunions with which he is to end.

The influence of romance is felt in this play not only in the develop-ment of the clearly romantic elements implicit in the structure of *Menaechmi* but also in the modifications made in the treatment of that play's comic substance. The comedy remains, but is given added weight and humanity by the interweaving of more serious material. Some of this is to be linked with the romance aspects of the play only because of the capacity of romance to include a wide variety of material—one thinks for instance of the theme, explored in a seriously comic way, of the proper relationships of husband and wife. Another theme that runs through the play, and that is both related to this previous one and also more clearly appropriate in itself to romance, is that of family relationships in general, involving the separation of the brothers, the apparent estrangement between Adriana and her husband, and the reunion of father, mother, sons, and servants in the last scene.

Also characteristic of romance is the notion, frequently stated or implied, that the events in the world of the play are subject to forces other than those of normal cause and effect; that there is some magical reason for the errors of the action. This serves a useful dramatic purpose in diverting our attention from the central personages' failure to deduce the true reasons for their mishaps; it provides a comic heightening of some of the situations; furthermore, by arousing a sense of wonder and even of fear, it helps to keep us in touch with some of the drama's more serious issues—that there is indeed a mystery about the human personality; that we depend for our sense of identity very much upon the reactions of those around us; that if everything familiar to us is taken away we are deprived of something inside as well as outside us (an idea prominent in *King Lear*); and that, more specifically, separation is a form of bereavement—'partir c'est mourir un peu'.

Conversely, of course, reunion is a renewal of life; and in this play both the poignancy of separation and the joy of reunion are concentrated on—though not confined to—Egeon. He had been condemned to death on the principle of strict tit-for-tat justice; it is perhaps no mere chance that the character who effects the happy resolution is an abbess, an explicitly Christian figure who brings with her the softening influence of a mercy that seasons justice—a redemptive mercy replacing death by life.

The last scene, with its multiple reunions so characteristic of romance, is no mere untangling of a farcical knot. Egeon's emotion on being rejected by the man whom he believes to be the son he has tended from birth is given full and wholly serious expression, and stands as the high emotional point. The background of suffering that has been genuinely if economically presented, along with the background of anticipated joy in union stated in Antipholus of Syracuse's declarations of love for Luciana, gives depth and reality to the joyful climax. It is still a climax appropriate to a comedy; there is enough improbability about the Abbess to keep us on the cheerful side of pathos; but pathos there certainly is. It is a romantic climax; comedy is subsumed in joy, bewilderment in rapturous wonder, the wonder of a dream—'If I dream not, thou art Emilia'—'If this be not a dream I see and hear'. The play ends with images of birth; on a serious level in the Abbess's final lines:

> Thirty-three years have I but gone in travail
> Of you, my sons; and till this present hour
> My heavy burden ne'er delivered.
> The duke, my husband and my children both,
> And you the calendars of their nativity,

> Go to a gossips' feast, and go with me.
> After so long grief, such nativity![14]

and more lightly from Dromio, in the final couplet:

> We came into the world like brother and brother;
> And now let's go hand in hand, not one before another.

It is unnecessary to labour the point that rebirth is a prominent theme of the last plays.

The conventions of romantic love are only one element in romance literature. In *The Comedy of Errors* the romance of courtship is present only between Antipholus of Syracuse and Luciana. The love of husband and wife is of course important; but equally important as a driving force in most of the major characters is a non-sexual love; the love of father for son, brother for brother, mother for son. Love in this sense is a major value of the play. None of the characters can feel complete in himself as long as he is apart from those he loves (the theme is particularly appropriate in a play so much concerned with twins, about whose psychology Shakespeare had more reason than most of us to be concerned). This emphasis on love that extends far beyond the romance of courtship is responsible for much of the emotional richness of Shakespeare's romantic comedies, including perhaps the greatest, *Twelfth Night*.

In one respect the plot of *Twelfth Night* is very close to that of *The Comedy of Errors*: twins—brother and sister this time—have been separated by shipwreck. The separation is recent, and Viola's grief is keen because she thinks her brother is dead. In some ways she resembles Antipholus of Syracuse, but she seems to be of a more buoyant temperament; also she is forced into a more practical state of mind by the necessity to earn her living. During the course of the action she does not, so far as we are told, spend much time thinking of her brother. But the possibility of reunion is built into the play to a much greater extent than in *The Comedy of Errors*. There it is always latent; is indeed by all dramatic laws inevitable; but it is scarcely made explicit after the opening scene. In *Twelfth Night* on the other hand we are explicitly reminded of the separation several times during the action. At the end of Act III, Viola is permitted to reveal the sort of deductive intelligence denied to

[14] 'nativity', the Folio's reading, is usually—perhaps rightly—emended. Globe reads 'festivity', Foakes, 'felicity'.

the Antipholuses when, hearing Antonio mistake her for her brother, she says:

> Prove true, imagination, O, prove true,
> That I, dear brother, be now ta'en for you!

And:

> He named Sebastian: I my brother know
> Yet living in my glass; even such and so
> In favour was my brother, and he went
> Still in this fashion, colour, ornament,
> For him I imitate: O, if it prove,
> Tempests are kind and salt waves fresh in love.

(Here too Shakespeare builds in an excuse for the similarity of costume that is presumed but unexplained in the earlier play.) These are not extended passages, but they are prominent, partly because they are in soliloquy, and partly because they are in a higher style than the rest of the scene. (Anyone who saw Dorothy Tutin's Viola will remember the moving radiancy of renewed hope with which she delivered these lines.)

Her brother, Sebastian, is reflected to us largely through his friend Antonio, perhaps the most seriously drawn figure in the play. Antonio regards Sebastian with unmistakable depths of selfless devotion. When the young man apparently denies him, he breaks into generalized remarks on the deceit of appearances comparable with for instance Claudio's anguish on hearing that Hero is false, or Othello's false judgement on Desdemona:

> But O how vile an idol proves this god!
> Thou hast, Sebastian, done good feature shame.
> In nature there's no blemish but the mind;
> None can be call'd deform'd but the unkind:
> Virtue is beauty, but the beauteous evil
> Are empty trunks o'erflourished by the devil.
> (III. iv. 399)

It is Antonio who suffers most as a result of the confusion of identities. In defending himself to Orsino he stresses the selflessness of his love:

> for his sake
> Did I expose myself, pure for his love,
> Into the danger of this adverse town.

This outburst of Antonio's is functionally very similar to Egeon's in the last scene of *The Comedy of Errors*. Both reveal a depth of suffering that casts into higher relief the joy to come. The twins' forthcoming reunion is invested with heavy emotional significance. Those who look for *Twelfth Night*'s climax in the coming together of Viola and Orsino are disappointed. The climax, effected in true romance fashion by chance and time, lies not in the union of lovers but in the reunion of brother and sister—the triumph of pure love. The radiancy that this sheds provides the emotional solvent in which all obstacles to understanding and union are dissolved. The long scene of reunion strikes with all the wonder and rapture of an achieved impossibility. Across a stage crowded with people, many of them deeply affected by the reunion, brother and sister confront each other. Each believed the other was drowned; the truth comes like a slow dawn:

> SEBASTIAN: Do I stand there? I never had a brother;
>   Nor can there be that deity in my nature,
>   Of here and every where. I had a sister,
>   Whom the blind waves and surges have devour'd.
>   Of charity, what kin are you to me?
>   What countryman? what name? what parentage?
> VIOLA: Of Messaline: Sebastian was my father;
>   Such a Sebastian was my brother too,
>   So went he suited to his watery tomb:
>   If spirits can assume both form and suit
>   You come to fright us.
> SEBASTIAN: A spirit I am indeed;
>   But am in that dimension grossly clad
>   Which from the womb I did participate.
>   Were you a woman, as the rest goes even,
>   I should my tears let fall upon your cheek,
>   And say 'Thrice-welcome, drowned Viola!'
> VIOLA: My father had a mole upon his brow.
> SEBASTIAN: And so had mine.
> VIOLA: And died that day when Viola from her birth
>   Had number'd thirteen years.
> SEBASTIAN: O, that record is lively in my soul!
>   He finished indeed his mortal act
>   That day that made my sister thirteen years.
> VIOLA: If nothing lets to make us happy both
>   But this my masculine usurp'd attire,
>   Do not embrace me till each circumstance

> Of place, time, fortune, do cohere and jump
> That I am Viola. (V. i. 233)

The style is measured, grave, requiring an adjustment in tempo. As at a comparable point in *The Comedy of Errors*, there is a suggestion of the supernatural; but the spirit becomes flesh, and brings a benediction with it.

Academic critics rarely give much prominence to this passage;[15] its importance is much more likely to be recognized in the theatre. Virginia Woolf wrote of an Old Vic performance:

> Perhaps the most impressive effect in the play is achieved by the long pause which Sebastian and Viola make as they stand looking at each other in a silent ecstasy of recognition. The reader's eye may have slipped over that moment entirely. Here we are made to pause and think about it; and are reminded that Shakespeare wrote for the body and for the mind simultaneously.[16]

And Alan Downer, writing of a performance in which the play had been translated and adapted by Jean Anouilh, and in which one actress played both Viola and Sebastian, made a similar point:

> For four and a half acts the complex structure of *Twelfth Night* prepares the audience for the confrontation of the twins. Shakespeare rewards our patience with seventy lines of anagnorisis, a long and gratifying tribute to the comic view of life. It is a *necessary* scene, and Shakespeare does not cheat even when improbability might have tempted him to do so. To share in the triumph of the improbable is the true delight of *Twelfth Night*, but Anouilh will be tinkering.[17]

Properly played, the scene creates a vision of harmony and concord in which are celebrated many aspects of human love; and at the end Feste remains to remind us that the romance vision is only, though beautifully, a dream.

When we turn from Shakespeare's romantic comedies to his last plays, we find much similar material. There are, however, important

---

[15] Cf. 'the confusion of twins which entertained us for five acts of *The Comedy of Errors* appears now as little more than an adroit device to bring about a happy ending' (Harold Jenkins, 'Shakespeare's *Twelfth Night*', *The Rice Institute Pamphlet*, January 1959, p. 20).

[16] *The Death of the Moth* (1942; Penguin Books, 1961), p. 45.

[17] 'For Jesus' Sake Forbear', *Shakespeare Quarterly*, Spring 1962, p. 228.

changes of emphasis in the way it is treated. *The Winter's Tale* is perhaps best approached by way of its main source. Here, Shakespeare was working closely from a prose romance written a generation earlier—Robert Greene's *Pandosto* (1588). No single source of real importance has been found for *Pandosto*, though many have been proposed. There are many analogues, not necessarily because Greene knew or remembered any or all of those that have been put forward, but because he was a conventionally minded writer who picked up his material where he could find it, with no concern for originality. *Pandosto* is a fabric woven from the common stuff of romance literature; predominant in their influence upon it are the Greek romances.[18] The romance background to *Pandosto* is relevant to a consideration of *The Winter's Tale* because it may remind us of some of the overtones that the play would have aroused in its own time, but that are no longer audible nowadays.

Although *Pandosto* is crudely constructed and on the whole badly written, it was popular for a phenomenally long time. It had been reprinted four times by the time Shakespeare wrote his play, and went on being read and reprinted regularly for at least a hundred and fifty years. It seems to have appealed especially to a not very highly educated class of reader. In Shakespeare's lifetime for instance it was said that a typical chambermaid 'reads Greene's works over and over', and it is a girl of the same class who is shown reading it, a hundred and fifty years later, in Richardson's *Clarissa*. Probably no Elizabethan novel had as long a natural life as *Pandosto*.[19] Its popularity can be explained only on the assumption that its readers enjoyed its presentation of basic human situations in an undemanding manner. The same quality may well have recommended it to Shakespeare as a source. A fully realized work of art would have left him no room to work in. *Pandosto* is a collection of clichés, of the well-worn themes and stock situations of pastoral romance. Greene had done Shakespeare an initial service by organizing these stereotyped elements into a pattern. In taking them over Shakespeare was of course well aware of their unoriginal nature

[18] Wolff studies this influence in immense detail. He is somewhat inclined to attribute any parallel between the romances and *Pandosto* to direct influence, without consideration of other writings that exhibit the same features. But he demonstrates beyond question that *Pandosto* has much in common with these works.

[19] The scholars took over from the chambermaids in the middle of the eighteenth century; the last references to the book as popular reading coincide closely with the beginning of interest in it as a Shakespeare source.

and improbable aspects. During the play we are reminded of the old-fashioned nature of the story we are watching. By a sort of alienation technique Shakespeare draws our attention to the nature of the fiction. Time the chorus says he will

> make stale
> The glistering of this present, as my tale
> Now seems to it;

and within the play itself, especially towards the end when marvellous events crowd upon each other, we have such remarks as the comment upon Antigonus' death:

> Like an old tale still,

and Paulina's remark that the fact that Hermione is still alive would be 'hooted at like an old tale'. It appears not only that Shakespeare was fully aware of the unrealities of the story, but that he deliberately played upon the audience's awareness too, inviting them to recall similar situations—even perhaps their memories of the source story itself, and also the centuries of tradition that lie behind it.

Shakespeare's handling of *Pandosto* is characterized at once by extreme freedom and by a remarkable willingness to turn to account even minute details of the original. He both takes over the episodic structure and draws attention to it in the long speech of Time as chorus. This emphasis seems designed to stress the romantic nature of the tale: in the non-dramatic romances, time is commonly the ally of chance and fortune in bringing about the changes of the actions. Time's speech is pivotal to the play. Shakespeare may have got the idea for it from Greene's subtitle, which is *The Triumph of Time*; and Greene's title-page bears the tag 'temporis filia veritas'. Certainly Shakespeare makes of the time element a poetic complex that helps in giving the play a richness of harmony without parallel in the novel. Showing how human beings can achieve at least the illusion of having triumphed over time, Shakespeare creates that illusion for us.

Leontes' comparatively unmotivated jealousy may be thought of as an intensification of the play's romance characteristics—motivation is not the strong point of most romancers; but the first scene is less than typical in emotional intensity that it generates. Leontes' sexual obsession is portrayed as a self-consuming, almost fanatical state of mind; impervious to suggestion, completely incapable of admitting the

E

possibility of error. This makes it appropriate that Shakespeare should have changed the business of the oracle. In Greene, the Queen asks her husband to send to the oracle, for the sake of their child. In the play Leontes sends of his own accord, merely to help to convince others of the truth of his suspicions:

> Though I am satisfied and need no more
> Than what I know, yet shall the oracle
> Give rest to the minds of others, such as he
> Whose ignorant credulity will not
> Come up to the truth. (II. i. 189)

Whereas Pandosto penitently accepts the oracle's pronouncement, Leontes at first denies it, pursuing his wilful course to the point of blasphemy:

> There is no truth at all i' the oracle:
> The sessions shall proceed: this is mere falsehood.
> (III. ii. 141)

Immediately there arrives the report of his son's death from an illness that Leontes had earlier attributed to shame at hearing of Hermione's disgrace—which was as if Leontes blamed himself. The news strikes home. 'Apollo's angry;' he says, 'and the heavens themselves Do strike at my injustice.' Thus Shakespeare greatly increases Leontes' implied responsibility for his son's death.

This emphasis on personal responsibility diminishes to some extent the part played in the action by those typical romance agents, chance, fate, fortune, etc. Shakespeare is humanizing his source, giving it greater relevance to normal life, making it a story of human beings rather than of puppets. To this extent the play is less of a romance than *Pandosto*. Shakespeare makes the baby Perdita's fate, too, less dependent on chance than in Greene, where she is simply left floating. Antigonus sails with the baby; we see him depositing her on the shore of Bohemia. But all evidence of where the baby is must be destroyed as otherwise it would be possible for the penitent Leontes to find his daughter. This no doubt is at least partly responsible for Shakespeare's introduction of the notorious bear that chases and devours Antigonus, and also for the less spectacular deaths of the sailors on his boat.

Shakespeare plays down too the element of chance in the matter of the lovers' return to Leontes' court. In *Pandosto* they are intent simply on getting away from the land ruled by the prince's father, who disapproves of their match; it is only because of a typical romance shipwreck that they land in Pandosto's country. In the play on the other hand the journey is carefully planned by Camillo, who suggests to Florizel that he may well be very welcome in Sicily, and says (in words that sound like a criticism of the lack of planning in *Pandosto*) that this is

> A course more promising
> Than a wild dedication of yourselves
> To unpath'd waters, undream'd shores.
> (IV. iv. 576)

In such ways does Shakespeare give greater credibility to his original. 'There is a strong web of realism running through the warp of the romance.' [20] But 'realism' is an even more dangerous word than 'romance'. It could be argued that Shakespeare's love scenes are more realistic than Greene's. In another sense they are far more romantic; they are suffused by a passion that is real in a poetic, not an everyday, sense. Certainly the sheep-shearing scenes represent an almost total transformation of the original. Greene's lovers are largely preoccupied by social considerations: the prince constantly astounded that he can feel anything remotely resembling affection for a lowly shepherdess, the girl equally shocked by her presumption in loving a prince. In Shakespeare of course all is on a much higher plane; and it is all much more deeply related to the main plot. It is significant for instance that Florizel's admiration finds expression in a sense of the timelessness of Perdita's actions:

> When you speak, sweet,
> I'ld have you do it ever; when you sing,
> I'ld have you buy and sell so, so give alms,
> Pray so; and, for the ordering your affairs,
> To sing them too: when you do dance, I wish you
> A wave o' the sea, that you might ever do
> Nothing but that; move still, still so,
> And own no other function.   (IV. iv. 136)

We remember Polixenes' description of the time when he and Leontes, the fathers of this pair, were 'Two lads that thought there was no more behind But such a day to-morrow as to-day, And to be boy eternal.' The lines look forward too to the illusion created by the last scene, that

[20] *The Winter's Tale*, ed. Pafford, Introduction, p. lxvi.

time the conqueror has been conquered: an illusion created partly by the presence of this same Perdita.

In the final episodes of Greene's novel, Pandosto is no different from his earlier self. He is violent and lustful; he throws the fugitives into prison and condemns all but the young prince to death. Leontes however is still penitent and intensely conscious of the wrong he did his wife. With terrible concentration he remembers her virtues and her beauty. This constancy of penitence may be regarded as a change in the direction of romance; certainly it is in line with, for instance, the inconsolable grief displayed by Pericles and by Posthumus. And it leads to the most important departures from the source. Greene has a tacked-on tragic ending—Pandosto, suddenly smitten once more with repentance, kills himself. Leontes of course remains alive, and, more important still, is reunited with his wife in the amazing statue scene, surely one of the most daring in Shakespeare. Here Shakespeare invests the familiar motifs of reunion and apparent resurrection with exceptional poetic and dramatic force. The scene is essentially of the theatre; the long wait before the statue moves is unfailing in its hold upon audiences. And Leontes' realization that Hermione lives, when art melts into nature, is one of those moments of silence in which in a sense Shakespeare leaves everything to the actor, yet in another sense has done everything for him. 'Silence', says Claudio, 'is the perfect'st herald of joy'; and here (as in the *Alcestis*) husband and wife do not address each other. But there must be (as the First Gentleman says of the reunion of Leontes and Camillo) 'speech in their dumbness, language in their very gesture'. If one considered the scene in purely literary terms it might seem perfunctory, especially when Hermione tells Perdita that she has preserved herself in order to see whether the oracle was right in suggesting that Perdita might be alive (this does not suggest any great affection for Leontes). But there is no danger of this in the theatre, at any rate when Leontes is performed with the intensity with which, according to Helena Faucit, Macready played the scene:

> At first he stood speechless, as if turned to stone; his face with an awe-struck look upon it. . . . Thus absorbed in wonder, he remained until Paulina said, 'Nay, present your hand.' Tremblingly he advanced, and touched gently the hand held out to him. Then, what a cry came with, 'O, she's warm!' It is impossible to describe Mr Macready here. He was Leontes' very self! His passionate joy at finding Hermione really alive seemed beyond control. Now he was

prostrate at her feet, then enfolding her in his arms. I had a slight veil or covering over my head and neck, supposed to make the statue look older. This fell off in an instant. The hair, which came unbound, and fell on my shoulders, was reverently kissed and caressed. The whole change was so sudden, so overwhelming, that I suppose I cried out hysterically, for he whispered to me, 'Don't be frightened, my child! don't be frightened! Control yourself!' All this went on during a tumult of applause that sounded like a storm of hail. . . . It was such a comfort to me, as well as true to natural feeling, that Shakespeare gives Hermione no words to say to Leontes, but leaves her to assure him of her joy and forgiveness by look and manner only.[21]

It is appropriate to the suffering we have witnessed during the play that there should be a strongly elegiac tone here. Shakespeare's changes of his source have increased the marvellous—or the miraculous. There is joy in the scene; but it is pregnant with sorrow:

> In the very temple of delight
> Veil'd melancholy has her sovran shrine.

Deep emotions have been stirred, and will not be satisfied by a conventionally cheerful ending. In the romantic comedies we are accustomed to final scenes that stress the restoration of the social order, of which the dance or feast is an appropriate symbol. In *The Winter's Tale* there are no macrocosmic implications. Emphasis is placed not on the group but on individuals whose suffering we have closely followed. The ending is not a vision of ultimate unity, as that of *Cymbeline* might be considered. There is sobriety as Leontes in his closing lines suggests how each may heal the wounds 'Perform'd in this wide gap of time since first | We were dissever'd'. It is not in fact a high romantic climax. The emphasis is not on the lovers, but on the older generation. We are reminded that Antigonus is dead, that Leontes has 'in vain said many A prayer upon' Hermione's grave, and that he needs pardon from both Polixenes and Hermione. The individuals must salvage what they can.

A late seventeenth-century edition of *Pandosto* is adorned with a crude woodcut illustrative of the story; one of the things represented is a cradle floating upon what appears to be a river but is presumably intended for the sea. It is a fitting emblem of the helplessness of humanity often implied in romance literature. Sometimes the forces against

[21] *On Some of Shakespeare's Female Characters*, New and Enlarged Edition (1891), pp. 389–90.

which mankind is helpless are external, sometimes internal. The baby Perdita is helpless in the face of her father's unreasonable passion; so is her mother; and so in a sense is Leontes himself—he is swept away by jealousy as a child might be swept away by the ocean. And the end of the play, focusing upon a few figures in their newly poised adjustments to each other, stresses the importance of human relationships as bulwarks against the forces of disaster. In his adaptation of *Pandosto* Shakespeare has produced a work that is far more powerful as a human document. He has done so not by denying the romance elements in Greene's book but by readjusting them—sometimes adding to them, sometimes toning them down with a modified realism, and always investing them with a poetic rather than a mundane reality.

That *The Tempest* employs basic romance material requires little demonstration. It begins with a shipwreck; Prospero and Miranda had themselves been cast up on this island after being exposed to wind and waves like the heroine of *Pandosto*; in the past Prospero had been separated from his brother; now Alonso is separated from his son and believes him dead; Miranda and Ferdinand are the handsome hero and pure heroine typical of romance; the supernatural plays its part; an air of deliberate unreality pervades the play; the story works towards reunion, reconciliation, and the happy conclusion of the love affair. But in form the play is very different from a typical romance. Shakespeare has chosen to begin his story at the end. The action is concentrated into a small space and a few hours. The sea-voyages and land-travels of *Pericles*, *Cymbeline*, and *The Winter's Tale* here can only be told in retrospect, or at most symbolized by the wanderings of the shipwrecked men around the island. Instead of being moved from a present which in the later acts becomes the past, we are throughout required to be conscious of the past in the present. The 'wide gap' of time in which we imagined the coming to maturity of Marina and Perdita has here become 'the dark backward and abysm of time' into which Miranda gazes with her father. The method is closer to that of *The Comedy of Errors* than to that of the other last plays; but Prospero is the centre of this play, whereas Egeon is present only in the framework of the earlier one. The tension that results from this combination of romantic material with 'classical' form helps to give this play its peculiar dynamic. The characters, as well as the audience, are often bidden to remember the past; our minds move with theirs. The result is perhaps, paradoxically enough, a more consistent and deeper consciousness of the effects of time than in plays in which a wider time-span is directly presented.

By sacrificing the large dimensions of space and time common in romance, Shakespeare clearly gains much in concentration. Nevertheless, it is a sacrifice. The romancer, typically writing a story in which little attention is paid to the sequence of cause and effect, depends a good deal upon time, and also chance or fortune (sometimes conceived of as an active god-figure) in order to render plausible those turns of the action or changes of character for which no explanation is given. In *Cymbeline*, for instance, Iachimo's sudden last-act penitence goes psychologically uninvestigated but is the more easily accepted in that we last saw him some time ago and in a different country. The story of *The Tempest* demands similar changes. Alonso has to be shown in penitence for his usurpation; and the penitence has to come about as the direct result of his experiences on the island. Shakespeare can (and to some extent does) hint that the Alonso we see at the beginning of the action is not as objectionable as he was twelve years before, but the actual process of conversion has to take place within the brief time-span of the play. This is made convincing primarily by being made the result of a conscious purpose. In a normal romance story, chance would have caused the shipwreck that puts Prospero's enemies at his mercy. In this play, though fortune plays her part (and Shakespeare is most subtle in his constant shifting of responsibility), it is Prospero himself who by his 'art' brings about the shipwreck. He is partly dependent on fortune, partly master of it. In a sense he is the 'god of this great vast' on whom Pericles calls. He has superhuman power, yet remains human. He is both god and man, a worker of miracles who finally accepts the full burden of humanity. At times it is difficult to distinguish him from a supernatural controlling force. It is partly by creating the wholly superhuman Ariel to act as the semi-independent agent of Prospero's will that Shakespeare has been able to keep Prospero human—perhaps the most remarkable technical feat of the play.

As the controlling agent of the play in which he has his being, Prospero himself resembles the narrator of a romance story. This is true not merely of the second scene, in which he tells Miranda of her childhood (with results, it would seem, resembling those of many romancers) but also of the methods by which he exercises his influence. Frequently and deliberately he tries to create a sense of awe, mystery, and wonder in the minds of those he is trying to influence. His use—generally through Ariel—of music is part of this. So is Ariel's tricksiness, such as his appearance to the mariners causing them to feel 'a fever of the mad', and the living drollery that reminds Gonzalo of the romantic travellers' tales he heard in boyhood. It is after the wonder induced by the appearance of the 'strange shapes bringing in a banquet' that Ariel makes his great speech of accusation against the courtiers; and in the last scene Prospero remarks:

> I perceive, these lords
> At this encounter do so much admire
> That they devour their reason and scarce think
> Their eyes do offices of truth, their words
> Are natural breath: but, howsoe'er you have
> Been justled from your senses, know for certain
> That I am Prospero.

To justle them from their senses has been part of his aim; but not all are responsive to this—just as Antonio and Sebastian had not responded to Ariel's sleep-inducing music. The cynical pair deny the wonder expressed by the perhaps over-credulous Gonzalo (e.g. II. i. *passim*).

If Prospero resembles a spinner of romance tales, his daughter is even more clearly the ideal audience for such tales. Belarius (in *Cymbeline*) describes such a person:

> When on my three-foot stool I sit and tell
> The warlike feats I have done, his spirits fly out
> Into my story: say 'Thus mine enemy fell,
> And thus I set my foot on's neck;' even then
> The princely blood flows in his cheek, he sweats,
> Strains his young nerves and puts himself in posture
> That acts my words.   (III. iii. 89)

Miranda too has all the open-mindedness, the willingness to be impressed, the capacity for wonder, that a story-teller could desire. She is all sympathy and eagerness to believe the best:

> O, I have suffered
> With those that I saw suffer: a brave vessel,
> Who had, no doubt, some noble creature in her,
> Dash'd all to pieces.   (I. ii. 5)

Her first sight of Ferdinand arouses similar awe:

> I might call him
> A thing divine, for nothing natural
> I ever saw so noble.   (I. ii. 417)

And the climax comes as Miranda looks up from her game of chess and sees the assembled group:

> O, wonder!
> How many goodly creatures are there here!
> How beauteous mankind is! O brave new world,
> That has such people in't!   (V. i. 181)

By this time in the play we know a number of these people rather well, and Miranda's innocence has a deep pathos, all the more pointed by Prospero's quiet comment, ''Tis new to thee'. But though Prospero's words provide an implied criticism of Miranda's attitude, they do nothing to destroy it. It is one of Shakespeare's greatest achievements that he can show the coexistence of opposed attitudes, making us aware of the tension between them but not forcing us to decide in favour of one or the other. Miranda's naïve innocence and Prospero's mature wisdom are both part of the truth; to counterpoint one against the other is to create a harmony that more than doubles the effect of each alone.[22]

Another quality typical of romance that Shakespeare might appear to have sacrificed by his decision to cast his play in an approximation to classical form is discursiveness: the provision of that 'variety of mirth and pastime' that Elizabethan romancers were so fond of advertising in their wares. But in fact he manages to cram a remarkable amount of material into this, the second shortest of his plays. He does so not by the multiplication of incident, the copiousness, the sheer length of many of his predecessors, but rather by an extraordinary multiplicity of suggestiveness—his power of creating a structure which looks different from every angle—his myriad-mindedness, as Coleridge put it. The enchanted island reverberates with sounds hinting at tunes that never appear fully formed. We can follow one strand through the work, but only by shutting our ears to the others; what we gain in line we lose in

[22] Cf. F. R. Leavis: 'Shakespeare's power to present acceptingly and movingly the unironical vision (for us given in Miranda and Ferdinand) goes with his power to contemplate the irony at the same time' ('The Criticism of Shakespeare's Late Plays: A Caveat', in *The Common Pursuit* (1952; Peregrine Books, 1962). p. 180).

depth. It is this of course that has made the play so happy a hunting ground for the symbol-seekers. 'Any set of symbols moved close to this play', wrote Mark van Doren, 'lights up as in an electric field.' [23] Prospero has frequently been seen as a self-projection of the author; the notion has been handled sensibly and persuasively by some, less so by others. Most critics find themselves driven to speak of Prospero in terms other than those in which Shakespeare has written of him. For some he is God; for others, the imagination. One sees him as Hymen or a masque-presenter; another as 'the genius of poetry'; yet another as both 'a close replica of Christ' and 'a matured and fully self-conscious embodiment of those moments of fifth-act transcendental speculation to which earlier tragic heroes, including Macbeth, were unwillingly forced'.[24]

Criticism of this play has its excesses; but we must recognize that the variety of available interpretations is the result of its extraordinary suggestiveness. The play invites consideration on different levels. Partly this comes from the resonance of the verse, which often takes us far beyond the immediate situation. Intimately connected is the fact that the characters lack the strong individuality of some—though by no means all—leading figures of the great tragedies. Depth of characterization is not a normal feature of romance. Generally this is because the emphasis is on event. The figures of the story are conventionalized. What happens to them is more important than what they are. In *The Tempest* there is less emphasis on event; there is indeed less event; but the characters also are representative rather than individual. They are comparatively little distinguished by variety of style. Miranda is not a Viola, a Rosalind, or an Imogen. But though she may lack these girls' vibrantly immediate impact, she gains in representativeness. Being less of a particular time and place, she becomes more of all time and everywhere. In this context, actions the more easily take on a symbolical value. It is not necessary to go outside the play to see Ferdinand's log-carrying as an expression of a theme that crops up at many points. On a realistic level, it is no hardship for a healthy young man to spend a few hours carrying firewood; but any hint of this attitude in performance is ruinous. Ferdinand's task must appear as one of the complex

[23] *Shakespeare* (1941), p. 323.

[24] Enid Welsford, *The Court Masque* (Cambridge, 1927), p. 339. D. G. James, *Scepticism and Poetry* (1937), p. 240. G. Wilson Knight, 'The Shakespearian Superman', *The Crown of Life* (1947, etc.), p. 208.

of actions and statements connected with the idea of control; a complex that begins in the first scene where the voyaging noblemen are seen powerless against the force of (as it seems) nature; which is further adumbrated in Prospero's control over nature, over Ariel, and over Caliban; in Caliban's failure to achieve self-control; in the falsely based power that Stephano and Trinculo achieve over Caliban; in their joint attempt to overcome Prospero's authority, which parallels Sebastian's and Antonio's plot to kill Alonso, which itself parallels Antonio's and Alonso's earlier usurpation of Prospero; in Prospero's ability to conjure up the masque, and in the explicit themes of the masque itself, which are clearly related to the self-control that Prospero regards as so important in his future son-in-law; and finally in Prospero's ultimate renunciation of power. By a variety of juxtapositions, hints, and poetic devices, Shakespeare makes his romance story a carrier of what might be regarded as a scheme of ideas on a philosophical topic.

And he even introduces contemporary matters. It is not fanciful to see in the play a whole set of correspondences to what for its original audience was a burning question of the day—the matter of colonization; it is no accident that among the few accepted minor sources are pamphlets on voyaging. There is little explicit reference to the topic; but there is enough for us to be sure that it was present in Shakespeare's consciousness. Caliban complains against Prospero's enslavement of him; and there is a kind of justice in his complaint. We are shown the totally irreconcilable situation that arises when civilizations clash. It is parallel to the situation of Shylock and Portia; and though we cannot but feel that Shylock and Caliban must be overcome, yet we feel too something of the anguish involved in a complex moral impasse.

While the unreality of *The Tempest* contributes towards the play's high suggestive power, it would be false to suggest that the total effect is unreal. The first scene is in prose so vivid and colloquial that with a few changes it could stand in a television script. But the opening lines of the next scene suspend reality as we learn that the storm was the effect of Prospero's art, and for the remainder of the play the alternation and balance between the palpably unreal and the illusion of reality is maintained. The romance is toughened by a strain of anti-romance. The unrealistic idealism of Gonzalo is countered by the callous cynicism of Antonio and Sebastian—just as, for instance, Autolycus adds astringency to the pastoral scenes of *The Winter's Tale*. The virtue of Ferdinand and Miranda is not taken for granted; it is thrown into relief by what we know of Caliban, by his suggestions that Stephano should make Miranda his queen, and by the care with which Prospero guards the lovers' virtue. Even Prospero's own virtue is not without its strains. It is easy to lay too much emphasis on the scene in which Ariel recommends him to have mercy on his enemies; the style does not suggest severe internal struggle. Nevertheless, we are reminded that he might have taken vengeance, that the travellers are in fact his enemies. He does not bear his responsibilities lightly; he is one of Shakespeare's worried rulers, for whom the burden of power is greater than the rewards.

In ways such as these the vicissitudes commonly undergone by inhabitants of the world of romance come to be seen, not so much as random happenings that they survive by the help of fortune, as events designed to test and, during the course of the action, to define them. The play has a moral seriousness uncommon in most romance literature —though least uncommon, perhaps, in Shakespeare's greatest immediate predecessors, Sidney and Spenser. *The Tempest* is a romance containing a built-in criticism of romance; not a rejection of it, but an appreciation both of its glories and of its limitations. Romance is associated with all that brings man nearer to Ariel than to Caliban. Responsiveness to nature and to art, the capacity for wonder, the ability to sympathize with those that suffer, the desire to shape experience in accordance with an imaginative and moral vision, the value of an attitude to life that denies cynicism even to the extent of creating a somewhat naïve credulity such as Gonzalo's—all these are included. When art guides nature, when the civilizing forces of self-control are dominant, then Gonzalo's vision may be realized—a vision that looks forward to the masque:

> Earth's increase, foison plenty,
> Barns and garners never empty,
> Vines with clustering bunches growing,
> Plants with godly burthen bowing;
> Spring come to you at the farthest
> In the very end of harvest!
> Scarcity and want shall shun you;
> Ceres' blessing so is on you.
>
> (IV. i. 110)

It is indeed 'a most majestic vision', and it is fitting that it should be celebrated in the form of a masque-like performance enacted by the spirits over whom Prospero has power. This was the great age of the masque—nothing could have been more suitable as an image of the results that man can achieve by the exercise of mind and imagination. The masque was at once a symbol of power and wealth—frequently used as such in the Jacobean game of power politics—and also of the highest achievements of civilization, in which the arts of music, dancing, painting, acting, and poetry combined in entertainments whose splendour was enhanced by their folly. Many thousands of pounds were lavished upon a single evening's entertainment by those who could not command unpaid spirits to enact their fancies. Thus the masque was an apt symbol too of the vanity of human greatness. The glittering bubble is easily pricked. The visions of a Prospero are at the mercy of the Calibans of this world. Power that can create can also destroy, and so, when Prospero learns of the evil being plotted against him, the vision vanishes, leaving not a rack behind. Prospero's famous reaction is one of acceptance rather than mourning. Though he is momentarily angered, he controls himself and consoles Ferdinand. The dream is recognized for what it is, but allowed the reality that belongs even to a dream—or to any other product of the imagination—a play, poem, or romance.

The Tempest takes the familiar material of romance but adopts to it an attitude firmly though sympathetically judicious. The creations of the fancy are subjected to the scrutiny of the imagination; and they do not emerge unscathed. The ending thus disappoints those who ask for a full romantic climax. It is true that Prospero's forgiveness, though nominally extended to all, lacks warmth at any rate when he speaks to his brother Antonio:

> For you, most wicked sir, whom to call brother
> Would even infect my mouth, I do forgive
> Thy rankest fault.   (V. i. 130)

But perhaps we should have the right to be disappointed by this only if Prospero had been presented as wholly superhuman. Since Antonio is not shown as penitent, it is not easy to see why Prospero should be expected so soon to show any warmth towards the man who had behaved to him somewhat as Macbeth had to Duncan. *The Tempest* is austere, and its final moments are muted; but it is not harsh in its total effect. Antonio's impenitence is balanced by Alonso's contrition; Prospero's world-weary emotional exhaustion by Gonzalo's ebullient recognition of the good that has come out of these events and also, in the younger generation, by the satisfactory conclusion of the love affair of Ferdinand and Miranda. If Caliban remains in bondage, he is at least temporarily the wiser for his folly; and after Prospero has taken care to ensure that the royal party will have 'calm seas, auspicious gales And sail so expeditious that shall catch Your royal fleet far off', Ariel is finally freed to the elements. One might even see a touch of humour in this reversal of the play's opening situation.

It would seem then that though the two 'last plays' on which I have concentrated make more use of the conventions of romance literature than do some of the romantic comedies, their total effect is by no means unqualifiedly romantic. In discussing romantic aspects of earlier plays I have had to omit much. These plays are of course more comic than the romances; but they are also more romantic, in the sense that their attitude towards the conventions of romance is less critical. Feste may cast his shadow over the bridal couples at the end of *Twelfth Night*, and Jaques has his sardonic contribution to make to *As You Like It*; but the mature Leontes, Hermione, and Prospero need no external safeguards against illusion; and the young lovers in both *The Winter's Tale* and *The Tempest* are surrounded by older and wiser friends and relatives. The world of romance is both tested against reality and itself shown to be a part of reality. The realization of the romance vision has involved suffering, self-discipline, even death. There is here none of the irresponsibility with which romance literature is often charged. But neither is there any of that portentousness with which it is only too easy to invest these plays. They are entertainments; that is to say, the response they demand is primarily imaginative.

The mood most characteristic of Shakespeare's later handling of romance material is perhaps one that fuses extremes of emotion. It can be felt in plays that are not predominantly romantic—in Cordelia's 'smiles and tears' on hearing news of her father, in Menenius' 'I could weep And I could laugh' when he welcomes home the victorious Coriolanus. In the romances, Pericles has to call on Helicanus to 'Give me a gash . . . Lest this great sea of joys rushing upon me O'erbear the shores of my mortality'; when Leontes and Polixenes were reunited, 'their joy waded in tears'; and every third thought of Prospero, his purpose accomplished, will be his grave. But more important than such formulations is the pervasiveness of this mood in the climaxes. These plays suggest a Shakespeare who has been able with clear eyes to contemplate extremes of imaginative experience. At the same time, each play has its own uniqueness; there is great variety within each, and within the romances as a group. Nothing is more indicative of the total control that Shakespeare maintained over his inherited material.

Note

First Editions. For *The Tempest* see the note to Chapter VIII. *Pericles* was entered in the Stationers' Register on 20 May, 1608, and published in Quarto editions twice during the year; Quarto editions followed in 1611, 1619, 1630, and 1635. The play was omitted from the First Folio of 1623 but included in the Third Folio of 1664. *The Winter's Tale* was entered in the Stationers' Register on 8 November, 1623, and first published in the First Folio.

Modern editions. *Pericles* was edited by J. C. Maxwell and J. Dover Wilson in the New Cambridge Shakespeare (1956), and by F. D. Hoeniger in the New Arden edition (1963). *The Winter's Tale* was edited by Sir A. T. Quiller-Couch and J. Dover Wilson in the New Cambridge Shakespeare (1931), and by J. H. P. Pafford in the New Arden edition (1963). Quotations from Shakespeare's plays in the following chapter are taken from the Folio text, and in the case of *Pericles* from Q1.

Scholarship and Criticism. Two chapters, on 'Shakespeare's Hand in *Pericles*' and '*Pericles*' are contained in K. Muir's *Shakespeare as Collaborator* (1960). K. Muir has also edited the related narrative, George Wilkins, *The Painful Adventures of Pericles, Prince of Tyre* (Liverpool University Press, 1956). *Shakespeare Survey* 11 (1958) was devoted to the theme of the last plays, and contains a retrospect review of modern criticism by Philip Edwards, an article on 'The Structure of the Last Plays' by Clifford Leech, and one on 'Six Points of Stage-Craft in *The Winter's Tale*' by Nevill Coghill. The mode of discussion initiated in Francis Berry's *Poets' Grammar* (1958) is relevant for the following chapter, which is included in the author's *The Shakespeare Inset* (1965).

IV

Word and Picture in the Final Plays

FRANCIS BERRY

★

In this chapter there will be an attempt to apply three pairs—each pair posing an opposition—of related concepts to Shakespeare's Final Plays in the hope that the application might be fruitful when these plays are considered as entities moving in time and *space*—which is exactly what they are during actual performance on the stage.

The first pair is usually referred to painting, though the reference could just as well be to a natural scene or, as we shall urge, to a theatrical scene. The terms defining this opposition are *foreground* and *background*, expressing nearness as against far-ness, of 'here' as against 'there'. Since the terms 'foreground' and 'background' are opposites, they assume an intermediate 'middle-ground', they assume the recognition of degrees of approach and recession, of varying planes in space, and the possibility of rendering these planes in pictorial art according to the laws of perspective. In the theatre there is likewise a 'down-stage' as opposed to an 'up-stage' (and there are the in-between planes), a nearness or a far-ness with respect to the audience. In the texts of Shakespeare's plays the movement of characters within the continuum foreground/background is everywhere presumed so that when, for example, in *Hamlet*, Gertrude says 'But look where sadly the poor wretch comes', it is likely that she is not on a stage-level with Hamlet as he enters, that she is likely to say this relatively down-stage on espying Hamlet entering relatively up-stage, and that she and Claudius withdraw up-stage before Hamlet encounters Polonius in the 'foreground'. In the texts such movement is presumed and, in the conditions of performing these texts in the theatre, a producer has constantly to mind these perspectives.[1] Thus in *The Winter's Tale* (I. ii) Leontes almost

[1] In this chapter the modern producer's terms 'up-stage' and 'down-stage' are used in default of our knowledge of the Elizabethan producer's standard

certainly has to watch from a position in depth (that he can only watch, not hear, precipitates the tragedy) the conversation of Hermione and Polixenes. Leontes, 'here' (foreground or down-stage), they 'there' (background or up-stage)—or *vice versa* whether removed from the audience, or in propinquity to the audience, Leontes observes those two 'paddling palms' *there*.

The first pair of concepts has to do with space, with pictorial composition: a half, or, if these things cannot be measured, a great part of any Shakespeare play during actual performance is 'pictorial'.

The second pair has to do with language. Just as the eye can realize nearness as opposed to far-ness in space, can distinguish here from there, advance or recession, in picture or in natural landscape, so grammatical inflexions distinguish nearness from far-ness, 'now' from 'then', advance or recession, not in space, but in time. The terms are: the 'present' as opposed to the 'past' tense. But as in painting or in stagecraft, degrees of distance from the viewer in the continuum of space are recognized by the term 'middle-ground' (or 'centre-stage'), denoting intermediacy between 'foreground' and 'background', 'down-stage' and 'up-stage', so the temporal scale is recognized. The 'past' stretches back, perhaps infinitely: very well, the language can distinguish degrees of temporal recession. Behind the 'now' of actions being presently and visibly performed are the actions which are completed or 'perfect' and, behind these, are actions performed yet more remotely in the past and these are expressed by the 'past'—or 'plu'-perfect tense. Clearly there can be correspondence or agreement between the space-time 'here/now' (foreground-present), on the one hand and the space-time 'there/then' (background-past perfect) on the other; but, intermediate between these, a 'middle-ground' (neither really here and now nor there and then) can correspond with the simple past tense.

The third pair has also, indeed, to do with language, but is less obviously concerned with language than with literary forms, or kinds. The opposition is the grand one between 'narrative' and 'drama'. They are opposed in that the narrative is tackled in the perfect (and past-

---

equivalents. In the Elizabethan public theatre, the existence of a tarras, or upper stage, meant that there was another dimension—the vertical—forming part of the pictorial composition. But this dimension is certainly presumed in only some of Shakespeare's texts, in others doubtfully, and in others not at all.

perfect) tense. The story-teller employs the third-person pronouns 'he' or 'she' or 'they'; he takes it for granted that, even if 'he' and 'she' are now happily living 'ever after', his persons' actions have been perfected (actions producing this abiding felicity), perhaps long perfected, before his telling. It is the case of 'once upon a time', of a 'then' and a 'there': 'Once upon a time there was a man, and his name was Leir, and he had three daughters. . . .' Opposed to the narrative form is the dramatic form. The dramatist shows the minute-by-minute unfolding present. The audience hears *and* sees it happening. The persons—Leir, his three daughters—come forward, here and now, to speak, each in his own person, each as 'I'. Here is the first person singular (or plural, if Goneril and Regan collude), the person here and now, choosing and embarking on actions with results of which they *are* ignorant, and which will not be perfect (in the grammatical sense) until the end of the fifth act. In the case of the narrative we know what happened, we know at least that the action is ended before the narrator reports, and are offended if the story-teller deviates from the sanctioned, from history. In the case of the drama we live in suspense at each showing of Lear and his three daughters. In drama it is still open for them to choose differently and perhaps we hope that they will; in narrative they couldn't have. In other words, the narrative mode generally agrees with the past tense (of our second pair of terms) and the background (of the first pair); the dramatic generally agrees with the present tense and the foreground. But only generally: for in Shakespeare, as in other authors, the general alignment of foreground (here) and present tense (now) of the drama, as opposed to background (there) and past tense (then) of the narrative, can break down, and does break down as one or other member of an alignment is transposed to the other side. In no phase of Shakespeare's career does this happen so often as in the Final Plays. To close this section with a single example. In *The Tempest* (I. i), Prospero *is* narrating to his daughter, Miranda, now aged about fifteen, a series of events which took place 'there' (Milan) and 'then' (in 'the dark backward and abysm of time') twelve years ago. The foreground picture, as the audience sees it, during performance, is Prospero's island, the time—now; but, as the narrative advances, Prospero backs out of his 'present', 'recedes', and he and both the audiences (the stage-audience, Miranda, and the audience in the theatre) recede with him as that past is invoked. This is a simple instance of a non-coherence between what the audience in the theatre sees (the characters on the island now) and what they listen to (about those characters long ago and elsewhere).

★　　　★　　　★

It will be clear that Hamlet's precept to the player to 'Sute the Action to the Word, the Word to the Action' so that the playing will show 'the verie Age and Bodie of the Time, his forme and pressure'— whether either the 'very age and body of the time' of the presentation, or of the lives of the characters, is meant—admits of exceptions as soon as remembered or past actions take the 'foreground' in place of the present business with its instantaneous accompanying gesture. The Final Plays of Shakespeare are charged with such exceptions because they are laden with memories, the memories of senior characters like Pericles, Leontes, Polixenes, Prospero. These memories can be drawn from the 'dark backward' of a time long anterior to the events now to be shown on the stage, and that 'past', that 'background', variously overcast, will now exercise its power on the present foreground action. Behind *The Winter's Tale* and *The Tempest* are phantom plots which Shakespeare did not dramatize but which he narrated (indeed the drama of the earlier part of *The Winter's Tale* has the narrative begun by Polixenes' 'We were as twyn'd Lambs . . .' behind it, and the latter part has Time's narrative behind it), and narrated to such purpose that, during their rendering, the 'there-then' masks, if not eclipses, the 'here-now'. The remote in time and space, parodoxically, becomes closer than the immediate in time and space.

It might be objected that the Histories are likewise always harking back, for is not Henry IV continually harassed by the memory of 'gentle Richard'? But history is different from private memory and, in the case of *Henry IV*, the memory only produces an intention—to go on a crusade—an intention not realized within or without the play; the Histories provide scant satisfaction of the private wishes of characters and poetic justice is subordinate to the facts of English history. In the Tragedies memories are short—Lady Macbeth's memory of 'giving suck' is used only to presently incite and, in the case of *Lear*, it needed a Gordon Bottomly to explain why Goneril and Regan were so cruel to their father.[2] And if Hamlet remembers his 'father as he lived', or Othello the manufacture of a handkerchief, or if Antony's lieutenants remember the prowess of a champion before he surrendered to the

[2] In his play *King Lear's Wife*.

fleshpots, in each case the reference is to a past which is not redeemed by the course of events shown in the foreground, in the action of the foreground play. In the Final Plays the memories are justified, the past marches forward and imposes a beautiful peace.

★   ★   ★

Pericles launched Shakespeare on to a new and experimental, albeit final, phase. Whether it is wholly Shakespeare's is a question that may never be conclusively answered. The present writer is inclined to share in the opinion that Shakespeare took over at III. ii.[3] But anyone taking over any kind of work, begun by someone else and left incomplete, is bound to be affected—unless he scraps it all and starts with fresh foundations—by what he takes over, even though he is likely to alter some or much of that for which he has now assumed the responsibility. I am prepared to believe that Shakespeare not only pondered another man's *Pericles*, I. i to III. i inclusive, but that he made it his own—as second-hand clothes *can* be made one's own not only 'with the aid of use' but after a shortening here or a lengthening there. Shakespeare's *Pericles* inaugurates a new phase in that it, *The Winter's Tale* and *The Tempest* not only dramatize the relations between generations, between parents and their children, but also dramatize the effect of parents' memories on those relations; and this differentiates the plays of the final period from *Lear* or even from *Henry IV*. By 'parents' memories' we mean their experience (Leontes', Polixenes' Prospero's) and experience is something which can only be acquired in the past. By making the past or background of the parents active in the present or foreground of their children, in the plot machinery of these plays, Shakespeare had to utilize, in terms of stagecraft and language, novel spatial and temporal perspectives. The novel conditions of Blackfriars probably favoured this experimentation. Nevertheless, the first compulsion to experiment came on this takeover of an unknown playwright's *Pericles*, I. i to III. i inclusive (the unknown playwright might have continued beyond III. i, but was still taken over at this point). Shakespeare, greatest of geniuses was, one suspects, a naturally lazy man (he could 'Waile his deare times waste'.), was a poet who required the

---

[3] But a case for Shakespeare's total authorship is presented by G. Wilson Knight with force and clarity in *The Crown of Life*, Chapter II.

shock or stimulus provided by the example of a competitor disclosing possibilities, which he himself had not considered, as a condition for a new advance in his development. Jonson had administered the shock of 1597, and the playwright of the abandoned (?) *Pericles*, the playwrights Beaumont and Fletcher, the prospect of having to write for the stage—and audience—of Blackfriars, provided the shake-up of 1608–9.

Pericles is 'framed'. The opening lines

> To sing a Song that old was sung,
> From ashes, auntient *Gower* is come,

pitch, or distance, it. Gower comes forward but only to pitch what he brings with him backwards. The opening lines pitch the 'Song' not simply into the fourteenth century, when now 'auntient Gower' was not 'ashes', as he is now,[4] but into a time which was hoary when this long-dead old man was alive, for

> *Et bonum quo Antiquius eo melius,*

there is profit, in these 'latter times' in a song that 'hath been sung at Festivals' where

> Lords and Ladyes in their lives,
> Have red it for restoratives.

The 'Song' of *Pericles*, from its foundations, foundations inherited by Shakespeare to build on, is not here, is not *now*, but is framed; it is remote; it is 'there/then'. Having thus framed, or placed, it in a remote perspective, Gower—and he must be down-stage to do this—tells this latter-day audience to mark the threatening aspect of Antiochus ('As yon grimme lookes do testifie').[5] Despite the position of the stage-direction in the Quarto, it is evident that 'Antiochus, Prince Pericles, and followers' had previously glided into the picture. Do 'Antiochus, Prince Pericles, and followers' form a tableau within the frame of an inner-stage at this point? We cannot positively know. We do know,

[4] In the church of St. Saviour's. Nearby, the remains of Edmund Shakespeare had been buried on 31 December, 1607.

[5] For an alternative interpretation, that the 'grimme lookes' refer not to Antiochus' aspect but to the heads of the unsuccessful suitors, see the New Arden *Pericles*, ed. F. Hoeniger (1963).

however, that it would be difficult to present the opening of *Pericles*, whether in the disputed Globe or the conjectural Blackfriars or on a modern stage (supposing here a fidelity to the text) in any manner other than the one hinted. Explicitly: 'Auntient Gower', risen from the ashes, addresses a latter-day audience from down-stage in archaic English, directing them to look up-stage, to look at figures in a frame who were *there* and *then*—ashes indeed—when he (Gower) was in the flesh; to look at figures (they will presently advance down-stage and talk) in a Song, that was remote in Gower's time, when 'Lords and Ladyes in their lives' (infinitely touching—those gay lords and ladies who had long been ashes when Gower was alive) 'red it for restoratives'. Infinitely touching! Yes, but the long perspective was established by a playwright, possibly dead himself, whose queer, abandoned, old-fashioned thing Shakespeare took up, took up to make new and modern in his own growth.

This perspective, established at the outset, whereby the audience are directed to see the old story re-enacted at a temporal and spatial remove from Gower, who was himself remote in time, tends to be modified, or shortened, between Gower's appearances: there is an alternate lengthening or shortening of focus. This is because it is the nature of drama to show a perfected action as still to come and 'still unsure'. Thus there is a swing in *Pericles* between Shakespeare's normal dramatic method and the method of the illustrated narrative—the dumb show or tableau in Act II is exactly such a pictorial illustration to a story. This swing did not exist in, say, *Romeo and Juliet*, for two reasons: first, the Chorus there makes fewer entrances,[6] does not become the expected *entr'acte* intruder and abridger of temporal gaps; and secondly, the Chorus there, far from placing affairs in the past, makes it all a 'live' issue, makes what was medieval renascent (i.e. modern), using present inflexions and urgently modern language in an up-to-date sonnet. Nor did it exist in *Henry V*. The Chorus in *Henry V* comes before each Act expressly to harangue and urge that what is all past is really about to happen *now*. But in *Pericles*, Gower is an *entr'acte* intruder, abridger, commentator, moralist; above all, he intrudes in order to relegate, to push or thrust back into the pluperfect, into the 'background' (veritably, at times, the inner-stage), a quaint old story that is obstinately liable to spill forwards in time and down-stage

[6] None at all in the Folio text. The difference between Q1 and subsequent Quartos, of the tenses of Chorus's sonnets, are notable.

unless Gower returns at intervals to refer it back to where it belongs—inside that frame.

So Gower relegates, and is assisted by the manner in which Act I proceeds. This manner might strike the reader as exceptionally ingenuous (reminding him of something as primitive as *Gorboduc*), but to the 1608 playgoer it probably seemed extremely sophisticated. It is a method adapted to the remote temporal-spatial frame that has been established. This method involves the passage of elements of the plot through three tenses: Gower had told us what we were going to see dug up; next we see it (I. ii); then (II. i) Pericles narrates ('Attend me then, I went to *Antioch*'), what we have just seen. What we have just seen is now projected into Pericles' past. Moreover, the whole business whereby Thaliard is employed by Antiochus to murder Pericles, only to find that he is too late at each station along the line to achieve his object, partakes of illustrated narrative rather than drama. A ripe dramatist, we might think, would not tell what he is to show, then show it, and then tell us he has shown it. To readers the first Act might appear almost a strip cartoon; surely Shakespeare could not, or, if he could, would not, at this point of his career, relapse into a dramatic method (or, rather, not a dramatic method but an illustrated narrative method) as primitive as the method of *Gorboduc*. He probably could and would not initiate the method; but, having taken them over, he adopted the first two Acts and was thereafter committed, committed to explore what were (to him) novel perspectives in a kind of theatre (Blackfriars) that demanded experiment.

That the results of the experiment were successful is attested by the title-page of the 1609 Quarto. *Pericles* 'hath been divers and sundry times acted by his Maiesties Servants at the Globe on the Banck-side'. The Globe. *Touché*, we have gone too far in presuming that Shakespeare was particularly envisaging novel conditions in Blackfriars. Accepting that *Pericles* was played in both houses, we must then additionally accept that Beaumont and Fletcher's plays, or Shakespeare's plays more particularly designed for Blackfriars, were also played in the Globe with the consequence that techniques adjusted to the conditions of the 'private' or winter house were extended to productions in the public theatre. Private theatre practice affected public theatre practice. Very well: in the setting of the Globe—and not at Blackfriars—consider the daring mixture of the archaic, or the affectedly archaic, combining with the novel temporal and spatial perspectives of Act II.

Act II begins with Gower reminding the audience of what they have
seen:

> Heere have you seene a mightie King,
> His child I 'wis to incest bring.

A hoarily distant past, in which there was a riddle to which the grim
answer is 'incest', lies now in the *audience's* recent past. They have *just*
seen. Three degrees of 'pastness'—the audience's, auntient Gower's, and
what was long past in Gower's age—are conflated. But the audience are
then ordered to bide their time, 'Be quiet then, as men should bee, | Till
he hath past necessitie'. The audience is to be patient until the old man
has finished telling (the language) and showing (the pictures) his tale,
but they are also referred to a future (theirs, the audience's, yet long
expired in Gower's time) when Pericles' sufferings will be judged to
have been worth while, 'I'le shew you those in troubles raigne; | Loos-
ing a Mite, a Mountaine gaine'. Stating that this prospect is before them
(a prospect that was a distant retrospect in the speaker's lifetime),
Gower immediately turns to the stage *present*, for 'the good [Pericles|]
Is still at Tharstill', although this present, like the future promised the
audience in that 'I'le', belongs to the *Vergangenheit*, the bygone-ness,
which Gower proclaimed at the start. Yet the 'now', the present tense,
contained and announced by the lines

> *Is* still at Tharstill, where each man,
> *Thinkes* all is writ, he spoken can:
> And to remember what he *does*,
> *Build* his Statue to make him glorious;[7]

this 'is', in the order of time, becomes peremptorily withdrawn, in the
order of space when, with the couplet 'But tidinges to the contrarie, |
Are brought your eyes, what need speake I', a 'Dombe shew' is introduced. The Quarto stage-direction reads:

> *Enter at one dore* Pericles *talking with* Cleon, *all the traine with them:*
> *Enter at an other dore, a Gentleman with a Letter to* Pericles, Pericles
> *shewes the Letter to* Cleon; Pericles *gives the Messenger a reward, and
> Knights him: Exit* Pericles *at one dore*, and Cleon *at an other.*

What happens is that the 'is' and the 'thinkes' and the 'does' of
Gower's language is immediately distanced, thrown back, by the

[7] The italics, here and later, except in the stage-direction quoted next, are
my own. I have de-italicized personal and proper names.

framed picture. We say 'framed': it is admittedly impossible to assert
that the 'Dombe shew' took place within the—in any case disputed—
inner-stage (and perhaps, though not certainly, the 'one dore' and 'an
other dore' make an inner-stage presentation unlikely), yet it is nevertheless 'framed'. Gower, unless from a pedestal, can scarcely remain
up-stage and address the audience over the heads of the participants in
the 'Dombe shew'. He must either be positioned aloft in the gallery or
upper stage (but how does this accord with a Blackfriars presentation?)
or, and this is the more likely, he must be positioned 'down-stage'.
Accepting the latter position, we have Gower, from one corner or the
other, addressing the audience and referring them to a spectacle
('tidinges . . . Are brought your eyes, what need speake I') more remote
from them in space, set in longer perspective, than from himself. In
this way what was erstwhile 'present' has receded out and become a
framed picture; the 'now' of a moment ago has travelled into the past.
That the stage picture has wrought this effect is evidenced by the verbs
that immediately follow the 'Dombe shew':

> Good Helicon that stayde at home, . . .
> Sav'd one of all, . . .
> How Thaliart *came* full bent with sinne,
> And *had* intent to murder him . . .

what was 'here' and 'now' a line ago—a single line plus the irruption of
the 'Dombe shew'—has become a 'there and then'; remote in time and
space. Thus in one line language, by the use of tense inflexion, has
caught up with the picture—but it catches up so that the discordant
spatial and temporal dimensions of auntient Gower's illustrated narrative become adjusted.

Nor do the daring and rapid alterations of temporal and visual focus
cease after the 'Dombe shew'. As soon as that spectacle, set or framed in
middle- or back-ground, is completed, Gower proceeds, but after
another change of tense. He now speaks of what 'had' been going on in
Tyre while Pericles 'is' in Tharsis. This reference to another time and
place, a narrator's abridgement, was no doubt unavoidable. But
Shakespeare's acceptance of the challenge forced him to be experimental, obliging him to pioneer in linguistic and pictorial terms to
project a long-term view of matters where more than one generation
was involved and where a merely tragic or a merely romantic comoedic
answer would be alike unreal. The inherited plot-line and scenario

defied the Unities in extraordinary degree. (Later, Shakespeare's total acceptance, in *The Tempest*, of all the Unities in answer to a challenge set by himself or by others as a consequence of experience of, or criticism of, *Pericles*, would also compel experiment.) Meanwhile, the *Pericles* experiment compels Gower, after the reference to past events at Tyre, to close the temporal gap once more:

> Good Helicon that *stayde* at home, . . .
> *Sav'd* one of all . . .
> How Thaliart *came* full bent with sinne,
> And *had* intent . . .
> He [Pericles] doing so, *put foorth* to Seas . . .
> For now the Wind *begins* to blow,
> Thunder above, and deepes below,
> *Makes* such unquiet . . .

that the storm

> *Threw* him a shore, *to give* him glad:
> And heere he *comes* . . .

and Gower retires after pointing, in these two lines, a past, a future, a present which are yet all housed in his own remote past. At his withdrawal: 'Enter Pericles wette' and, in his own person speaks, either Shakespeare's, or the indubitably Shakespearian, *Lear*-like two-and-a-half lines:

> Yet cease your ire you angry Starres of Heaven,
> Wind, Raine, and Thunder, remember earthly man
> Is but a substaunce . . .

Whether Shakespeare's lines or not, for the speech beginning auspiciously degenerates, Shakespeare at this point was poetically interested. And he was possibly the more interested, the more struck, if these lines were Shakespearian rather than his own, Shakespeare's. He was interested enough at this point to become committed as a poet; and, to find that his own plays, his own exercises in time and space, word and picture (to concentrate the matter on the levels of a dramatic poet's techniques) heretofore had been chastely constrained, would additionally interest. Old habit means that from III. ii to the end there is a gradual 'close-up' as the different 'I's speak their 'here' and 'now'. But still there are unusual departures from habitual practice, largely governed by a plot and scenario which ranged widely in space and swung backwards and forwards in time. At the conclusion, all is sealed up and distanced again by that 'auntient' fourteenth-century poet, whose bones in Southwark Cathedral lay near Edmund Shakespeare's.

And William Shakespeare's interest engaged the interest of the 1609 audience at the Globe, that Globe audience reflecting the interest of the Blackfriars audience. That audience could listen to and watch 'the whole Historie, adventures, and fortunes' of Pericles, knowing that he would end successfully, because they watched and heard from a vantage position, so long after the 'Lords and Ladyes' had heard the Song 'in their lives'. The audience was fascinated (Fortuna rewards in the end, the stars are lucky), the play *Pericles* was successful, variants in scenic presentation and delivery at Blackfriars survived transference to the Globe.

★   ★   ★

The dramatic poet, who had taken over, in *Pericles*, someone else's or his own much earlier play and made it—or remade it in the light of twelve or fifteen years' experience—his own, and who had found—in the process of making it his own—that a plot which spanned a wide arc of time demanded novel perspectives in its showing, would have been ready to deal with Greene's *Pandosto*. Ready, even eager, for the distension asked of Shakespeare's powers in *Pericles* had been both dramatic and linguistic. Now, when sixteen years were to be covered or accounted for, a period sufficient for an infant daughter to grow to the point where she becomes nubile, memories—the pressure of the parent's past on the destiny of the child—are involved. The memories which act on the future in *Pericles*, *The Winter's Tale*, and *The Tempest* are those of the father of a girl. It is as though *King Lear* were, in the final plays, to be made plainer by means of an autobiography of Lear and a biography of Cordelia. In the Final Plays this autobiography and the biography engage in a dialogue. The illustration of the power of the memories (either of past actions or past sufferings) of the father on the destiny of the daughter had required of Shakespeare in *Pericles* technical experiments. Technical discovery can restore, we may suppose, joy to a writer when the discovery is the instantaneous expression of an enlarged vision of life—even if the enlargement came by chance.

Add therefore Blackfriars, the up-and-coming Beaumont and Fletcher, and the need somehow to harmonize word and picture when the strategy of the task, the plot, often insisted that those be at variance, and it is apparent why the test of *Pericles* should lead to *The Winter's Tale*. For they have much in common.

They have much in common but they have this difference. Instead of scenes 'from the life of' Pericles, all set at a remove by Gower, *The Winter's Tale* is to be managed in two halves. Time, as the Chorus, is to apologize for, and try to bridge, between Acts III and IV, a period of time which in *Pericles* was shown at spaced intervals. But though the purpose of 'Time, the Chorus' in *The Winter's Tale* is copulative—to prevent one play becoming two plays—yet, if he succeeds in his purpose, the major consequence of his success is to place (or set) the scenes in Bohemia in a curious relation to the spectators. *If* Time succeeds, and it is a critical point whether 'he' does, then an audience, which for all of three Acts has been experiencing a heady and violent *here and now*, thrusting towards its apparent satisfaction in tragedy, have to adjust the perspective and perceive the Bohemia scenes—not with the immediacy with which they perceive, or perceived, comico-tragic scenes in Shakespeare's Romantic Comedies with their temporal aura of an eternal or continuous present tense—through the lens of the tragedy-determined first half. If Time succeeds.

If Time *does* succeed—to the extent that, though they 'had slept between', as Time pleads, they yet remember what had happened before they slept—the audience is confronted by a pastoral romance (IV. iv) in Bohemia which is judged in one way by the lovers and in a very different way by themselves. Whereas Florizel and Perdita live in their 'now', in the forepeak of time, their place an everywhere—exquisite, romantic, comoedic—and see themselves as the lovers in the Romantic Comedies see themselves, the audience sees them in the light of their parents' (especially of Leontes') experience. Because he is in love, Florizel wishes, and can imagine, each moment as eternal:

> When you speake (Sweet)
> I'ld have you do it ever: When you sing,
> I'ld have you buy, and sell so: so give Almes,
> Pray so: and for the ord'ring your Affayres,
> To sing them too. When you do dance, I wish you
> A wave o'th Sea, that you might ever do
> Nothing but that: move still, still so:

And owne no other Function. Each your doing,
(So singular, in each particular)
Crownes what you are doing, in the present deeds,
That all your Actes, are Queenes.

but an audience, informed by Time of the 'slide | Ore sixteene yeres',
and remembering the events of the first half of the play, will frame
these 'present deeds' and, if not distrust, yet distance them—will project them, so that they are not accepted as all in all, as absolute (as
Florizel or Perdita in their state of euphoria might accept them), but
instead recognize them simply ('simply'—to term them 'mere' would
be to speak as a complete 'square' about the central illusion of existence)
as components within a dimension of time, of a reading of life which
comprehends the lovers' Innocence, Leontes' Experience, Leontes' and
Polixenes' age of Innocence which long antedated Perdita's and
Florizel's. The audience will take the lovers' ecstasy not at the lovers'
valuation (that their love is unique and should, and therefore may, last
forever) but at another, and possibly higher, valuation, knowing—as
they do, if Time as Chorus has been effective—that the lovers' moments
ought indeed to be protracted infinitely (because they are priceless
while they last) but that they most certainly will not under a temporal
dispensation which includes Age, Experience, and Authority as well as
Youth, Innocence, and Love. This consciousness of the audience—at
variance with the lovers' consciousness as the consciousness of the
audience was not so at variance with the lovers' consciousness in the
Romantic Comedies—frames the Bohemian pastoral romance, places
it so that it is contemplated through the lens of the lovers' parents'
experience, projects it, projects it far and away—for the Golden Age,
the time of Leontes' youth, of the audience's own youth and innocence
(after what it has lived through during the earlier Acts) are all remote.[8]
From within this 'inset', the Shepherd, with memories of occasions
when his 'old wife liv'd', and Perdita, with her mere teenager recol-
lections of traditional 'Whitsun pastorals' scoop—or disclose—deeper
vistas.

[8] Perdita's speeches, on youth and age, while distributing flowers to her
foster-father's guests, are *inspired* since she cannot have experienced what she
prattles about so sweetly. That the speeches, unknown to her, directly touch on
what the audience (who were in the theatre before she was born) has had to
learn the hard way, is evidence of her—and Shakespeare's—inspiration.

With Act V the Bohemian excursion ends. It has been an 'inset', revealing a 'golden age' being enjoyed by Florizel and Perdita and which had once been enjoyed by their parents. The Sicilian 'here and now' returns with Act V but, until the final scene, this 'here and now' conflicts, in the audience's mind, with the Bohemian dimensions of space and time. But with Hermione's resurrection the two orders are drawn together and harmonized. When the effigy of Hermione becomes a living Hermione, and she advances from her up-stage (inner stage?) chapel to the foreground and to a new 'here and now', experience of the Bohemian excursion is subsumed or incorporated.

In retrospect, it will be realized that success or failure of the play as a whole will depend, in the theatre, on the measure of conviction that Time the Chorus secured during his narrative speech. It is also, I believe, fairly evident that there would have been no *Winter's Tale* (as we know it) but for Shakespeare's previous 'takeover' of *Pericles*, which resulted in a play not rudimentary in its methods but highly experimental and which, combining as it did narrative and drama, compelled the trying out of new visual perspectives to match the temporal scheme with its many and rapid changes of tense.

★   ★   ★

Whereas the action of *Pericles* straggles over the years, and the action of *The Winter's Tale* has its temporal hiatus to allow for the growth of a new generation, the visible action of *The Tempest* represents a time-span scarcely greater than the time needed for its showing. Whether or not in response to criticism of its predecessors, it observes the Unities. Here, as with its two predecessors, Shakespeare chooses a plot involving a father and his daughter and, throughout its unfolding, it has points of contact with either *Pericles* or with *The Winter's Tale* or with both. All three plays end with the restoration of a father, who has been changed by his suffering, to his possessions, his fortunes, or his rights, and the happy marriage of his daughter. In all three plays the father–daughter relationship recalls some aspect of the Lear–Cordelia relationship. But with all the resemblances of story there is this main difference in tactical handling: *The Tempest*, though it supposes a period of time (here twelve instead of sixteen years) sufficient for a female infant to grow to marriageable age, renders that period, and the tragic events leading to it, entirely in narrative terms. Who can doubt that Shakespeare's choice here was partly, if not entirely, conditioned by the experience gained in the making of *Pericles* and *The Winter's Tale*? In any case, this choice obliged Prospero in I. ii to narrate to Miranda, and through Miranda to the audience, the events of twelve years ago, and in so doing creating an imaginative picture which is in the strongest contrast to the actual spectacle the audience beholds. The audience sees an old man and his daughter seated side by side, and alone, on a luxuriant island; but, while they see this, they hear of violent, bustling, middle-of-the-night activity in which the passive victims are not—and yet, also, *are*—the Prospero and Miranda they physically behold, but rather a middle-aged Prince of Milan and a baby. Memory is powerful in Prospero while he tells Miranda the reason for the present tempest. To what extent does the picture from the past (for memories can only refer to the past) advance, obtrude upon, even superimpose itself upon, the present stage-picture offered to the audience?

Now there are three forms of expressing the perfected past in an English verb where the Latin has but one form: *amavi* may be translated as (*a*) I *loved* or (*b*) I *have loved* or (*c*) I *did love*. Grammarians differ among themselves in their use of terms, but we can call (*a*) the Simple Perfect, (*b*) the Present Perfect (since the auxiliary *have* possesses a Present inflexion and conveys a measure of its Present meaning to the past participle *loved*), and (*c*) the Emphatic Present Perfect (*did* expresses past-ness but, variably according to context, emphasizes the verb qualified—*love*—which has a present inflexion). Thus there is in English a choice of forms denoting a scale of remoteness or urgency within a past they all express; and at one end of the scale is a form in which the past is so relived in its telling that it becomes—in a manner—present. If Prospero's narration of the events which precipitated him, and his baby daughter, from Milan twelve years ago creates a picture which gradually closes up on the audience till it mingles with, even supersedes, the stage-picture physically exposed to them, it is because of Shakespeare's playing on this scale—that and an earlier insistent use of the historic present and present participles. The whole of Prospero's narrative is so charged with energy, not so much because of the frequency of verbs but because of the changes of tense that the verbs undergo (contrast Egeon's narrative in *Comedy of Errors* where, despite the excitement of the events abstractly considered, there is a dead flatness of tone and monotony of tempo, unvaried perspective—all attributable to the employment of a single tensal inflexion) that it demands reference to the whole of the episode to bear out the truth of these remarks. We can give here but a few examples.

Following the pluperfect of half-remembrance there is the abrupt tense-change that makes this dream-like past an 'is' that 'lives':

> MIRANDA: 'Tis farre off:
>   And rather like a dreame, then an assurance
>   That my remembrance warrants: *Had* I not
>   Fowre, or five women once, that *tended* me?
> PROSPERO: Thou *hadst*; and more Miranda: But how *is* it
>   That this *lives* in thy minde? . . .

Next a firm placing in the 'dark-backward':

> Thy Mother *was* a peece of vertue, and
> She *said* thou *wast* my daughter; and thy father
> *Was* Duke of Millaine . . .

which 'dark-backward' is to be drawn forwards in the light of these Historic Presents, Infinitives, or Participles:

> he [Anthonio] *needes* will be
> Absolute Millaine . . .
> He *thinks* me now incapable. *Confederates*
> (So drie he *was* for Sway) with King of Naples
> *To give* him Annuall tribute, *doe* him homage
> *Subject* his Coronet, to his Crowne and *bend*
> The Dukedom yet *unbow'd* (alas poore Millaine)
> To most ignoble *stooping*.

So the King of Naples '*hearkens* my Brothers suit' that he '*should presently extirpate* me and mine'. Whereon

> A treacherous Armie levied, one mid-night
> Fated to th' purpose, *did* Anthonio *open*
> The gates of Millaine, and ith' dead of darkenesse
> The ministers for th' purpose *hurried* thence
> Me, and thy *crying* selfe.

and, after the Present Perfect of 'the very rats | Instinctively have quit it', the Present Emphatic Perfect enters in force, for the 'did Anthonio open' is followed by 'Wherefore did they not | That howre destroy us', by 'to sigh | To th' windes, whose pitty sighing backe againe | Did us but loving wrong', by 'Thou was't that did preserve me; Thou didst smile', by 'Gonzalo | . . . did give us . . .' so that Miranda, experiencing the original horror consciously for the first time, can properly exclaim:

> I not remembering how I cride out then
> Will cry it ore againe:

and then—innocently enough till she learns of the names on the ship's passenger-list—turn to enquire of her father,

> And now I pray you Sir,
> For still 'tis beating in my minde; your reason
> For raysing this Sea-storme?

In *The Tempest*, Shakespeare rejected the method of illustrating a narrative at spaced intervals; equally he rejected the composition of a play in two halves. He decided in *The Tempest* to narrate the matter of most of *Pericles* and three acts of *The Winter's Tale* within much less than half of a single scene. But the decision owed much, if not all, to his experience of inheriting, or adopting, the script of an unknown playwright or of his earlier forgotten self. This inheritance, or adoption, compelled him to face the opposing claims and methods of narrative and drama, of past and present, of time and space, of language and picture (all in relation to the physical conditions of the Blackfriars Theatre as well as to the familiar ones of the Globe) and, at the last, to hit on a mode which reconciled these opposing claims as completely as possible. Looked at in this light, the interest of *Pericles* is considerable.

*   *   *

There remains the task of considering, in the shortest of space, the Betrothal Masque in *The Tempest*, IV. i. This Masque has connections with those Fourth Act scenes with an emphasis on Nature or flowers in other later plays—*Hamlet, Othello, King Lear, Cymbeline*. But what more concerns us here is to note the Masque's function in the design of *The Tempest*, to compare and contrast that function with the function of IV. iv (the Sheep-shearing Festival scene) in the design of *The Winter's Tale*, and to observe a certain similarity of mechanics.

First to point to the obvious and yet important similarities and dissimilarities. In both the Sheep-shearing Festival of *The Winter's Tale* and the Betrothal Masque in *The Tempest* there is a celebration of the fertility of the earth. In the Festival this celebration has an autumnal note; it takes place in late summer or early autumn and it recognizes the foison that has *been* given: in the Masque the blessings of

Earths increase, foyzon plentie,
Barnes, and Garners, never empty,

are rather *pro*spective, Juno asking that these riches should attend Ferdinand and Miranda *in their future*. Next, in the Festival, the deities Flora, Jupiter, Apollo, Dis, Phoebus, etc., though they are referred to in the dialogue, do not appear in person; in the Masque, Iris, Ceres, Juno appear in person. In both Festival and Masque, the dramatist includes, at some point, dances in his stage-picture; in both Festival and Masque, the poet calls in the non-linguistic art of music to accompany some of the words. In both Festival and Masque, the audience sees, as an essential in the two stage-pictures, the mixture or confrontage of youth with age. In both Festival and Masque, the audience is made aware, both through words and pictures, of the young lovers in their present delight and with a future before them, and of their parents' generation burdened with remembrance, who perceive in their children a kind of re-enactment. In both scenes there is a presentation of past and future, of memory and desire.

Now, in the Festival of *The Winter's Tale*, we noted that the rapture of Florizel and Perdita is to the audience—is indeed to Polixenes—distanced or 'framed' because of the experience of the early tragic acts of the play. In *The Tempest*, no less, the Betrothal Masque (whatever its practical usefulness may have been to the poet-dramatist as a temporizer—as something to occupy ear and eye of the audience while Caliban's 'foule conspiracy' gets under weigh) effects a change in the temporal, and probably the pictorial, perspective of the audience when it occurs. Granted that remorse or remembrance or vindictive feeling

on the part of the ship's passengers or Prospero have weighed continuously on the action until the Masque, and have coloured that action,
yet—with the Masque—some characters become, like ourselves, an
audience, an audience within an audience. This applies to Ferdinand
and Miranda, and Prospero too 'had forgot' his role as character during
the time he, with Ariel as a sort of Inigo Jones, is absorbed as author,
producer, and spectator of the Masque. During the Masque there is an
escape or withdrawal from the temporal dimensions of the play's plot,
an escape of the kind anyone and everyone has experienced by an
intense absorption—whether in a work of art, in a Test Match, or in
anything else sufficiently compelling to participant or observer or
listener.

In the Masque, the goddesses of heaven (Juno) and earth (Ceres) and
of their *liasone*, Iris, appear or descend, and speak, and are followed by
'certaine Reapers' and 'Nimphes' who dance. All this may be mere
illusion, conjured by Prospero's 'so potent Art', but it entertains
Ferdinand and Miranda (for the future son-in-law is not simply
flattering with his 'most magestick vision'?), and it holds, as we are
informed, the author-producer himself spellbound. During the playing-
time of the Masque, until it is broken off abruptly, a *time* and a *space*—
other than the time and the space of the plot of *The Tempest*—
are imported: imported, they occlude the time and place of the
plot.

What time and what space? That belonging to the goddesses of
fertility which is outside mortal first-hand experience. How was the
Masque performed? And where was the inner audience of two positioned. We do not know enough about the structure of the Globe or
Blackfriars, or of the winching gadgets of either, to know, or to be
sure whether the audience, consisting of Ferdinand and Miranda, sat
with their backs or their faces to the paying audience in the theatre.
But, whatever the original disposition of the inner audience in relation
to the divine performers of the Masque, the fact that the paying
audience—whether in the Globe or in Blackfriars or in a modern
theatre—beholds the Masque through the eyes of that inner audience,
rather than directly, results in an adjustment of focus to correspond
with the peculiar linguistic (rhyme, some octosyllabics, a special mode
of heightened delivery suitable to goddesses who are putting on a
show) properties of the Masque. For this method of harmonizing the
pictorial with the verbal in an 'inset'—a deposit within a play fairly

sharply demarked from its context—Shakespeare might well of course have learned something from the Court Masques and the 'perspectives' of Inigo Jones. Equally well, as far as the Masque in *The Tempest* is concerned, he was profiting from the composition of *The Winter's Tale* and his recollection of the experimental *Pericles*.

Note

Fools and Clowns. Biographical facts may be sought in E. K. Chambers, *The Elizabethan Stage*, 4 vols. (1923), G. E. Bentley, *The Jacobean and Caroline Stage*, in progress, 5 vols. to date (1941–   ), and E. Nungezer, *A Dictionary of Actors* (1929), which last often cites the evidence in fuller form than Chambers or Bentley.

Fools and laughter have been studied in a European context by Enid Welsford in *The Fool: His Social and Literary History* (1935), and Barbara Swain, *Fools and Folly during the Middle Ages and the Renaissance* (1932); W. Kaiser's *Praisers of Folly* (1964) considers Erasmus, Rabelais, and Shakespeare comparatively. W. Farnham's 'The Medieval Comic Spirit' in *J. Q. Adams Memorial Studies* (1948) is useful and stimulating within brief compass.

Studies of the fools of Shakespeare include R. H. Goldsmith, *Wise Fools in Shakespeare* (1955), and L. Hotson, *Shakespeare's Motley* (1952). Most useful, for their wider base in Elizabethan and Jacobean dramatic writing in general, are Olive M. Busby's *The Development of the Fool in Elizabethan Drama* (1923), and L. B. Wright's compendious article, 'Variety-Show Clownery on the Pre-Restoration Stage' in *Anglia*, XL.

Comedy and Laughter. A general and popular introduction is M. Willson Disher, *Clowns and Pantomimes* (1925). For a more particular approach R. Findlater's *Grimaldi: King of Clowns* (1955) may confidently be chosen.

The causes of laughter have been variously examined; two contrasting approaches, one scientific and one pragmatic, are S. Freud, *Jokes and their Relation to the Unconscious*, in *Complete Psychological Works*, ed. J. Strachey, viii (1960)—this establishes the similarities between joking and dreaming—and M. Eastman, *The Enjoyment of Laughter* (1930).

V

Laughter in the Last Plays

JOHN RUSSELL BROWN

★

AGAINST the rare example of plays like *Richard II* or Chapman's *Bussy D'Ambois*, or Jonson's always unpopular tragedies, Elizabethan and Jacobean dramatists exploited laughter. Total laughter was strong in their dramatic inheritance. Although miracle and morality plays presented issues of life and death, destiny and choice, good and evil—themes which in other ages have proved inimical to laughter—they had been given comic servants and midwives, coarse jokes, horseplay and grotesque combats; successive revisions augmented rather than pruned the low comedy. The later interludes on moral and social subjects were often most dramatically alive (and most effectively didactic) in incidents of parody or ignoble conflict. And when theatrical conditions became more stable and individual dramatists emerged, this comic vitality was sustained without diminution. Pathos, propaganda, heroics and romance all coexisted with full-bodied laughter. In 1565, *The Excellent Comedy of the Two Most Faithfullest Friends, Damon and Pythias*, introduced a parasite, witty pages, and a clownish Grim the Collier among events depicting tyranny and endurance in the face of death. Wager's *Enough is as Good as a Feast*, which brought Satan, Heavenly Man, Precipitation, Plagues, and a Physician on to the stage, was recommended on publication as '*very fruitful, godly and full of pleasant mirth*'. A few years later a witty 'vice' and a team of three comic clowns were exploited in a play by a Fellow of King's College, Cambridge; its title-page announces '*A Lamentable Tragedy, mixed full of pleasant mirth*'.

Of course 'poison in jest' and moral earnestness mixed with jest were often dismissed from serious consideration. Sir Philip Sidney hoped they represented a passing imperfection and his magisterial rebuke in *An Apology for Poetry* (1585) of those who 'thrust in clowns by head

and shoulders to play a part in majestical matters, with neither decency
nor discretion' was echoed by other critics more closely involved (and
more generally approving) in theatrical matters. The prologue to
Henry VIII is in this tradition and the prologue to Marlowe's much
earlier *Tamburlaine* with its scornful dismissal of 'such conceits as clown-
age keeps in pay'. The Parnassus plays, performed in Cambridge about
1600, follow Sidney more exactly, with a stage-direction '*Enter* Dromo,
drawing a clown in with a rope' followed by the mocking comment:

> Why what an ass art thou! dost thou not know a play cannot be
> without a clown? Clowns have been thrust into plays by head and
> shoulders, ever since Kempe could make a scurvy face . . .
>
> (ed. J. Leishman, *I, Return*, ll. 661–7)

But to criticize and to offend are distinct functions. All the reproach
had little effect, and comedy continued on its broad path. It was not an
early crudity that needed to be outgrown. Shakespeare, whose Hamlet could reprove clowns for speaking more than was set down for
them, continued to use clowns; and all his respect for the single judicious auditor did not banish fools, fights, and merry bawdy incidents
from his plays. From the slapstick incidents of *The Comedy of Errors*
and *The Taming of the Shrew* to the subtle and elaborate foolery in
Twelfth Night, or from the crazed and cruel humour of *Titus Andronicus*
and *Henry VI* to the intensities of Lear's Fool and his own madness,
there is an obvious refinement and deepening of comedy; but that
should not be allowed to obscure the prat-falls and absurdities of his
neatest comedies—Maria promises that Sir Toby shall 'laugh himself
into stitches'—or the tripping-up and abuse of Oswald by Kent in *King
Lear*. If *Henry VIII* is wholly by Shakespeare he there introduced two
comic porters with a pushing crowd in despite of the play's prologue
that scorned both 'fool and fight': here are blows enough, and the usual
bawdy jokes about 'the Indian with the great tool', about women,
honour, and cuckoldom—and all this by way of preparation for the
great prophetic concluding scene. Clearly the continual criticism of
broad humour in Elizabethan and Jacobean days is not a sign of a falling
off in the dramatists' taste for it; rather it is a mark of continuing and
sometimes undesirable exploitation.

The King's Men, in common with other Jacobean acting companies,
would have been quick to find how to get laughs from Shakespeare's
plays. Each company had good comics—enough to play Malvolio, Sir

Toby, and Sir Andrew as well as Feste, or to bring Jonson's *Bartholomew Fair* to its abundant life—and the chief clown[1] was often its most important member. Richard Tarlton of Queen Elizabeth's Men, who died in 1588, was the first of a line of comedians who could claim to be the funniest men in England. The succession passed to the Chamberlain's Men and then to the King's in the clowns William Kempe and John Armin. In notoriety these men surpassed the heroic and romantic actors like Alleyn, Burbage, and Perkins. Professor Nungezer, who has collected eye-witness accounts in his *Dictionary of Actors . . . in England before 1642*, found that:

> No other Elizabethan actor has been the object of so many notices in contemporary and later writing as Tarlton, or has been remembered with such various and practical tokens of esteem.   (p. 355)

His face was instantly recognizable and inns were named after him; as Joseph Hall satirically announced:

> O honour, far beyond a brazen shrine,
> To sit with Tarlton on an ale-post's sign!
> (*Satires* (1599), vi, l. 204)

The great clowns were star actors, capable of thriving on their own verbal wit or their own projected personalities. Tarlton was famous for solo 'jigs' (or song-and-dance routines) and for extemporizing verses on themes proposed by members of his audience. Kempe left the Chamberlain's Men about 1599 to exploit his individual talents, as by dancing from London to Norwich and writing a book about it. Armin, who was known as a writer before succeeding Kempe, wrote a play, *The Two Maids of More-Clack* (1609), in which he could act himself—taking three distinct parts, not counting the occasion when in his second role he pretended to be in his first. These clowns were prepared to succeed without much help from the literary art of others. If we merely read the roles they accepted we shall get a dull and unvaried impression: as in low comedy at all times, falls, blows, knavery, mimicry, stupidity, and surprise provided constantly recurring jokes. There was, indeed, good reason for clowns to say and do more than was set down for them; they needed new ways of sustaining old routines; they had to be

---

[1] In this chapter 'clown' indicates a kind of actor: a star, 'personality' comic. This corresponds to Elizabethan and Jacobean usage; for example, Feste, the professional fool in *Twelfth Night*, is designated 'Clown' in the speech-prefixes of the Folio text.

individual and original to succeed. In a crazy, exaggerated, and energetic art, Tarlton, Kempe, and Armin established themselves—themselves rather than their authors or their roles.

Certainly the individual art of the chief clowns helped to sustain the ubiquitous comedy in the plays of Shakespeare's time; and guaranteed popularity. Jo. Cooke's *The City Gallant*, performed by the Queen's Men in 1611, was known by an alternative title, *Greene's Tu Quoque*, in honour of the famous clown who created the role of Bubble. In the text Bubble was given a fool's puff for his creator:

> GERALDINE: Why, then, we'll go to the Red Bull: they say Greene's a good clown.
> BUBBLE: Greene! Greene's an ass.
> SCATTERGOOD: Wherefore do you say so?
> BUBBLE: Indeed I ha' no reason; for they say he is as like me as ever he can look.

Shakespeare must also have been aware of the talents of his company's clowns. In four of the plays originally printed from his autograph manuscript, or a good copy of it, the names of actors found their way into the speech-prefixes or stage-directions, usurping the character they were meant to sustain. Twice it was the thin man of the company, John Sincklo, who in *Henry IV, Part II* played the Beadle described as an 'anatomy' or skeleton, but twice the actors named were clowns. In *Much Ado About Nothing*, Kempe appears in IV. ii instead of '*Dogberry*' or '*Constable*', and Cowley for '*Verges*', '*Headborough*' or '*Con. 2.*' In *Romeo and Juliet*, IV. v, the direction '*Enter Will Kemp*' appears instead of '*Enter Peter*'. In each case the actor seems to have dominated the character in Shakespeare's creating mind; none of the straight actors of the company ever took over his role to similar effect.

In looking for the laughs in Shakespeare's plays the art of these clowns must be appreciated. First there must be opportunities for impressing a dominant personality. Often a role will begin with a solo entry, without much reference to the existing dramatic situation and often without reference to any other character. This is varied by immediately providing the chief comedian with an obvious foil or 'feed'. Often the textual provision is most detailed at this point, as if Shakespeare felt the need to insist on the clown taking some colour from his author's conception on the all-important first impression. Verbally the comic parts tend to peter out when a sufficient head of dramatic energy

has been established; at the end of a successful low comedy performance the actor's hold over an audience ensures that a very little material
will go a sufficiently long way.

Whatever the demands of plot or theme the clown needs to be able
to use his traditional business, and the author's words will stand more
chance of being respected if they invite this usual co-operation. Any
reference to an ugly face, for example (or ironically, its opposite good
looks) would be taken up at once, for clowns, then as now, exploited
out-of-the-ordinary features. Henry Peacham used the effect of this as
an almost mythological simile:

> As Tarlton when his head was only seen,
> The tirehouse door and tapestry between,
> Set all the multitude in such a laughter
> They could not hold for scarse an hour after . . .
> *Thalia's Banquet* (1620)

Other clowns used a 'scurvy face' as a circus clown uses exaggerated
make-up. Grimaces were invented and grotesque gestures. Thomas
Goffe wrote in the Praeludium to his *Careless Shepherdess* (1618–29):

> I've laughed
> Until I cried again to see what faces
> The rogue will make. O it does me good
> To see him hold out's chin, hang down his hands,
> And twirle his bauble. There is nere a part
> About him but breaks jest . . .

Silent by-play was often accompanied by trite words. In the 'bad'
Quarto of *Hamlet*, the prince takes his complaint of clowns a step
further than in the authoritative text:

> And then you have some again, that keep one suit
> Of jests, as a man is known by one suit of
> Apparel, and gentlemen quote his jests down
> In their tables before they come to the play, as thus:
> 'Cannot you stay till I eat my porridge?' and 'You owe me
> A quarter's wages', and 'My coat wants a cullison',
> And 'Your beer is sour'; and blabbering with his lips
> And thus keeping in the cinquepace of jests,
> When, God knows, the warm clown cannot make a jest
> Unless by chance, as the blind man catcheth a hare.
> (Sig. F2)

Many authors provided running gags of this sort for their clowns, as popular radio or television programmes today have their marks in 'Don't forget the diver' or 'Hullo . . . Eth!' or 'Yeah! Yeah! Yeah!'

The clowns also had more normal skills. They were pictured playing on tabor and pipe. They were active and nimble, Tarlton being a fencing master and Kempe a notorious dancer. In Chettle's *Kind-Heart's Dream* (1592), Tarlton is recognized by 'his suit of russet, his button'd cap, his tabor, his standing on the toe, and other tricks'. In Greene's *James IV* (1591), Slipper the clown dances to entertain, and after performances of plays the clowns often took over to entertain the audience with a jig. They were skilled, too, in mimicry, becoming sad or gay on demand, and were often given speeches which allowed them to imitate different kinds of behaviour within a short compass, as in Touchstone's party-piece on the various degrees of quarrelling. In this way they could show their imitative skill and project shrewd and compendious social comment. When the Clown enters in Thomas Heywood's *Rape of Lucrece* (1609) and is asked for news, he offers court-news, camp-news, city-news, country-news, and news-at-home, and is asked for them all (C2^v–3). The Porter in *Macbeth* probably mimicked the walk and talk of the farmer, equivocator, and tailor whom he imagined at the castle gate; so played the scene is still continuously funny today.

One of their greatest strengths was an ability to call forth abnormal responses, to make pathos, villainy, wisdom, or cowardice both funny and acceptable. This goes beyond the licence of the idiot-fool, being descended from the revelry of Saturnalia and Feasts of Fools, and from the didacticism of the praise of folly.

As Launcelot Gobbo mocked his blind and mistaken father in *The Merchant of Venice*, the servant-clown in *The Miseries of Enforced Marriage* (1607) mocked his own misery:

> Well, I could alter mine eyes from filthy mud into fair water; you have paid for my tears, and mine eyes shall prove bankrupts and break out for you; let no man persuade me, I will cry and every town betwixt Shoreditch Church and York Bridge shall bear me witness . . . (C2^v)

Later the audience is invited to enjoy his weeping in place of a performance on tabor and pipe. Thieving is a common occasion for enjoying the clown's skill: Mouse, the clown in the long-popular romance

Mucedorus, steals a pot of ale and a stage-direction follows to describe his subsequent engagement with the ale-wife:

> *She searcheth him, and he drinketh over her head, and casts down the pot. She stumbleth at it, then they fall together by the ears; she takes her pot and goes out.*

Often these escapades were mixed with an element of cowardice, as when Cuckedemoy in Marston's *Dutch Courtezan* (1603–4) picks the pocket of Malheureux as he is going to execution. Sometimes two divergent responses were called forth together, notably bawdy enjoyment with some piece of social criticism or a mocking imitation of some unamorous activity; the school lessons in *The Taming of the Shrew* are examples of this, or the clown's tilt at pedantry in his disavowal of any intention to flirt with Lucrece's maid in Heywood's play:

> If ever I knew what belongs to these cases, or yet know what they mean; if ever I used any plain dealing or were ever worth such a jewel, would I might die like a beggar; if ever I were so far read in my grammar as to know what an interjection is, or a conjunction copulative . . . why do you think, madam, I have no more care of myself, being but a strippling, than to go to it at these years; flesh and blood cannot endure it. I shall even spoil one of the best faces in Rome with crying at your unkindness . . .   (D4f.)

Here too is the obvious lie, superlative overstatement, mock weeping, and ugly face. And here is the clown's deliberate and two-faced concern with sexual virility: so Touchstone complained that Corin brought the 'ewes and rams together' and betrayed a 'she-lamb of a twelve-month to a crooked-pated, old, cuckoldly ram', and then justified his attachment to Audrey in that as 'horns are odious, they are necessary'.

The strangeness and licence of the clowns' humour is well illustrated by their liking for animal disguises. *Ram Alley* (1607–8) by Lording Barry has a clown who dresses as an ape to do lewd dances; Fletcher's *Mad Lover* has a dog-barking episode by a clown who had been in a masque of beasts. A tract called *This World's Folly: or a Warning-Piece discharged upon the Wickedness thereof* written by I. H. and published in 1615 has much to say about 'obscene and light jigs, stuff'd with loathsome and unheard-of ribaldry, suckt from the poisonous dugs of sin-swell'd theatres'. This critic singled out Greene of the Queen's Men for his 'stentor-throated bellowings, flash-choaking squibbles of absurd vanities' and his speciality of dancing as a baboon, 'metamorphosing human shape into bestial form'.

★ ★ ★

Performances of the clowns or fools of Elizabethan and Jacobean theatres are well documented compared with those of their fellow actors, but even so our knowledge is fragmentary. It needs to be amplified by a study of later-day comics who have left detailed memoirs. Fooling is timeless and so three extracts, in place of many, can show the unchanging form of clowning and suggest something of the actors' art behind the brief facts that have survived from Shakespeare's time.

The clown's 'scurvy' face and comic dress has always been sufficient cause of laughter. *The Life of the Late Famous Comedian, Jo. Haynes* (1701) tells how:

> There happen'd to be one night a play acted call'd *Catiline's Conspiracy*, wherein there was wanting a great number of senators. Now Mr. Hart, being chief of the House, wou'd oblige Jo to dress for one of these senators, altho' Jo's salary, being then 50s. per week, freed him from any such obligation. But Mr. Hart, as I said before, being sole Governor of the Playhouse and at a small variance with Jo, commands it and the other must obey. Jo, being vex'd at the slight Mr. Hart had put on him, found out this method of being reveng'd on him: he gets a Scaramouch dress, a large full ruff, makes himself whiskers, from ear to ear, puts on his head a long Merry Andrew's cap, a short pipe in his mouth, a little three legg'd stool in his hand, and in this manner follows Mr. Hart on the stage, sits himself down behind him, and begins to smoke his pipe, to laugh and point at him. (p. 23)

A century later *Oxberry's Dramatic Biography* (new series, i; 14 April, 1827) gave a compendious picture of Grimaldi that illustrates how a clown can centre attention on his assumed character no matter what is happening elsewhere on the stage and can make the audience laugh at actions that would usually evoke an anxious concern:

> The hopelessness of one who knows not what to do next, he hits to a nicety—he always appeared to us to represent a grown child waking to perception but wondering at every object he beholds. Then, his exuberance of animal spirits was really miraculous—what a rich ringing laugh!—the very voice of merriment! Then, the self-approving chuckle, and the contemptuous look, half pity, half

derision, that he gave to the dupe of his artifice—his incessant annoyance to *Pantaloon*—and his feigned condolence for the very misfortunes of which he was the author—his amazement and awe of Harlequin—his amorous glances at *Columbine*—and his winks at the imbecility of the doting, and the dandyism of the young lover— his braggadocia blustering—his cautious escapes from detection— and his ludicrous agony during fustigation, an operation duly performed on *Clown* by all the personages of the motley drama— were all his, and HIS ALONE. He was the very *beau idéal* of thieves— robbery became a science in his hands—you forgave the larceny, for the humour with which it was perpetrated. He abstracted a leg of mutton from a butcher's tray, with such a delightful assumption of *nonchalence*—he threw such plump stupidity into his countenance, whilst the slyness of observation lurked in his half-closed eyes—he extracted a watch, or a handkerchief, with such a bewitching eager- ness—with such a devotion to the task—and yet kept his wary eye upon the victim of his trickery; he seemed so imbued with the spirit of peculation, that you saw it in him, merely as a portion of his nature, and for which he was neither blameable or accountable. His pantomimic colloquies with the other sex, too, were inimitable— his mincing affectation, when addressing a dandizette—his broad bold style, when making love to a fisherwoman—were all true to Nature.

A clown's struggles to be funny have been disclosed in some memoirs. In *Grock, King of Clowns* (tr. 1957) the great twentieth-century circus artist has contrasted himself with a straight actor:

> Unlike an actor who has his set part to play, a clown can vary and embroider his part every night if he chooses. The chief thing is that what he does makes a hit. (p. 83)

He is free to improvise for each new audience and he is also imprisoned by the absolute need to raise a laugh. Grock tells the story of how he invented his 'piano-lid trick'. At each routine joke with the piano, his feed, Antonet, had been saying 'Do you think that was funny? . . . Do you really think that was funny?' and so had killed his effects. Grock became truly enraged and took off the piano lid to strike Antonet:

> My costume and make-up must have made my genuine rage in- credibly funny. The public shrieked with laughter. I came to my senses and pursued Antonet no further.

Grock returned to the piano to put the lid on, but failed to do so:

> Something had to be done to amuse them now that I was alone in
> the ring. But what on earth was I to do? I rested the lid against the
> left-hand side of the piano, sloping to the ground from the end of
> the key-board. At the sight of it, the idea came to me to let my hat
> slide down it. No sooner thought than done. My hat tobogganed
> merrily to the ground. I was just going to pick it up and put it on
> when the great inspiration came! Why not toboggan down after
> my hat? I climbed up on to the piano, slid down the slope straight
> to my hat, which I put on and then walked proudly off. The effect
> was stupendous!   (pp. 85–6)

Anger and a ludicrous face; obvious child-like pleasure; unexpected
and disproportionate behaviour; the simple action of putting on a hat;
these can raise stupendous laughter and applause, given a clown's
agility, resilience, and sense of scale and timing.

★   ★   ★

Read with the eyes of a clown Shakespeare's plays offer abundant
cues for business and improvisation. *The Winter's Tale*, which E. M. W.
Tillyard has called a presentation of 'the whole tragic pattern from
prosperity to destruction, regeneration, and still fairer prosperity'
(p. 40), can be taken as an example.

For clowns Autolycus is the star part. He enters with a solo song,
with no immediate dramatic task beyond the establishment of his
assumed *persona*. The words Shakespeare has given him invite mimicry
and business on the four times repeated 'With heigh!', the 'tirra-lirra'
for lark-song, and the contrasting references to thrush and jay. A brief,
prose speech serves to connect the character with 'Prince Florizel' and
so, vaguely, to the plot; and, at the same time, makes pointed reference
to his comical rags, being 'out of service' like himself, and provides an
excuse for imitating a superior person dressed in 'three-pile' velvet. At
once he has another song, contrasting in mood with the first:

> But shall I go mourn for that, my dear?
> The pale moon shines by night; . . .

But an imitation of the forlorn lover is quickly revalued as a prelude to
mischief when a second stanza presents Autolycus again as an adven-
turer, this time with a reference to punishment in the 'stocks'; and even
here there is a usual twist, for he will 'avouch' his account in the stocks

as if formally claiming right while being punished for wrong. With his prose speech that immediately follows Autolycus is established by name and by his thieving; and as something of a coward and also an indolent innocent:

> beating and hanging are terrors to me; for the life to come, I sleep out the thought of it. (ll. 29–30)

With the entry of the shepherd's son, he lets the audience share his hope of successful trickery and at once goes into a new imitative routine: this time he is a poor robbed and beaten man—'O that ever I was born' —crying out for death. Tears will bring laughter here; and so will his dexterity in picking the young shepherd's pocket while talking of a 'charitable office'. The comic business has its surprises, for his victim offers to give him money and so threatens to discover the robbery. Autolycus himself nearly spoils everything, for as he pretends in his assumed role to talk about his real one he gives himself away by calling his vices virtues. Before he successfully shakes off the shepherd's son the joke of imitation is taken a step further as he has to pretend to be a bigger coward than the coward he really is. Alone again, he raises expectation for his next appearance at the sheep-shearing—and makes the obvious word-play in hoping that the 'shearers prove sheep'. With a further glance at 'virtue' he leaves the stage with a third song which again invites stage-action and picks up the pace of the performance:

> Jog on, jog on, the footpath way,
> And merrily hent [jump] the stile-a; . . .

It also justifies his villainy by the merriment it brings and gives a further opportunity for mimed action:

> A merry heart goes all the day,
> Your sad tires in a mile-a.

A master-clown would use this introductory scene to show off many of his tricks and gain the connivance of the audience.

His next entry is a further transformation. Now a pedlar he enters with yet another song, this time giving opportunity for by-play with his audience on the stage and a run of sexual innuendoes. After telling tall stories to the credulous rustics he 'bears' his part in a song for three voices:—'you must know 'tis my occupation', he says, with a clown's extra-dramatic statement about his own interests and a glancing jest at

H

the expense of puritans whose accustomed phrase this was. He leaves the stage to follow his dupes with a brief aside to keep the audience aware of his intentions ('And you shall pay well for 'em') and with another song asking questions of 'My dainty duck, my dear-a' and, finally, telling even his victims that 'Money's a meddler'.

His second appearance in IV. iv begins with another soliloquy, as Camillo, Perdita, and Florizel talk aside. Autolycus is in full triumph after his 'sheep-shearing', but when he thinks he is overheard he has only one thought: 'hanging'. Camillo supplies a spoken stage-direction in case the actor does not see the cue for yet another transformation:

> How now, good fellow! Why shak'st thou so? Fear not, man; here's no harm intended to thee.

As Camillo continues, the audience enjoys the rogue's slow revival:

> I am a poor fellow, sir.
> I am a poor fellow, sir. [*Aside.*] I know ye well enough.
> Are you in earnest, sir? [*Aside.*] I smell the trick on't.

He is being asked to exchange his poor clothes for Florizel's and is given a tip to 'boot'—a clown brings out bad puns from others as well as himself. He enjoys a show of reluctance:

> Indeed, I have had earnest: but I cannot with conscience take it.
> $\qquad\qquad\qquad\qquad\qquad\qquad\qquad$ (ll. 635–6)

When his benefactors leave him outwardly transformed to a courtier with a 'Farewell, my friend', he is ready for his new role in 'Adieu, sir:'—comically he is only *just* ready, for he is still wearing his pedlar's false beard (cf. l. 702).

In soliloquy he congratulates himself on coping with business somewhat out of his usual line of pickpocketing; and he is allowed to kick the joke of the boot around a little further. Here is another verbal glance, too, at the traditional art of the clown: 'Sure, the gods do this year connive at us, and we *may do anything extempore*'; he, the clown as well as Autolycus, proclaims himself 'constant to my profession'. Then more 'matter for a hot brain' enters with shepherd and his son; more 'work' for a 'careful man' he claims, indulging a clown's customary transference of values.

A few preparatory asides and the business of taking off a false beard and he is then ready to encounter the rustics as a full-fledged courtier.

Here the clown can satirize the familiar distinctions between town and country, and would give himself away to anybody but fellow clowns by picking his teeth and, despite the assumed 'gait' with 'the measure of the court', by wearing his clothes 'not handsomely' (ll. 738 and 742). The necessary plot-development being complete, the episode ends with Autolycus terrifying the shepherd's son with a description of tortures and at the same time assuming the role of outraged and self-secure morality. The others leave Autolycus behind for a soliloquy in which he expostulates about his embarrassment of riches:

If I had a mind to be honest, I see Fortune would not suffer me; she drops booties in my mouth.

The last scene in which Autolycus appears (V. ii) would seem an anti-climax to any actor but a clown. He is now in Sicilia and at first he is but one of an audience for the news of Perdita's reunion with her father. But his presence from the start of the scene ensures that he can react to the new situation and allows him a soliloquy immediately before the shepherd and his son enter dressed in new finery. He is dejected:

Now, had I not the dash of my former life in me, would preferment drop on my head . . .

His 'merry' philosophy has let him down and he is even envious:

Here come those I have done good to against my will, and already appearing in the blossoms of their fortune.

But dejection for a clown is a new ploy, even if it appears unassumed. The actor will take advantage of the silence with which he answers the first overtures of the now irrepressible shepherds; and will give a dawning irony to his belated response: 'I know you are now, sir, a gentleman born' (l. 130). After hearing further chat he is ready to make a cumbersomely humble approach. His last words promising to 'prove' a tall fellow is no large conclusion for Autolycus, but that is provided by the last words of the shepherd's son: 'Come, follow us; we'll be thy good masters.' Autolycus makes his exit after them and, for a clown, this is an invitation to provide his own idiosyncratic business: simple mimicry, or a renewed picking of pockets (this became a stage tradition, with words added from David Garrick's version of the play) or, more comprehensively, using grimace and gesture, a rehabilitation of the clown's hopefulness, his nose catching the smell of new trickery—a dawning satisfaction at the prospect of his old comfortable discomfort, his old virtuous vices. With a good clown as Autolycus—and the part calls for one—the mere call to *follow* the others off-stage ensures that he has the last laugh. As Grock would say: 'The chief thing is that what he does makes a hit.'

Autolycus does not attract much attention from readers of *The Winter's Tale* and most literary critics pay only passing recognition. Even in performance he can fall flat. *Punch* of 1 February, 1933, said of an Old Vic production:

> There was little in this dark gymnastic gipsy of Mr. Geoffrey Wincott to suggest that here was one of the great Shakespearean characters. It is not a part which plays itself . . .

Comment in other papers agreed with this, and with the *Manchester Guardian's* judgement of 7 July, 1948, that a Stratford-upon-Avon production had a 'rather too zealously grotesque Autolycus'. The part comes to life only when a clown contributes his own art and personality, and takes up most of the cues that Shakespeare has given him.

In the great age of English pantomine, Garrick's *Florizel and Perdita* held the stage instead of Shakespeare's play. Besides curtailing the action of the play this version gave considerable prominence to Autolycus and the shepherds. But a prompt-book for Kean's revival of Shakespeare's play at the Princess's Theatre in 1856 (now in the Folger Library) shows another way with Autolycus—to cut him down in the interest of stage spectacle and narrative clarity: here, for example, he makes no appearance in Act V. In the theatre Autolycus must be a clown's star performance, or nothing. At almost the same date he was given full scope at Sadlers Wells (as another Folger prompt-book shows): here he enters in IV. ii, '*accompanied in the Orchestra*' and amplifies his role with business, especially when terrifying the shepherds with talk of hanging or amazing the peasants with his ballads.

A very well-documented production was one sponsored by a famous clown at his own theatre and for his own Autolycus. A published *Collection of the Critical Opinions . . . of 'the Winter's Tale' at Burton's Theatre, New York* gives some idea how Simon Forman, a Jacobean playgoer, came to note in his diary after seeing a performance: 'Beware of trusting feigned beggars or fawning fellows.' The New York *Sunday Times* said of William Burton:

He seems to have entered completely into the spirit of the thing; he is so jovial a vagabond, so amusing a specimen of rascality, and commits petit larcenies and small swindling transactions in such a funny, jolly sort of way, that one cannot help enjoying the entertainment he creates as a set off against his natural and unconquerable depravity. . . . The rags are worn with such a jaunty, swaggering air, and he is altogether a most magnificent specimen of the 'bummer' of antiquity. One can hardly help admiring the lazy nonchalance and consistent independence of the honest labor with which he gains a questionable livelihood. . . . In an age of large financial speculation, he would have been a great capitalist, and we admire and respect him accordingly.

The *Albion* also saw contemporary point in Burton's Autolycus— successful clowning is timeless and therefore free to mirror the concerns of any particular age:

He is the embodiment of the vulgar idea of success and the sharpest satire on the worship of the almighty dollar. His 'revenue is the silly cheat.' O, Wall Street, behold thy King! 'Hanging and beating are terrors to him; for the life to come, he sleeps out the thought of it!' Comfortable nodder, in the deep wall pew, behold thy ancestor!

The *Sunday Despatch* described the effect of this Autolycus on the play as a whole:

Our only regret is that Master William Shakespere does not send that rogue Autolycus upon the stage before the fourth act, when, in reality, that life which alone can give general popularity to the play only begins. Burton is grand, rich, unctuous, racy, roguish, and funny all at one and the same time in the part. . . .

Burton had much the same creative qualifications for the role as an Elizabethan clown. Like Tarlton and Armin, he had published his *Waggeries and Vagaries*; and he wrote several farces. 'Mirth', it was said, 'came from him in exhalations', and 'the resources of by-play, grimace, and mimetic effect, were his at command' (W. Keese, *Actors and Actresses*, iii (1886), p. 224):

The secret of Burton's power did not lie in any single gift; it was not only his mirth-provoking face, his ability to infuse character and comicality together into his countenance, though doubtless this was the most peculiar of his talents; he had others. . . . Burton had a creative faculty. He did more for many of the characters he played

than the author of the piece. His *Toodle* and *Sleek* were absolute
creations, and indicated an ability quite akin to that of a great
dramatist. . . .

(The *Sunday Times*, New York, 12 Feb., 1860)

A full clown's performance in *The Winter's Tale* importantly affects
the theatrical life of the play. In a story that moves from prosperity
through destruction to regeneration, from separation to reconciliation,
the clown presents a character who is both a failure and a success. In an
intensely felt narrative he evokes from the audience laughter, connivance and appreciation, relaxation and admiration. In a drama about
the influences of time, he provides a timeless artistry and remains unchanged at the conclusion. He brings topicality to a fantastic tale, an
escape from the consequences of knavery to a moral confrontation,
and a grotesque embodiment of irresponsible fears and aggressions, of
vigorous and sexual activity, to a shapely and often refined romance.

Some implications of his role can be appreciated through particular
points of contact with the rest of the play. Before and during the sheep-
shearing, Autolycus establishes the trickery of disguise, the sport of
thieving and the easy excitement of 'summer songs . . . While we lie
tumbling in the hay.' Verbal connections indicate the relevance of all
these exploits to the main plot: Florizel calls Perdita a goddess, as
Autolycus sings his wares 'as they were gods and goddesses'; Polixenes
calls her a 'knack', as he had called Autolycus' pedlar's wares; Perdita's
'blood looks out' at Florizel's whisperings, after Autolycus had hailed
the 'red blood' that reigns in the 'winter's pale'; and Florizel had dis-
appeared from court, as Autolycus' ballad promises:

> Get you hence, for I must go
> Where it fits not you to know.

Later the very clothes for disguising Florizel are taken from Autolycus'
disguise, and the fearful trembling of this clown, and later of the
shepherd's son, is here a reminder of the dangers everyone risks at this
juncture of the plot.

But Autolycus' contribution to the play is greatest at its most general.
His heightening of the 'mirth of the feast'—the licence of instinctive
and irresponsible enjoyment—enables Shakespeare to present Florizel
and Perdita without stiffness and yet with contrasting carefulness; it
also enables the dance of the wild 'men of hair' to make its contrast
with the earlier decorous dance with immediate acceptance as another

divertissement. The last exit for Autolycus in Act V, with its climactic and possibly silent humour, is an important device to relax the critical attention of the audience immediately before Hermione is revealed as a painted statue. Grock used to play Verdi on a diminutive concertina at the end of his act, and it always seemed powerfully seductive to the audience; and so here, the audience's contentment at the invincible humour and roguery of Autolycus disposes it to accept the strange, severe and sweetened (cf. l. 76) theatricality of the concluding scene. Laughter and dreams alike release our fantasies from the restrictive control of our censoring minds; so, having joined everyman's laughter at the undeserved and unfounded resilience of Autolycus, the audience will more readily accept the dreamlike conditions of the final scene, the living statue that

> Excels whatever yet you look'd upon
> Or hand of man hath done. (ll. 16–17)

Laughter has contrived the relaxed and uncritical condition suitable for the acceptance of a further and solemn fantasy.

'Dreams are toys' argues Antigonus in III. iii, and at the end of *A Midsummer Night's Dream* Puck asks that the whole comedy should be accepted as an idle dream. So much Shakespeare certainly knew about the connections between fantasy and humour, and his contemporaries accepted it too. The total solemnity of much criticism of the last plays that is current today would strike Elizabethans and Jacobeans as pompous and restrictive. Romance, for them, spelt wonder, delight, *and* mirth. The prologue to the romantic comedy *Mucedorus* expresses this directly:

> Mirth drown your bosom, fair Delight your mind,
> And may our pastime your contentment find.

In *The Winter's Tale* there is more 'pastime' than Autolycus. The two shepherds are traditional rustic comics, with muddled meetings and muddled speeches; they mix comedy and pathos in discovering the disastrous end of Antigonus; they mistake meanings, labour slowly in witticisms, attempt mimicry, and, like Autolycus, leave the play with more troubles obviously to come. There is comedy, too, in the earlier scenes of the main plot, especially in the contrasts between the forthright Paulina and the timid jailor and courtiers, and the two husbands, Antigonus and Leontes. All the comedy contributes to the final effect of the play, by its fantasy and freedom, obviously; but also by the individuality and robust vitality that are required to perform the more comic roles. Laughter brings release, warmth, engagement, enjoyment, and spontaneity, and invites an almost limitless extension of the audience's fancy.

★   ★   ★

Shakespeare's other romances raise laughter too, in various ways, according to their narratives and themes. *Pericles*, that is probably not wholly by Shakespeare, has least comedy. In the last three Acts, where the authorship is less disputed, humour is concentrated in the brothel scenes, allowing a kind of ease and delight to incidents out of tone with the thrusting and evocative narrative of the rest of those Acts. Boult, the clown's part, is dominant here, but the whole incident takes some colour from him, notably in a short scene (IV. v) with the memorably exaggerated line, 'Come, I am for no more bawdy-houses. Shall's go hear the vestals sing?', with which an anonymous Gentleman suggests a zany impracticability in sudden conversion. Boult remains unchanged when he leaves the play, but subdued to Marina's purposes and having voiced, perhaps in unusually solemn tones, the clown's usual defence of his misdeeds—that is, that the fault lies in the world, or with 'others':

> What would you have me do? Go to the wars, would you, where a man may serve seven years for the loss of a leg, and have not money enough in the end to buy him a wooden one?
> (IV. vi. 168–70)

In *Cymbeline*, the jailor is the only outright clown's part, but his clown's defence, 'I would we were all of one mind, and one mind good' (V. iv. 200), is an important, verbal preparation for the Soothsayer's final:

> The fingers of the pow'rs above do tune
> The harmony of this peace.   (V. v. 464–5)

But here the humour is dispersed throughout the play. Cloten looks at first to be a loutish clown, amusingly and coarsely interrupting the courtly scenes and then becoming the foolish wild-man of the woods who ineffectually tries to ravish Imogen and kill Posthumus. But in his two soliloquies, 'I love and hate her' and 'Meet thee at Milford Haven!' (III. v. 70 ff. and 131 ff.) he is presented with too strong an impression of pent-up and self-conflicting feelings to remain either a clown or a comic villain. His end is funny, like a typical braggart's combat, but Belarius reminds the audience of the risks he has so far taken:

> not frenzy, not
> Absolute madness could so far have rav'd
> To bring him here alone.   (IV. ii. 135–7)

and he differs from other braggarts in actually taking the initiative in the last engagement—'Yield, rustic mountaineer'—and actually, though off-stage, dying. In *Cymbeline* the relaxed enjoyment of comedy is seldom unalloyed; the Queen, Posthumus, Iachimo, Pisanio, Belario, Guiderius, Arviragus, Cymbeline himself perhaps, and certainly Imogen, all raise laughter at times, as does the contrivance of the plot, and yet all these characters, at times, command the audience's closest and directest sympathy.

When Imogen mistakes Cloten's headless body as Posthumus', laughter and tears are brought together most sharply. For Imogen the experience is specifically like a 'dream':

> The dream's here still. Even when I wake it is
> Without me, as within me; not imagin'd, felt.
> A headless man? . . .
>   O Posthumus! alas,
> Where is thy head? Where's that? Ay me! where's that?
> Pisanio might have kill'd thee at the heart,
> And left this head on. How should this be?

The apparent reality as expressed here is so absurd that very few actresses have dared to use all the words provided. Bernard Shaw recognized that Shakespeare had successfully created the 'dim, half-asleep funny state of consciousness' but he nevertheless advised Ellen Terry to cut 'A headless man' from her performance:

> This is what I cannot understand; and I believe it is an overlooked relic of some earlier arrangement of the business.[2]

The whole soliloquy so mixes abrupt comedy with deepest feeling that, temporarily, the comedy is entirely subdued, becoming part of the terror of Imogen's nightmare-dream. Only out of dramatic context, without the passion and uncertainty of the 'felt' situation, are the lines

---

[2] *Ellen Terry and Bernard Shaw; a Correspondence*, ed. C. St. John (1949), pp. 45–6.

at all funny; trust the mixture of absurdity and fantasy and the scene becomes wholly affecting.

In the last scene the persistent mingling of comedy and affecting dramatic narrative is smoothly resolved. The characters file off-stage together, no one drawing all sentiment to himself but all moving at the bidding and with the reassurance of the Soothsayer, Philarmonus. All are 'o'erjoy'd' (l. 401): 'joy'd' that others are what they are, and prepared to 'laud . . . the gods' and wonder at the new 'peace' (ll. 424 and 474–83). It would be wrong to cut from this last scene its hints of comedy, the laughter that can so readily be raised by Posthumus' 'Shall's have a play of this?', Cymbeline's 'Does the world go round?', the Doctor's 'I left out one thing . . .', Belarius' 'My boys, There was our error' and 'Not too hot . . . I am too blunt and saucy', and the sudden reappearance of the Doctor for the ludicrously neat 'By the Queen's dram she swallow'd'. At these and other points the contrivance of the play's conclusion can appear hilariously complicated; and the laughter that will undoubtedly come during rehearsals must be prized and its occasions carefully retained and possibly augmented in order to help present the delight and fantasy of the happy ending. This romantic play uses laughter as an entry and support for fantasy, and so gains moments of feeling that are all the sharper for contrast, and it arrives at a conclusion that in performance can seem sublime because it is not always perfectly serious and so not always obviously impossible.

The conclusion of *The Tempest* is the most grave and considered of all. But in this play, too, the importance of laughter can be underestimated. The last arrivals when Prospero stands revealed as the rightful Duke of Milan are a drunken jester and butler, and a 'thing of darkness': such emphatic placing alone requires respect. Obviously Trinculo and Stephano seeking shelter or profit from Caliban is a normal comic ploy, and singing of 'Freedom' or 'Scout 'em and flout 'em', or falling-out about the finery Prospero sets as a trap, are incidents inviting team work and embellishment. And Caliban himself as a strange 'monster' is partly a clown's role; even his attempted rape of Miranda and attack on Prospero, together with his care for the island's beauties, are in the comic tradition. Bremo, the wild-man in *Mucedorus*, tries to woo Amadine, offering like Caliban to Stephano:

> If thou wilt love me thou shalt be my queen;
> I'll crown thee with a chaplet made of ivory,
> And make the rose and lily wait on thee.

I'll rend the burly branches from the oak,
To shadow thee from burning sun,
The trees shall spread themselves where thou dost go,
And as they spread, I'll trace along with thee . . .

(IV. iii)

and much more. William Burton played Caliban in his own theatre, along with Autolycus, Bottom, Belch, Falstaff, and a host of his farcical creations:

> The most superb performance of Burton's which I remember was his *Caliban*. A wild creature on all fours sprang upon the stage, with claws on his hands, and some weird animal arrangement about the head partly like a snail. It was an immense conception. Not the great God Pan himself was more the link between the man and beast than this thing. It was a creature of the woods, one of nature's spawns; it breathed of nuts and herbs, and rubbed itself against the back of trees.
>
> (*New York Times*, 20 June, 1875)

To give Caliban to a clown does not mean underplaying the obvious pathos and power of feeling in the role:

> His Caliban we have tried to forget rather than remember; [wrote W. L. Keese in his memoir of Burton] it terrified us and made us dream bad dreams; but for all that, we know that it was a surprising impersonation. (p. 175)

There are, in fact, changes in Shakespeare's use of his comics: from the beginning of this play their characters carry a more than usual burden of immediate and inescapable feeling. They are closer to Cloten than to Autolycus or the shepherds. Trinculo and Stephano are afraid of the storm, the monster, the island and strange noises, without having the compensating resilience of a clown; they are saved by mutual recognition (II. ii. 92–3) and later by Caliban's 'Be not afeard. The isle is full of noises . . .' (III. ii. 130 ff.). And the coward revealed under Trinculo's jesting and the bully under Stephano's good cheer are displayed at last without a chance of laughing the consequences away. The last appearance of the trio raises an obvious laugh from the callow Sebastian, but their ludicrous debacle produces a muddled exhortation that is more surprising than the jailor's or Boult's last resort, less obviously hypocritical than that of Autolycus:

> Every man shift for all the rest, and let no man take care for himself; for all is but fortune. (V. i. 256–7)

In the confrontation that follows wit serves the severe moral tone of
Prospero's judgement, not the irresponsibility of fooling:

> TRINCULO: I have been in such a pickle since I saw you last that, I
>   fear me, will never out of my bones. I shall not fear fly-blowing.
> SEBASTIAN: Why, how now, Stephano!
> STEPHANO: O, touch me not; I am not Stephano, but a cramp.
> PROSPERO: You'd be king 'o the isle, sirrah?
> STEPHANO: I should have been a sore one, then.
> ALONSO [*pointing to Caliban*]: This is as strange a thing as e'er I
>   look'd on.
> PROSPERO: He is as disproportioned in his manners
>   As in his shape. Go, sirrah, to my cell;
>   Take with you your companions; as you look
>   To have my pardon, trim it handsomely.
> CALIBAN: Ay, that I will; and I'll be wise hereafter,
>   And seek for grace. What a thrice-double ass
>   Was I to take this drunkard for a god,
>   And worship this dull fool!

Each of the trio makes a forced jest at their own expense; but not as a
comic escape route. Nor do the despatching words suggest a funny
exeunt:

> PROSPERO: Go to; away!
> ALONSO: Hence, and bestow your luggage where you found it.
> SEBASTIAN: Or stole it, rather.

Nor do they encourage sympathy. Laughter has been aroused by the
earlier meetings and conspiracy; but its perpetrators are not laughed
off. Remembering them, Prospero had been so disturbed that his
daughter had never seen him 'touch'd with anger so distemper'd'
(IV. i. 144-5).

Shakespeare has tightly reined all the laughter in this deliberately
judicial play. Miranda's first encounters with Ferdinand cause her to
'prattle something too wildly', to ask outright 'Do you love me?', to
announce unbidden 'I am your wife'. Prospero's comment when he
finds them together suggests the incipient comedy: 'Poor worm, thou
art infected! This visitation shows it'; but within forty lines he is
caught into a very different response:

> Fair encounter
> Of two most rare affections! Heavens rain grace
> On that which breeds between 'em! (III. i. 32-76)

In the last scene too, Miranda's 'Sweet lord, you play me false' and

> How beauteous mankind is! O brave new world
> That has such people in't!   (V. i. 172–84)

may well bring laughter for their ironical innocence; but even more
quickly than at the end of *Cymbeline*, this comedy is lost in wonder and
in the joy of reconciliation.

Antonio and Sebastian's jesting with Gonzalo turns awry as 'Widow
Dido' is introduced and Alonso, for whose ease the wit was encouraged
by Gonzalo, is forced to think anew of his lost son and daughter.
When the lords mock the idealism of Gonzalo's utopian discourse, the
jesting gives place to a conspiracy to kill Alonso.

Ariel has some flashes of Puck-like humour, as in:

> The King's son have I landed by himself,
> Whom I left cooling of the air with sighs
> In an odd angle of the isle, and sitting,
> His arms in this sad knot— (I. ii. 221–4)

and he seems to relish joining the clownish quarrels of Trinculo and
Stephano. But Ariel is also, from the first, a 'moody spirit', and one
who is busy in order to win freedom from contact with everyone in
the play. Once he does sing '. . . merrily. Merrily, merrily . . .', but
that is only when his own freedom is in sight. He does not answer
Prospero's 'I shall miss thee' (V. i. 95) and he is almost silent on his last
errands. Dismissed in the very last speech of the play he has no words
of farewell to Prospero; perhaps he should laugh 'merrily' after he
has left the stage.

Shakespeare gave laughter to all his romances, mixing mirth with
delight and dreaming. But for the one which ends with a solitary man
wanting:

> Spirits to enforce, art to enchant;
> And my ending is despair
> Unless I be reliev'd by prayer, . . .

he banished laughter too before its conclusion; it is lost in punishment,
in wonder and joy, in conspiracy and treachery, and in the escape of
Ariel.

Note

Early performances. Pericles, Cymbeline, The Winter's Tale, and *Henry VIII* were acted at the Globe Theatre. *Pericles* was performed at Court in 1619, and *Cymbeline* in 1633. *The Tempest* was performed there in 1611, *The Winter's Tale* in 1612, and the last two were among plays chosen for performance during the wedding festivities for Princess Elizabeth and Prince Frederick in 1613; and it has been suggested that *Henry VIII* was intended for the same repertoire. *The Two Noble Kinsmen* was performed at Blackfriars in 1613, and possibly at Court in 1619. All these plays were of mixed theatrical provenance, capable of being presented at the Globe, or Blackfriars, or the Court.

Scholarship and criticism. Recent studies of the public and private theatres of Shakespeare's time include G. E. Bentley's 'Shakespeare and the Blackfriars Theatre', in *Shakespeare Survey* 1 (1948), A. Harbage's *Shakespeare and the Rival Traditions* (1952), and W. A. Armstrong's *The Elizabethan Private Theatres—Facts and Problems* (Society for Theatre Research, 1958).

Among accounts of Elizabethan acting styles are M. C. Bradbrook's *Themes and Conventions of Elizabethan Tragedy* (1935), especially chapters ii–iii; Bertram Joseph's *Elizabethan Acting* (1951; revised 1964); *The Tragic Actor* (1959), and *Acting Shakespeare* (1960); A. Harbage offers a more inclusive suggestion on the 'formal' aspects of Elizabethan acting in *Theatre for Shakespeare* (1955), Appendix B. J. R. Brown's 'On the Acting of Shakespeare's Plays', *Quarterly Journal of Speech* (1953), opposes a categorically 'formal' approach. See also R. A. Foakes, 'The Player's Passion', *Essays and Studies* (1954), D. Seltzer, 'Elizabethan Acting in *Othello*', *Shakespeare Quarterly* (1959), and B. Beckerman, *Shakespeare at the Globe 1599–1609* (1962); a 'naturalistic' approach is strongly taken by M. Rosenberg's 'Elizabethan Actors: men or marionettes?', *P.M.L.A.* (1954). The writer of the present chapter is engaged on a book on the subject. References to some of the above articles are given by authors' names only in this chapter. Line references are from the Globe text, and quotations from Shakespeare, unless otherwise noted, are from the Variorum editions of First Folio plays: for *Pericles* quotations are from W. W. Greg's Shakespeare Quarto Facsimile (No. 5) of the 1609 Quarto; for *The Two Noble Kinsmen* quotations are from J. S. Farmer's Tudor Facsimile Text (1910) of the 1634 Quarto.

VI

The Staging of the Last Plays

DANIEL SELTZER

★

WHEN Shakespeare's company leased in 1608 the empty theatre at Blackfriars, it is natural to assume that these actors, including their most important playwright, took into immediate consideration the nature of the new stage—its potentials and its limitations—and planned accordingly what was in the main a new repertory. We have no reason to assume that occupation of the theatre at Blackfriars was a move which caused the company trouble or worry, however; on the contrary, to have obtained it as a second house was a cause for rejoicing. Surely Professor Bentley is right in his assumptions that the new lessees made adjustments, and made them eagerly; for good artistic and commercial reasons, much discussion and thought must have been expended just before and during the King's Men's first performances in their private theatre: the suitability of certain plays to a different audience, the necessity to have new ones written (the children had taken their scripts with them), the potential of the acting company as it was then composed, the fact that the commercial future 'lay with the court and the court party in the private theatres'. Each of these considerations must have played a part in plans for the future; and that the Shakespearian repertory in the years which followed was, at any rate, somehow 'different' has been the judgement of several generations of scholars and critics. Many reasons for the difference—whatever that may be—have been advanced, and it is not the purpose of this chapter to review or to discuss them in detail. But we must at least ask ourselves whether the new stage now used by the King's Men as well as that at the Globe may not have accounted for some aspects of the often-remarked alteration in mood and style. We know that James Burbage, father of Cuthbert and Richard, had transformed certain rooms in the old priory 'into a play house wth great charge & trouble',[1] but although

[1] *Malone Society Collections*, II: 3 (1931), p. 371.

certain characteristics of these stage facilities may be inferred, probably with some accuracy, from the texts of the plays performed there, we actually know less about the King's Men's stage at Blackfriars than about their physical situation in the Globe. And since the company continued of course to perform in the Globe as well as Blackfriars, we know even less about the exact theatrical provenance of the plays Shakespeare wrote after the private house was leased. None of the records fixes any one of them as a work planned specifically for one stage or the other, and those critics are certainly correct who observe that they could have been performed in either.

It is important to keep this in mind when one endeavours to isolate aspects of staging in Shakespeare's late plays—at Blackfriars, at Court, or at the Globe. The natural tendency is to seek innovation; but actors, especially when they belong to a highly successful repertory company, can be remarkably conservative. And we must remember that during a period when many new plays were quickly learned and rehearsed, and some revived which had been out of the current list for some time (even if Blackfriars required fewer new plays than were needed at the Globe), many completely new techniques would have been impossible. I do not suggest that the style of Elizabethan acting itself did not develop; there is some evidence that this took place in any case, regardless of the auspices of performance. But because the moral and literary qualities of the last plays are 'different' does not mean that the staging which articulated them was necessarily new in any drastic way.

On the other hand, Shakespeare wrote always in a manner which made best use of the theatrical facilities available to him. It would be folly to ignore aspects of private production which, although practicable in the Globe, are given interesting significance in the last plays. The ways in which these theatrical matters become significant does suggest that Shakespeare's intentions in these plays might be made tangible perhaps more conveniently or more directly at Blackfriars than in the public theatre, although one feels that Professor Harbage's judgement is nevertheless correct, when he observes that 'the plays . . . in [this] period, contrary to a common critical assumption, are popular in type' (p. 86). Bentley suggests that after 1608 Shakespeare wrote 'with the Blackfriars in mind and not the Globe', for 'the Globe could be left to take care of itself with an old repertory as the Blackfriars could not' (p. 46). Granting the truth of this statement (the opinions of Harbage and Bentley are not incompatible), it is necessary to remember as well that whatever the theatre in Blackfriars contained—whether we consider the demands of its audience, the nature of its stage, or its potential for visual and musical elements—the plays Shakespeare wrote for it represent a natural development of his art. This development, as it shaped his last plays, is inseparable from the theatrical situation in which it thrived. We must try to avoid any interpretation of data concerning these plays and the private theatre in Blackfriars which implies between them a cause and effect relationship. The fact that almost all of these plays seem to have been performed with success at the Globe (and, indeed, in the cases of four of the six, our earliest reference to performance is to staging at the Globe), probably points to the truth of the matter: Shakespeare did not begin writing in a special way only because Blackfriars had become available, any more than the King's Men decided to lease Blackfriars because Shakespeare's plays were gradually altering in scope and in tone; rather, just as in the previous decades the development of the great public theatres both answered the needs of the popular drama and were richly served by it, so in the last part of his career, the needs of the playwright's art and the development and availability of theatrical facilities answered each other.

Any consideration of the staging of these plays must involve examination of acting style as well as the theatrical use of music, dancing, and, in all six plays, stage spectacles such as processions, dream visions, and theophanies. I exclude from treatment here discussion of artificial lighting and painted scenery. In both cases, documentation is meagre, and one is too easily tempted to speculate. No doubt some stage structures, some painted scenes, and some costuming at Blackfriars resembled some of these elements in the Court masques; but although the rich collection of designs by Inigo Jones, preserved at Chatsworth, allows one to reconstruct some of the Court's costumes and scenery quite specifically, parallels with the décor in performances of Shakespeare's plays are necessarily open to question.[2] Music, dancing, and spectacle of various kinds are other matters, however. Notation for these, although it may be very incomplete, is usually either explicit or may be inferred, with caution, from the texts of the plays.

It is possible to examine with some accuracy two aspects of style in the staging of these six plays. The first has to do with the techniques of the actors, and the second with the frequency and means with which

[2] Cf. A. Nicoll, *Stuart Masques and the Renaissance Stage* (1938), p. 150.

I

spectacle or music were introduced into the acted representation of reality. It is pertinent also to ask why a certain technique or spectacular element is appropriate to the play or plays in which we find it. As has been suggested, one enters such a study with the expectation of a style somewhat altered from that of Shakespeare's 'Globe plays' previous to 1608; it is natural to anticipate that a different sort of play (if not a different stage and audience) would produce some changes, and even the most casual reader can tell that most of these plays contain (for example) more music, strategically located in the action, than had been included in the earlier plays. But it is just as important to note those aspects of staging which apparently did not change in any way when the King's Men established a repertory at Blackfriars.

Almost all our information concerning the style of Elizabethan acting is implicit in the lines of the plays. Occasionally, a piece of writing about the players is revealing, but although the Elizabethans produced many eulogies to actors, much descriptive satire about the behaviour of some types of spectators, and a remarkable number of records (considering how many have been lost) concerning the conduct of the acting companies, they hardly ever left for us specific descriptions of technique and method.[3] Their judgement that the art of acting, when it was well executed, was 'realistic' really does not help us much; every age has always maintained that the goal of its representational arts was to mirror nature accurately. As E. H. Gombrich has observed succinctly, 'What we call *seeing* is invariably coloured and shaped by our knowledge (or belief) of what we see',[4] and it is for this reason that a study of Elizabethan acting techniques, as part of an over-all style of staging, can help us understand a bit more about habits of perception in Shakespeare's time. The important question remains, of course, *how* the mirroring of reality was effected. Although it is not one of the heavily embattled areas of modern criticism, the subject of this acting method has elicited a number of opinions; to date, the body of evidence necessary for an accurate estimate has not been collected, but the opinions of the opposing camps are easily summarized. A number of critics hold that Elizabethan acting was highly 'formal', that is, that its range of movement, gesture, and vocal expression was more or less

---

[3] See J. Cocke's Character of 'A common Player', 1615 (qu. Chambers, *Elizabethan Stage*, IV, 256), and Nashe, Prologue, *Summer's Last Will and Testament* (McKerrow ed., Works of Thomas Nashe, III, 236).

[4] *Art and Illusion* (1960), p. 394.

categorical, corresponding to a range of rhetorical attitudes capable of being described objectively, and prohibiting (therefore) factors we might wish to call 'inspiration' or 'individual interpretation'. The opposing opinion maintains that much in the style was specifically 'realistic', even 'naturalistic', that certain details of action would have been executed as they might be today, and that there was every reason for a performance by a great actor to exhibit personal inspiration, in every modern sense of the word. Other critics believe the acting technique was a mixture of rhetorical forms and precise naturalism; and some suggest that this style gradually changed from the early days of the Theatre to those of Blackfriars presently under discussion.

This matter cannot be settled here, of course; but a selected number of pertinent facts relative to acting in Shakespeare's late plays add to the potential usefulness of the more extensive collection still needed. It should be observed in passing, however, that those critics who speak of the 'formal' aspects of Elizabethan acting are only commenting upon ways in which it may have appeared different from ours (that dangerous theatrical adjective, 'stylized'—meaning 'mannered'—has come into use only in our own day, and the Elizabethans would not have known what is meant by it). Critics who find evidence for a 'realistic' style, on the other hand, propose simply that much Elizabethan acting looked like ours. Neither mirror image can be entirely correct. That the acting at its best was considered 'realistic' there can be no doubt whatever, but even without accumulated evidence there is no more reason to assume that some aspects of it would resemble our own styles, than to expect any other form of Renaissance art to resemble its modern equivalent.

Documentation of acting techniques in Elizabethan plays may be divided in three categories. The first is composed of those printed stage-directions which actually tell us how something was done on stage— excluding that sort of direction commonly called 'literary', which may describe (for example) a setting which might not have been manifest in the playhouse. Some of the original directions, however, do indicate order of entrance, properties, physical placement of the actors on the stage, and the like. Two categories of information may be called 'implicit stage-directions', since they derive, on the one hand, from lines in which one character will describe what another on stage is doing, or how he is doing it. (We are lucky to find such evidence of action; it is naturally rare in any period of dramatic writing, since it is seldom necessary for anyone on stage to describe activity which the audience can observe just as clearly. The Elizabethans—either for emphasis, or because some part of the audience in fact could not see the action, or for some other reason—did include such description in their scripts.) Great care must be exercised in drawing conclusions from the second category of implicit directions. These indicate the spatial relationships among actors on stage—that aspect of staging a modern producer or director usually calls 'blocking', or the 'moves' of an actor. The possibilities of movement at any given juncture in stage action are numerous, but ultimately there are only so many ways an actor, alone or with one or more others, can move—in address (to them or to the audience) or in silence. Most of the time this form of evidence is impossible to isolate; but occasionally one spatial relationship, precisely defined, could have taken place only in sequence with another, usually immediately preceding it. Sometimes, if rarely, it is possible in this way to reconstruct two or three such arrangements, and in these cases a tangible picture of stage movement emerges.

From this body of information one may draw some conclusions about four aspects of acting style; these categories are reasonably inclusive, and together cover everything an actor can do (physically) on stage.

(1) *Business.* The term includes all stage actions relating to the actor who originates them and to others involved in them; I append to this category of action all gestures and smaller details of stage movement not properly included under the head of 'blocking'. Walks and other action carried out while speaking are also a form of 'stage business', as distinct from those movements interesting to us because they help reveal the placement of actors about the stage. Included as well are facial expressions.

(2) *Voice.* Primarily, pitch and volume; occasionally, special uses such as imitation or parody, drunkenness, and the like; and also the dramatic pacing of speeches, such as indications of special pauses, extra speed, and tonal quality.

(3) *Blocking* (*stage movement*). The actor's moves from one part of the stage to another; his location when alone on stage; the spatial relationships between two actors or among more than two; the areas of the stage apparently considered 'strongest' and those utilized for different kinds of action.

(4) *Address*. Literally, the direction of the actor's speech—when he is alone on stage (as when, in a meditative speech, he may, as it were, address 'himself' only; or, in an explanatory or descriptive vein, or in a comic routine, address the audience; or, in a speech of apostrophe, usually in strong emotions, address an imaginary hearer—see Beckerman, *op. cit.*, pp. 183–6) or with other actors (when he may speak to one or more at a time, or speak without actually addressing any, or in asides to the audience, or alternate among actors, or between them and the audience; also when his speech covers the exit or anticipates the entrance of another actor).

STAGE BUSINESS

In 2 *The Return from Parnassus* Kemp is made to criticize the academic actors who 'never speake in their walke, but at the end of the stage, iust as though in walking with a fellow we should never speake but at a stile, a gate, or a ditch, where a man can go no further' (cited by Brown, *op. cit.*, p. 487). The observation is good evidence that a natural manner was common practice, and plays from earlier decades contain enough evidence of it to prove it no innovation. The late drama of Shakespeare, however, is particularly full of explicit and implicit directions to walk or carry forward other business while speaking.

A few examples must suffice. As might be expected, the range of business possible while speaking was great. Glasses are filled and food is eaten (*Per.*, II. iii); Ariel sings while dressing Prospero in the robes of Milan (*Temp.*, V. i. 87 S.D.), and his master speaks as he adjusts the robes ('but yet thou shalt have freedom: so, so, so'); Ferdinand speaks, in all likelihood, while carrying logs (III. i. 1–17); and Palamon and Arcite joke boisterously while drinking (*Two Noble Kins.*, III. iii). During the highly detailed business involved in adjusting armour, the two knights conduct a dialogue questioning each other about the fit of each piece, and anticipating their combat (III. vi). Because the handling of costumes and properties took place during the lines, these would necessarily have been delivered directly to each other, timing speech to each item of completed business; one cannot escape the impression, therefore, of great flexibility and natural pace of delivery.

> ARC: . . . doe I pinch you?
> PAL: Noe.

> ARC: Is't not too heavie?
> PAL: I have worne a lighter.
> But I shall make it serve.
> ARC: Ile buckl't close.
> PAL: By any meanes.
> ARC: You care not for a Grand guard?
> PAL: No, no, wee'l use no horses, I perceave
> You would faine be at that fight.
> ARC: I am indifferent.

After more in this vein, Palamon turns to help Arcite, and as he does so, they recall battles of earlier days.

> ARC: When I saw you charge first,
> Me thought I heard a dreadfull clap of Thunder
> Breake from the Troope.
> PAL: But still before that flew
> The lightning of your valour: Stay a little,
> Is not this peece too streight?

The same ease and natural pacing appear in an episode, containing identical business and use of properties (but with much greater pertinence to the thematic concern of the play), in *Antony and Cleopatra*; apparently whatever alteration of platform area was entailed in using the Blackfriars stage required no real difference in method for this intimate type of action.

> ANT: ... Come.
> CLEO: Nay, I'll help too, What's this for?
> ANT: Ah, let be, let be! thou art
> The armourer of my heart: false, false: this, this,
> CLEO: Sooth-[la] I'll help; thus it must be.
> ANT: Well, well, we shall thrive now.
>
> . . . .
> CLEO: Is not this buckled well?
> ANT: Rarely, rarely. . . .   (IV. iv. 5-11)

There is in *Henry VIII* a scene which is an almost complete book of directions for action intended to convey deep confusion, fear, and anger; it serves here as evidence for detailed movement during a partial soliloquy, but also indicates precisely a series of gestures which are most suggestive in any consideration of an over-all style of acting. Norfolk, Suffolk, Surrey, and the Lord Chamberlain have been discussing events relative to the King's divorce, when Wolsey and Cromwell enter. Immediately, Norfolk says, of the Cardinal, 'Observe, observe, he's moody' (III. ii. 75); nothing has been said, but Norfolk —and the audience—have seen the Cardinal frowning (see below, on facial expression). Wolsey speaks to Cromwell of the letters the King has opened, not observing the others on stage, and, after his servant is dismissed, the Cardinal's speech informs the audience of his plans and fears.

> It shall be to the Duchess of Alençon,
> The French king's sister; he shall marry her.
> *Anne Bullen*? No: I'll no *Anne Bullen* for him,
> There's more in't than fair visage. *Bullen*?
> No, we'l no *Bullens*. Speedily I wish
> To hear from Rome. The Marchioness of Pembroke?

The lords on stage have not, of course, 'heard' Wolsey, but Norfolk observes, 'He's discontented'. After the others comment, the Cardinal resumes:

> The late queen's gentlewoman?
> A knight's daughter,
> To be her mistress's mistress? The queen's, queen?
> This candle burns not cleer, 'tis I must snuff it,
> Then out it goes. What though I know her vertuous
> And well deserving? yet I know her for
> A spleeny Lutheran; and not wholesome to
> Our cause, that she should lie i'th'bosom of
> Our hard rul'd king. Again, there is sprung up
> An heretic, an arch-one, *Cranmer*; one
> Hath crawl'd into the favour of the king,
> And is his oracle.

For the third time Norfolk comments on Wolsey's state of mind: 'He is vex'd at something.' Here the King enters, reading (as he moves into the acting area) the inventory of Wolsey's possessions, and, not noticing the Cardinal (which indicates that Wolsey has moved to one corner of the stage, probably diagonally opposite whichever door used by Henry for his entrance), asks for him. Norfolk replies:

> My lord, we have
> Stood here observing him. Some strange commotion
> Is in his brain: he bites his lip, and starts,
> Stops on a sudden, looks upon the ground,
> Then lays his finger on his temple: straight
> Springs out into fast gait; then stops again,

> Strikes his breast hard, and anon, he casts
> His eye against the moon: in most strange postures
> We have seen him set himself.

Norfolk's catalogue of movements and gestures must be accurate, of course; the audience has just seen whatever it was the actor playing Wolsey did, and even if the playwright is anxious for us not to miss how troubled the Cardinal is, any added emphasis in Norfolk's description would be built upon the action just ended. Wolsey's business was evidently categorical action for great perturbation; biting the lip, for example, had long been a standard piece of business (e.g. Catesby, *Rich. III*, IV. ii. 27: 'The King is angry, see he gnaws his lip'; Desdemona, *Oth.*, V. ii. 46: 'Alas, why gnaw you so your nether-lip?'). In addition we have sudden movement into a fast walk, and sudden stops, quick alteration of looks upward and downward, pressing the finger against the temple, and striking the breast; 'There is a mutiny in's mind', Henry observes.[5] Following Norfolk's summary, it would almost be possible to insert stage-directions for the lines of Wolsey's speeches in this scene; in any case, this acting style clearly involved more than a few gestures and must have eschewed small or over-subtle facial expression. It demanded considerable movement across the stage. It was, to say the least, a 'large' style.

Henry VIII contains more evidence for walking on lines than any other play in this group. For some reason, such walks are frequently made explicit in stage-directions—but this does not mean, of course, that they occurred only at these moments. We know, for example, that Queen Katharine, early in I. ii, has allowed Henry to bring her to his side, where she is seated; after the discussion of taxation is over and the matter of Buckingham raised, however, the King says to her, 'Sit by Us, you shall hear | . . . of him | Things to strike Honour sad' (I. ii. 124–6). The only explanation is that during her long speeches on the royal commissions and the subjects' discontent, Katharine rose and moved across the stage, remaining there during Wolsey's defence of the policy. There is no doubt that speech took place on movement, and not only between moves; this scene itself begins with the stage-direction, '*Enter King Henry, leaning on the Cardinal's shoulder . . .*' Although the first speech is Henry's, it could have begun before actually arriving at the throne. Later, in III. ii, after discovering

[5] A similar range of attitudes and gesture may have been used by Burbage as Othello; see my article, *op. cit.* pp. 208–10.

Wolsey's plots, the King is to leave the stage (frowning upon the Cardinal as he does so), and the nobles are to '*throng after him smiling, and whispering*' (S.D. at 203). One of the most satisfactory uses of the move, and one of the most natural, occurs during Henry's interview with Cranmer, late in the play. Meeting the Archbishop, the King says, 'Come, you and I must | Walk a turn together' (V. i. 92 ff), obviously taking Cranmer by the arm and conducting the conversation as they walk about the platform; again, when Cranmer kneels to him, Henry says quickly, 'Give me thy hand, stand up, | Prythee let's walk', and the business continues (116 ff.). There is evidence for walking on lines in plays throughout the period before 1608, although one finds it less frequently in the earlier plays of the 1590's. As we may infer from Kemp's remark (the *Parnassus* play in which it occurs could not have been performed later than Christmas, 1602—see Leishman, *op. cit.* p. 24), it was fairly common practice. In Gower's second chorus in *Pericles*, for example, the dumb show direction has, '*Enter at one door* Pericles *talking with* Cleon, *all the train with them*'. Later in the play, Dionyza explicitly instructs Marina to walk about with Leonine ('Come *Leonine* take her by the arm, walk with her', IV. i. 29–30; and see ll. 27–8, 47), indicating that Marina's longish description of her birth at sea (54–66) is meant to be spoken as she walks about the stage with Leonine. (Note, by the way, how this stage business, as naïve as it may seem to us, increases the suspense an audience must feel, wondering exactly when and how the hired murderer will begin his work.)

On the whole there is no indication in evidence of stage business in these plays of any new techniques or manner markedly altered from business which took place in earlier periods. There was—as there had always been—much pantomime speech *ad lib.*, while more important dialogue took place (e.g. *Cymbeline*, I. v. 33–44, and cf. V. v. 119; *Wint. Tale*, IV, iv. 241–2, 304–5; *Temp.*, IV. i. 124–6; and cf. the banquet scenes in *Per.*, II. iii and *Henry VIII*, I. iv). In I. ii and II. i of *The Winter's Tale* there is considerable evidence of that kind of intimate stage business which reveals a remarkable degree of flexibility during speech, here, on the one hand, between Leontes and Mamillius, and, on the other, between Hermione and Mamillius. In both scenes, there is ample evidence of many small details suggestive of modern 'realistic' pacing and gesture; but such evidence is by no means unique in the late period of plays. All of the texts abound in implicit directions for 'small' business, balancing the impression of a rather 'large' style, inferred from such lines as Norfolk's description of Wolsey. These details range from comic routines (drunken staggering, for example, *Temp.*, II. ii. 75–6) to business connected with costume disguises (*Wint. Tale*, IV. iv. 637–49); sometimes, although the detail of business is 'small', the style with which it was apparently rendered would seem to us 'large', even exaggerated—the roughness with which Pericles may have pushed back Marina (V. i. 88), for example, or Leontes' pinching of Antigonus (*Wint. Tale*, II. i. 153). For each example of stage business, however—reading, weeping, preventing the speech or action of another, manifestations of physical weakness, and so on—there are equivalent examples in earlier plays; none of them throw light specifically upon an acting style in the late period not evident earlier. Leontes' description of some courtly manners, displayed by Hermione and Polixenes as Leontes speaks in half-soliloquy, while grotesquely misinterpreted, of course, must nevertheless have been acted out in some way (*Wint. Tale*, I. ii. 115–18, 125–6, 284–8), and the description provides valuable evidence of this sort of action (cf. *Wint. Tale*, IV. iv. 358–9; *Temp.*, IV. i. 51–2)—but such action of 'dalliance' would not have been unique in the last plays.

There are certain descriptions in these plays, in fact, which while they tell what is being done by an actor, fail to tell us how the business was executed, but create the impression nevertheless of a style rather more 'formalized' in our sense of the word, broader and more expansive, than one might have anticipated; for example, Pericles' *'mighty passion'* (IV. iv. dumb show), Alonzo's *'frantic gesture'* (*Temp.*, V. i. 57), or Katharine's gesture with *'which (as it were by inspiration) she makes (in her sleep) signs of rejoycing, . . . [holding] up her hands to heaven'* (*Hen. VIII*, IV. ii. Vision), as well as more specifically described action, such as Imogen's sad hand-writing (*Cymb.*, III. vii. 78, and see 75–9), and Palamon's bent fist in rage (*Two Noble Kins.*, III. i. S.D.), all might be called emblematic gestures, large enough to form a part of a stage picture as they occur. They seem to represent action, rather than to perform it—much as one character occasionally will describe the action of others narratively, the action having taken place 'off-stage', the description retaining nevertheless a scenario of business (see *Hen. VIII*, I. ii. 203–6, or the Gentleman's description of the reunion in *Wint. Tale*, V. ii. 46–53, 71–6). The point here is not that such passages suggest evidence of a newer style of business (Ophelia's recounting of Hamlet's visit to her chamber, II. i. 77 ff., is the same in kind); on the contrary, since such descriptions may give us a fairly accurate summary of an acted stage picture had the events actually been performed, the logical inference is that even in the very late plays, stage business mixed highly detailed nuance with something which can be described only as pictorial emblems.

FACIAL EXPRESSION

So often do Elizabethan characters comment upon the frowns or stares on others' faces, one begins to wonder if for some reason it was necessary to make sure the audience understood what perhaps it could not actually see at all times. On the other hand, the cumulative impression left by such repeated references is one of a convention of facial 'gesture' big enough to motivate response and, often, comment. This must have been the case, at any rate, much of the time. The late plays are remarkably full of such evidence; again, *The Winter's Tale* provides typical description—in this case, of Leontes' angry, deranged countenance. Polixenes tells Camillo of the King, who 'hath on him such a countenance | . . . even now I met him | With customary complement, when he | Wafting his eyes to th' contrary, and falling | A lip of much contempt, speeds from me' (I. ii. 368, 370–3); and Hermione, asking her husband if he is 'mov'd', observes his 'Brow of much distraction'. There is no reason to assume that Polixenes' account is anything but a literal description of the more or less standard facial 'gesture' for haughty dislike. Note that it covers the details of expression in a quick shift of the eyes and use of the mouth, as well as a change of movement into a fast pace.

The brow, however, is almost always that part of the physiognomy to which the observing actor refers; when Lear notes Goneril's 'frontlet', he refers in fact to her frowning—as distinct from other 'smaller' facial expressions which might indicate anger. Pericles addresses Helicanus: 'thou hast | Moovd us, what seest thou in our looks?' The reply is, 'An angry brow, dread Lord'. Pericles' terminology makes the whole expression emblematic, and yet the description is probably quite literal: 'If there be such a dart in Princes frownes, | How durst thy tongue move anger to our face?' (I. ii. 50–4). After Cymbeline's refusal to pay the Roman tribute, the Queen observes Lucius' exit: 'He goes hence frowning . . .' (III. v. 18). When Arcite promises to bring Palamon fresh clothes and food, the latter tells him to 'doe the deede with a bent brow, most [cer]taine | You love me not' (*Two Nobl. Kins.*, III. i. 101). By far the greatest number of such allusions to facial expression is in *Henry VIII*; they occur both in stage-directions and in the characters' lines. Here is a sampling:

> S.D. I. i. 114: '*The Cardinall in his passage* [across the stage], *fixeth his eye on Buckingham, and Buckingham on him, both full of disdain*' (Note the characters' lines on these stares; Wolsey's threat: '*Buckingham* | Shall lessen this big look' [119]; Buckingham's answer: 'I'll follow, and out-stare him' [129].)
>
> S.D. III. ii. 203: '*Exit King, frowning upon the Cardinal* . . .'
>
> V. i. 87–8, Cranmer observing Henry: 'I am fearful: Wherefore frowns he thus? | 'Tis his aspect of terror.'
>
> V. ii. 11–12, Cranmer of Butts: 'as he past along | How earnestly he cast his eyes upon me . . .'
>
> S.D. V. iii. 113: '*Enter King frowning on them, takes his seat.*'

The frequency of the direction in this play makes one wonder if there was need for it in some aspect of characterization we are unable now to perceive entirely; more likely, since all categories of stage-directions in *Henry VIII* are remarkably full, this one only becomes more noticeable.

In listing evidence for other sorts of expression, I do not imply that each was, categorically, always the same; indeed, the range of expression (sometimes with accompanying action) indicates greater variety.

Sadness

> *Cymb.*, I. vi. 83–5, Imogen to Iachimo: 'You look on me: what wrack discern you in me | Deserves your pity?'
>
> III. iv. 4–6, Imogen to Pisanio: 'What is in thy mind | That makes thee stare thus? Wherefore breaks that sigh | From th' inward of thee?'
>
> V. v. 22, Cymbeline to the Queen's ladies: 'There's business in these faces: why so sadly | Greet you our victory?'
>
> *Winter's Tale*, IV. iv. 454–5, Florizel to Camillo after Polixenes' stormy exit: 'Why look you so upon me? I am but sorry, not affear'd. . . .'

Threat

> *Cymb.*, III. iv. 10–12, Imogen to Pisanio (note the alteration of expression implied in the course of six lines; see above, III. iv. 4–6): 'What's the matter? | Why tender'st thou that paper to me, with | A look untender?'

Worry

> *Temp.*, **IV.** i. 143–4, 146–7, Ferdinand and Prospero observe each other's expression 'your father's in some passion | That works him strongly'; 'You do look (my son) in a mov'd sort, | As if you were dismay'd . . .'

Perplexity, amazement

> *Cymb.*, V. v. 108, 110, 114, Lucius and Cymbeline to the disguised Imogen, who stares at Iachimo: 'Why stands he so perplext?' 'What would'st thou boy | . . . Know'st him thou look'st on? Speak . . . | Wherefore ey'st him so?'
>
> *Temp.*, II. i. 299–300, Alonso, suddenly awakening, and surprising Sebastian and Antonio: 'Why are you drawn? | Wherefore this ghastly looking?'
>
> III. iii. 89–90, Prospero of Alonso and the rest, after the banquet has vanished: 'these (mine enemies) are all knit up | In their distractions . . .'; Gonzalo to Alonso, at the same time: 'I'th name of something holy, Sir, why stand you | In this strange stare?'
>
> S.D. V. i. 214; The Master and the Boatswain are to enter after Ariel, '*amazedly following*'; cf. V. i. 240.
>
> *Henry VIII*, S.D. III. ii. 372: '*Enter Cromwell, standing amazed.*'

Very few of these examples indicate exactly how the varying expressions were accomplished. One thing is certain, however, and that seems to be the emphasis in all on *staring*, or expressive use of the eyes. Now although the stricture would probably not apply in Blackfriars, nuance of expression about the eyes of an actor could not have registered well in the large public theatre—in the jargon of the modern actor, would not have 'read' adequately. Perhaps the impression of such facial expression was achieved at least in part through the stance of the actor. Some of the directions above imply, in fact, posture as well as facial 'gesture'. For example, Lucius wants to know why the disguised Imogen '*stands* so perplext', and Cromwell, struck powerfully by the news of Wolsey's fall, is instructed to enter, '*standing* amazed'. Perhaps there was something in the way these actors managed the total presentation of the emotion which complemented the expression of the face, and particularly that of the eyes.

VOICE

It is difficult to document what must have been the vocal styles of

Elizabethan actors; matters of pitch and volume, dramatic pacing, and certain special effects are all pertinent, but frequently only volume elicits from another character the sort of response which, in turn, serves as evidence. There is evidence of great variety of style in the late plays, but although a similar range existed in the earlier period too, it may be useful to note the categories of documentation available.

Sometimes in high emotion and sometimes for mildly comic effect, characters would 'speak thick', that is, quickly, crowding one phrase rapidly upon the one preceding, sometimes creating the effect of being out of breath (see *Wint. Tale*, III. ii. 47–58; *Two Noble Kins.*, I. iii. 54–82, and Hippolyta's observation following; cf. *2 Henry IV*, II. iii. 24). Possibly the actor could in fact '[stop] the career | of laughter with a sigh' (whether or not Hermione actually did so); there is ample proof that the style encompassed weeping during speech (*Cymb.*, V. v. 352) and punctuating speech with sighs (*Per.*, V. i. 84), sudden interruption by another character, a detail which necessarily involved modulation of pitch and pacing (*Per.*, IV. vi. 39–40; *Cymb.*, IV. ii. 230) —modulation which might be inferred as well from the compressed syntax and involved sentence structure of almost any part of Leontes' long half-soliloquy in the second scene of *The Winter's Tale*. Techniques of modulation could handle self-interruption (*Cymb.*, I. vi. 89–91), sudden changes of tempo (*Temp.*, I. ii. 77–9), and quick alteration of pitch and tonal quality (*Hen. VIII*, II. iv. 74–5).

One can come to no fixed conclusions concerning Elizabethan voice production. If it is true, as Bertram Joseph suggests, that this 'voice production involved what is known nowadays as a sustained tone' (*The Tragic Actor*, p. 15), such alteration of pace implicit in the examples quoted above relied more upon shifts of pitch than upon varying stress. I find it difficult to agree with Joseph either that such tone has necessarily 'more melody in it than the ordinary modern speaking voice used off and on the stage today', or that 'when an actor does not use a sustained tone, or does not sustain it sufficiently, he finds that he has to make use of pauses when he wishes to enable an audience to become aware of the structural complexities of verse and all the nuances of a line packed with meaning'. Surely both pitch and stress were—and are—of great importance in the rendering of Elizabethan verse; especially in Shakespeare's late verse, such complexity must be made intelligible to the ear as had never before been the actor's task. But there appears to be ample evidence—in the lines themselves, if nowhere else—that the first actors of these plays had to rely on their ability to negotiate complex tempo within each line, as well as shifts of pitch, in order to articulate the sense. It is hard to see in any case how one could separate the two requirements.

BLOCKING

Evidence of stage movement and address pertain directly to the over-all style of acting. When we think (to use Gombrich's excellent phrase, in terms of our own 'vocabulary of motif') of a 'formal' or of a 'naturalistic' style, we tend to imagine, perhaps first of all, the *way* in which an actor talks to another, how he shows that he is aware of another presence on stage, or how often he moves from one area of the stage to another, appearing to know as he does so that standing in a certain place will increase the power of what he has to say. Although the conventions of Elizabethan stage movement are harder to document, patterns of stage address are, on the other hand, more often than not implicit in the lines themselves. It is difficult to consider one category of acting style without touching upon the other—an actor cannot at times alter direction of his address without effecting some alteration in his stage position. On the whole, however, all that one can say about 'blocking'—in Shakespeare's last plays or in any others of the period—depends upon certain inferences concerning the distribution of actors on the stage platform.

While there appears to have been considerable flexibility in this distribution, the fact that it is hard to discover a great deal of evidence for such detailed 'small' moves as exist from moment to moment of stage-time in the modern theatre, leads one to wonder if there *were* many such moves on the Elizabethan stages. Evidence for two small moves of this nature—each creating a different impression in the modern reader—should be noted. The first is from *Pericles*. After the hero pushes Marina from him, he begins to review certain phrases she has spoken, and asks her to repeat them. 'I said my Lord, if you did know my parentage, you would not do me violence', she replies; 'I do think so', Pericles says, 'pray you turn your eyes upon me' (V. i. 100–2). Now Marina has had an aside a few lines previous—'I will desist, but there is something glows upon my cheek, and whispers in mine ear, go not till he speak' (96–7)—and it is possible that the actor was to turn away from Pericles on this; but it is clear in any case that Marina speaks her next lines turned from him—a very 'modern' way to render them. In *The Two Noble Kinsmen*, after the three queens have presented their requests to Theseus, he says, 'Troubled I am', and the stage-direction next to the line reads: *'turns away'* (I. i. 77). Hippolyta observes that her 'Lord is taken | Heart deep with your distress: let him consider', and Theseus very likely remains in this stage position until his own exit order, 'Forward to'th temple', closing the scene. This detail of movement, in contrast to the one from *Pericles*, strikes us as rather 'formal', effecting on stage an almost emblematic tableau of the pleas of subjects to a benevolently distressed ruler. The fact that Theseus apparently holds the position so long (there is no indication that, except for this, he has moved since making his entrance) emphasizes the pictorial quality of the stage rendering, while it is possible that in the example from *Pericles* the lines spoken by the character, although holding a comparable position, create (for us) an impression of psychological reality. Perhaps the truly important point to be made, however, is that these are the only two examples of such a turn which can be documented in the texts of the six plays under discussion here. Surely there were more, and of course we must not assume that the only action which took place on the Elizabethan stage is that for which we can isolate descriptive evidence. Lear may have turned his back on Cordelia, or Othello his upon Desdemona, or, with other emotions, Hamlet his upon Ophelia. At some point, Imogen must have turned from Iachimo, as Leontes must have done from Hermione. But that habit of *stage*-conscious description which one finds in so many Elizabethan texts ('Look how she rubs her hands'; 'see he gnaws his lip'; 'Then lays his finger on his temple') leads one to expect more examples than in fact there are; and it is at least possible that the very paucity of documentation for this category of staging points to the truth of the matter, and that such small moves, externalizing a deep emotion in the character—such turns, for example, as executed by Marina and Theseus, were few and far between.[6]

★   ★   ★

After examination of several hundred plays from the Tudor and Stuart repertory, it is possible to come to some tentative conclusions

[6] Note that one example is from a play the origin of which was definitely the Globe, and that the other is from a play almost certainly a Blackfriars piece exclusively.

about general use of the stage area, and to try to determine the larger category of moves made upon it. (1) It was not uncommon for more than one acting area to be in use simultaneously; but this was not a new development, and there are many examples of such practice among the earlier Tudor interludes: (2) the 'strongest' place on the stage—for the speaking of a 'big' soliloquy, for example—was not far down-stage, on the lip of the apron, but at a point roughly in the centre of the stage, or even a bit up-stage of centre; (3) action seems to have spread across the stage area, with some positions held without many subsidiary moves, in two major patterns—one which might be described as a linear pattern, forming points of action from one side of the stage to another, and the other circular, with a point of attention (for the actors as well as the spectators) in either the centre of the stage or, further up-stage, in or near (and in some cases, *above*) the 'discovery' area. The first of these patterns of movement may stem from arrangements suitable on platforms set up for plays at the end of long halls, while the second, implying as it does an axis of movement emphasizing the depth of the stage, may have developed in terms of the projecting apron stage in the large public theatres. Neither pattern was ever exclusive of the other, of course; and much movement may have taken place about which the texts tell us nothing, or which pertained to a habit of mirroring reality lost to our own perception and therefore unrecognizable in the fabric of a play.

Any time a character or a group of characters is meant to overhear the action of one or more others, the stage accommodates, obviously, at least two and sometimes three acting areas. The scene in *The Winter's Tale* in which Mamillius moves from Hermione to the group of ladies, and back to Hermione, for whom he begins his ghost story, continuing it in pantomime as Leontes and his lords enter, is such an episode. There seems little doubt that the ladies ('Yond Crickets') stood up-stage, that Hermione's chair or stool was down-stage, but towards one corner of the platform, and that Leontes and the rest entered and remained up-stage (left or right) until he ordered the boy taken from her (II. i. 56). Whether the King moved towards Hermione during his speeches (partly addressed to her, partly to his lords), is impossible to say; it is fairly certain that three points of attention altered to two after Leontes' first words to Hermione: the husband, near or with the lords who seek to lessen his anger, and the wife, whose ladies, perhaps, come nearer to her (or she to them) as the accusation is made clearer. No other

K

movements are apparent in the text, and, in point of fact, none seem necessary. Basically, the scene takes place along both axes, with Mamillius moving between points up- and down-stage, and, afterwards, Leontes (with the lords) and Hermione (perhaps with the ladies) addressing each other from positions linear in relationship. The movement was fluid and altered easily between sections of the episode.

The progress of many episodes in this drama indicates a pattern of movement from one basically linear to another which filled the depth of the stage, and was perhaps basically circular (cf. *Per.*, end of II. ii to beginning of II. iii, in which the passage of the knights across the stage must alter almost at once to Simonides' banquet, an arrangement oriented to an up-stage centre, and *Hen. VIII*, I. iv. S.D., indicating a similar positioning for Wolsey's 'State', the word 'under' perhaps implying here our sense of 'down-stage of').

It is interesting that the use of two stage areas simultaneously did not necessarily imply relative importance for one area over another, as similar usage implies in modern staging (where an up-stage position— in proscenium production, at any rate—is considered the 'stronger' placement). Different positioning implies an arbitrary adjustment of stage space to meet the needs of particular dramatic situations; a character diagonally up- or down-stage of other action observes it, executing in the meantime little or no business of his own (e.g. *Per.*, II. i. 1–57, *Wint. Tale*, I. ii. 209), two characters conduct dialogue with another across the stage, again with no apparent need for separate stage moves (*Temp.*, I. ii), although sometimes actors were to '*stand in convenient order about the stage*' (*Hen. VIII*, II. iv. S.D.) while one of them is given a move which confirms the generally circular distribution of the others ('*the Queen makes no answer* [to the Cryer's summons], *rises out of her chair, goes about the Court, comes to the King, and kneels at his feet*'). Some scenes automatically required an alteration from full distribution about the stage to a generally circular one, as attention would be directed to the playing area near the 'discovery' place (*Wint. Tale*, Hermione's statue; *Per.*, the 'dead' Thaisa during the storm; *Temp.*, the charmed circle is suddenly shown the lovers' chess-game). Whether or not we infer great flexibility of 'blocking' from the apparent ease with which different areas of the stage were used simultaneously depends in some measure upon our own perceptions of 'stronger' and 'weaker' positioning. But it is possible that the actors in Blackfriars—and the Globe—thought more in terms of episodic units of narration than we do (even when we produce Elizabethan plays), and that for them the exact position of one actor or group of actors relative to another was less important than the simple progress of characters in a sequential plot.

ADDRESS

The flexibility with which an actor alters direction of his address implies, as had been suggested, some alteration of stance as well. It is often impossible to say what tangible shape such alteration may take, but it is valuable, in trying to describe a general style of acting, to know at least the number of levels of address possible within the convention. Examples of great flexibility abound in these plays—perhaps more so than at any other point in the previous drama; the ease with which a character can encompass a number of different directions of address—and, therefore, tones—within a single speech is typical, of course, of a number of other dramatists whose work was becoming important during these years. In Shakespeare especially, this quality was more and more prominent. One can locate in the earlier plays long sections of solo speech and dialogue containing many modulations of address, but the consistency with which the last plays reveal such modulation is remarkable.

When the chest containing Thaisa's 'body' and Pericles' jewels is washed ashore and found by Cerimon, this lord has one scene of quick movement, great modulation of tone and address, and considerable stage business. Most of this is implicit in the lines themselves:

> look how fresh she looks
> They were too rough, that threw her in the sea.
> Make a fire within; fetch hither all my boxes in my closet,
> Death may usurp on nature many hours, and yet
> The fire of life kindle again the o'er-press'd spirits:
> I heard of an Egyptian that had nine hours lien dead,
> Who was by good appliance recovered.

> *Enter one with napkins and fire.*

> Well said, well said; the fire and clothes: the rough and
> Woeful music that we have, cause it to sound, beseech you;
> The violl once more; how thou stirr'st thou block?
> The musick there: I pray you give her air:

Gentlemen, this queen will live,
Nature awakes; a warmth breath[es] out of her;
She hath not been entranc'd above five hours:
See how she gins to blow into life's flower again.

                                        (III. ii. 78–95)

Cerimon, without altering his position on stage, changes his stance and address as he speaks to his lords, reprimands an attendant, looks carefully at the reviving Thaisa, and muses to himself for a line or two; Henry VIII toasts Anne Bullen, and addresses a whole company (I. iv. 94–7); the old shepherd modulates address from calls to his son, remarks to the audience, and lines directly to the infant in his arms (*Wint. Tale*, III. iii. 60–76); Imogen berates Cloten, calls to Pisanio off-stage, returns to answer Cloten's outbursts (*Cymb.*, II. iii. 101–36). While other techniques of acting in the late period reveal only infrequently new manners and methods, such flexibility of address does seem to be more often the rule rather than the exception.

One of the more common forms of alteration of address in the drama of the period occurs when a character on stage speaks to another who is leaving the acting area (usually covering the exit, and, in fact, giving us the opportunity to know exactly when the second actor leaves the individual or group), or sees the entrance of another and comments upon it, covering in a similar way the new actor's movement towards the acting area. This form of address can be delivered just as easily, of course, by the actor who is leaving or approaching. Frequently it involves address over the shoulder, or coming to a short stop in the exit walk, which is resumed after the line or lines. In the earlier period, up to, say, 1580, this form of delivery covered, when it occurred, on an average, six lines. Usually these lines involved some descriptive comment on the approaching character, delivered either to another character already on stage or, in many cases, to the audience. The average number of lines used in such 'anticipatory' or 'covering' address in the major period covering roughly 1580 to 1605 is closer to three lines for each occurrence; and, although mathematical exactness is probably not only impossible but subject to varying line readings by each student of the subject, the average seems to drop off still more in plays such as those under consideration. Moreover (and more interesting, perhaps), the use of the convention itself seems to decrease. In these six plays, for example, the average number of lines used in this category of address is only two; and such address occurs infrequently.

In earlier plays, the use of such address was twofold; mainly it served the practical purpose of covering stage-time while a character left or approached an acting area, but occasionally, and more important, it served an expository or narrative purpose: the character making the address would speak about the other, or explain what event might take place next—in terms, let us say, of what the character leaving was to do, or what the one remaining had already done. More often than not, this would lead directly into solo speech by the actor still on stage; the joining of episode to episode, in many early plays of the period, was accomplished purely in terms of explanatory soliloquy. In this sort of speech, action—even thought—would be *described*, and not acted, or truly 'thought'.

Adequate discussion of the technique of the soliloquy would require many pages. The convention was old in the early days of Tudor drama, and many critics have observed the different kinds of material which could be included in such speech. From the early interludes onwards examples of purely introspective or explanatory soliloquies are plentiful. There are also many speeches which one might call 'apostrophic'. Frequently, these modes of address blended. Students of the subject have always wanted to know how often this sort of speech was in fact delivered directly to the spectators, but the general opinion that such address took place quite frequently is difficult to document. It is easiest to find evidence for direct address in the solo speeches of the early 'Vice' characters, since here the actor will sometimes actually pick out a member of the audience for specific address, or refer again and again to 'you', as a collective object of his plot descriptions.

One suspects that other forms of soliloquy—the hero's meditations or laments, for example—were also addressed at times to the spectators; but this is harder to prove, especially as dramatic writing improved and the characters were given personalities in terms of action instead of external description (whether by themselves or others). Nevertheless, there is good evidence of audience address in some introspective speeches from early plays; the writing is unpolished, the machinery creaks, and the manner of the actor is in some cases much clearer. In Garter's *Susanna* (*c.* 1568), for example, Joachim comments on the lack of moral government, partly in meditation as he looks about the stage for the judges, but partly in audience address, as he prays for blessings upon each spectator as well as for himself (ll. 836–51). That part of the speech which is clearly set in direct address is mainly a device to help the actor get off-stage, but without it, and the explanatory tone in the beginning, one could only observe that much of the sententious tone of the lines rings of explanation to a group of listeners. The speech proves that no strict rule prohibited such a mixture. In an even earlier play, *Calisto and Melebea* (c. 1527), Calisto prays for Sempronio's good fortune, then says,

> To pas the tyme now wyll I walk
> Up and down within myne orchard,
> And to my self go [commune] and talke,
> And pray that fortune to me be not hard,
> Longyng to here whether made or mard;
> My message shall return by my servaunt sempronio;
> Thus, farewell my lordys, for a whyle I wyll go.
>
> (ll. 306–12)

The tone here is not sententious but personal. The character presents, in fact, the subject-matter for a soliloquy which the playwright apparently did not wish—or did not know how—to attempt. Although the speech is, in its own terms, 'introspective', it rings of explanation; in this period of the drama, individual emotions may be verbalized even if they are not 'acted out', and it may be said that Calisto *announces* what his emotions are, but does not actually express them. They are, in a sense, presented—much as Joachim, in *Susanna*, presents *sententiae* upon moral government.

Similarly, in the interlude of *Impatient Poverty* (c. 1547), the Summoner speaks to the audience before Poverty himself appears—'Rowme, syrs, auodaunce, | That this man maye do hys penaunce'—and then, 'with a candell in his hande', Poverty also addresses the audience as he moves about the platform: 'The pouertie and trouble that I endure | I cannot to you in fewe wordes expresse' (ll. 994–5, and ff.). In this case the feelings of the character are acted out, as Calisto's are not; his walk brings the character of Poverty face to face with all areas of the audience, and his words, although they do little more than describe his 'blocking', are introspective. A later development, in *The Rare Triumphs of Love and Fortune* (a play acted around 1582 by the Earl of Derby's men, and sometimes associated with *Cymbeline*), reveals audience address in an 'apostrophic' soliloquy by the exiled Bomelio, lamenting his fortune. After he states his sad case, he addresses the spectators: 'list, Lordinges, now my tragedie begins' (l. 589), and he proceeds to list his woes individually, three lines beginning, 'Beholde me, wretched man'. Were it not for the single phrase indicating direct address, this is precisely that sort of speech we might categorize as addressed to an 'imaginative rather than actual, mute rather than responsive' auditory (Beckerman, p. 184); and yet apparently much of the soliloquy was oriented towards the audience. Later in the same play, Bomelio's son, Hermione, having found his father's books of necromancy, describes in solo speech his fear of such matters, ending, 'Gentlemen I pray, and so desire I shall, | You would abhor this study, for it will confound you all' (ll. 1370–1).

These examples have been chosen rather arbitrarily; coming from a period so much earlier than the one under discussion, they can indicate only in the crudest fashion certain conventional practices. One might add to them speeches from *Clyomon and Clamydes*, from *Cambises*, *Horestes*, and *Appius and Virginia*, from plays performed in schools, at court, and upon public stages, in which direct address occurs in all types of soliloquy—usually with the Vice's common intention of explanation, but more and more often in purely introspective, meditative speech. The point here is not to elaborate the various sorts of soliloquy possible in this drama, but to indicate that there is every reason to assume a certain amount of direct address *whenever* a character was alone on stage, that it frequently took place in the execution of asides, and that there is no evidence for less use of the convention in the great plays of Shakespeare, whenever soliloquy occurred. Indeed, Joachim's observations on the insolence of office require direct address neither more nor less than Hamlet's do; and Poverty's walk about the platform, and his speech to the audience delivered as he moved, may be the mould not only for all the prodigal sons of the Tudor interludes, who hawk their wares in similar walks, as Mater and Pater occupy another part of the platform, but for such soliloquies as Ferdinand's as he bears Prospero's logs, while the magician and the princess stand nearby. It is well to remember J. R. Brown's observation that any sort of direct speech in this drama was not addressed to the audience 'as if it were in another world' (p. 479)—but that a sense of reality in these plays moved in both directions across the edge of the platform. Since an actor will usually project speech to a listener as though some sort of response were possible, and even forthcoming, we may perhaps conclude that audience address in the plays of this period placed the spectator in a truly creative relationship with the actor. This relationship existed not only during solo speech on stage, but would have been reinforced as actors directed asides to the audience while other characters were in the scene. Thus the total action of the play would be punctuated at frequent intervals with speech which literally included the audience in the narrative action or introspective thought.

In the early period of Tudor drama, a conservative estimate indicates that about eight per cent of each play was addressed either entirely to the audience, or contained speeches, beginning with audience address which were then directed back to a stage area. This estimate is based upon a figure of 1,900 lines, on the average, in each play, with some manner of solo speech in which direct address occurred taking place (again on the average) five times in the course of each play, each speech averaging about thirty lines. This set of figures does not change much as one moves into the greater period of the drama, although of course certain plays, considered individually, range far from the norm. Nor is there evidence, as the years pass, that direct address was associated more or less with solo speech than it had been in the earlier period. What does take place—and must have had a profound influence upon the appearance of Shakespeare's last plays in performance—is that the frequency of soliloquy itself diminishes dramatically. When it occurs, even in the late plays of Shakespeare, it is usually possible to recognize the 'kind' of solo speech which is in each case the archetype— sometimes, as I have suggested, recalling a form used in the very early years of the period; but it occurs much less often.

The less frequent appearance of the device does not coincide, however, with the availability of a private theatre. Although Shakespeare's art in the composition of soliloquies reached its height during the period 1600-6, when the major tragedies were written, there was already some indication that certain kinds of action did not require the convention as often. Except for Angelo's *tour de force*, we do not remember *Measure for Measure*, *Troilus and Cressida*, or *All's Well That Ends Well* for their soliloquies; in *Troilus*, in fact, there are no speeches which really qualify to be so called. In *Othello*, Shakespeare maintained the oldest of the old categories of solo speech—that of the Vice—in distributing Iago's brilliant soliloquies of explanation and planning (many of them couched explicitly in a form of direct address; e.g. 'And what's he then, | That saies I play the Villaine?'), but the hero has really only one speech which may be called a soliloquy (III. iii. 262-81); his long speeches before and after the murder of Desdemona in the last scene are only in part private addresses. There may be much audience address in *Lear* which takes the form of asides or short speeches which bridge episodes of action, and a large part of I. ii is given over to Edmund's solo speeches, one apostrophic (1–22) and one a prose speech of character 'explanation' (111–27). Considering the play as a whole, however, there is very little use of the device. *Macbeth* is a different matter, for the action of the play progresses in direct proportion to the development—or disintegration—of the hero's mind; and Macbeth's soliloquies, performing their proper function in such a concentrated drama, account for a little under ten per cent of the play's stage-time (and this does not take into account the solo speeches of Banquo or Lady Macbeth). In *Antony*, the way in which the device is used in the last plays begins to take shape. The play has only one big set-piece—Enobarbus' lamentation on his desertion—but such meditative moments as Antony's 'I must from this enchanting queen break off' pass quickly into another sort of action; this, for example, is embedded in a nine-line 'soliloquy' on the death of Fulvia— matter which, in an earlier play, would have suggested a full-blown speech.

An examination of *Pericles*, *Cymbeline*, *The Winter's Tale*, *The Tempest*, *Henry VIII*, and *The Two Noble Kinsmen* indicates on the whole a curious diminishing of emphasis upon the soliloquy. Counting all speeches spoken by a character alone on stage—including Prologues, Epilogues, and Gower's choruses—and by characters in asides longer than five lines each, there are in *Pericles* 389 lines of 'solo' speech, 401 in *Cymbeline*, 146 in *The Winter's Tale*, 87 in *The Tempest*, 69 in *Henry VIII*, and—a wholesome warning against superficial or quick judgements!—210 in *The Two Noble Kinsmen*. For what the observation is worth, there are only fourteen lines of solo speech, aside from Gower's, in the last three acts of *Pericles* (the acts generally agreed to be Shakespeare's); the relatively few lines of solo speech in *Henry VIII* occur as often in the so-called 'Shakespearean' scenes as in the 'Fletcherian'. The question of authorship in *Two Noble Kinsmen* is too complicated to make any distinctions; but whichever playwright is responsible for the mad scenes of the Gaoler's daughter is responsible for the sudden alteration in the pattern.

It is possible to underestimate the theatrical effect of this gradual change in the plays. It is an alteration in the very texture of the stage artifice, in the means used by the playwright to advance action. The actual response of the spectators, taken in sum, would be altered commensurately, for, as I have tried to suggest in terms of earlier plays, a special habit of response was rendered less and less central to the actors' projection of plays with fewer soliloquies, each of them, therefore, containing less direct address. One of the effects of this would be to lend greater emphasis to those soliloquies which were composed, to under-score the importance of material set forth in them. A comparison might be made to the late operas of Verdi, starting in portions of *Aïda*, but mainly to *Otello* and *Falstaff*. In these works, the composer and his librettist, Boito, achieved a method of concentration of materials in which a melodic line, for example, would be compressed to the barest essentials, and elaborated through a wealth of detail which was always subordinate to the movement of the whole; a movement in which no single detail would itself stand complete. It was a technique which implied, as Edward Cone has written, 'the living development of expressive means . . . the activity of a total organism rather than a mere "containable" substance'.[7] Detail, in short, became subordinate to phrase. Just as there remain in *Falstaff* and (perhaps more often) in *Otello* musical fragments suggestive of the large set arias and concerted numbers of earlier operas, so in the last plays of Shakespeare there remain several soliloquies, some of them truly in the old style (Posthumus', for example, on women, *Cymb.*, II. v. 1–35), and many half-soliloquies, usually spoken with reference to others actually on stage. But considered as a whole one's impression of these plays as theatrical pieces has a distinctly new emphasis. This emphasis corresponds to the critical opinion, widely held, that the last Shakespearian romances have 'lost' the focus and the concentration of the major tragedies, and that this concentration is replaced by other dramaturgical factors—which nevertheless leave some portions of the last plays diffuse and somehow less 'dramatic'.

At least part of the focus in the major tragedies was achieved, speaking for a moment purely in theatrical terms, through the skilful use of soliloquy. This device aided in gradual concentration inward upon the mind of the hero, always shown to strive painfully towards understanding, always true to the agony of a vision limited by mortality. The hero's *self*-exposition at regular points in the course of the play, especially true of Hamlet and Macbeth, actually effects one element of action. In the last plays, the dramaturgy must concern itself with a

[7] 'The Old Man's Toys: Verdi's Last Operas', *Perspectives U.S.A.* (1954), p. 125.

fabric of action at once shallower and more complex: shallower in point of character, since the sequence of cause and event is more important than internalized motivation; and more complex in plot-line, which must spread more widely, with greater speed, involving as it does so more characters. And of these characters it is more important to know where they are geographically, and where they are about to go, than to know, at length, what they are thinking. Here, of course, a comparison with Verdi ceases, for Verdi achieved in the last operas a deeper articulation of character than ever before in his career —an articulation to which the traditional forms of aria and ensemble were, at this stage in his development, probably inimical. Shakespeare's development—beginning perhaps most noticeably in *King Lear*—had been towards a more generalized vision, a fabric in which the total effect would be more important than the probing in depth of an individual mind. But just as Verdi had been able to compress the long melodic lines of his earlier method—melodies which had sometimes been longer than their content required—into tighter phrases and motifs, full of potential for detailed development, so Shakespeare had developed ways to compress the rhythms of human speech so that much of the elongation implicit in the device of soliloquy was now not only unnecessary, but would have changed his new characters into the sort of personalities destructive to the dramaturgy of romance.

Leontes' soliloquy, early in *The Winter's Tale*, is the best example of the developed form in these plays. It is really a half-soliloquy, since it is spoken with other actors on stage. From the point of view of physical staging, it would probably not differ much from many others except that this soliloquy does not strongly suggest any kind of direct address. But vocally it is entirely different, and although some of its techniques are anticipated here and there in *Cymbeline* (if that play was indeed the earlier), it seems to present an entirely new way of using the voice.

In the earlier portions, it requires great modulation of address, from the scene across the stage to a stance of meditation, to the boy standing nearby. As the speech progresses, its tempo and stress change suddenly, and the language mirrors the chaos in Leontes' imagination. It is instructive to compare this speech, for general method, with another which also attempts to parallel in certain aspects of its syntax, a tortured sequence of thought, such as Hamlet's first soliloquy. It will be seen that Shakespeare's approach has changed entirely. The process in the *Hamlet* soliloquy is one of self-interruption, the subject-matter moving from the specific to the general and back again. To render it adequately required—as is true today—an ability to modulate tone and tempo within the individual line; but there is nevertheless a regularity about it missing from Leontes' speech. There is a swifter alteration of specific address in Leontes', for one thing, with interruption representative not only of a change of subject, but of *degree* of the character's very ability to articulate it. When this articulation is meant to be more difficult, the diction itself becomes more abstract; and to render this theatrically, implying the concentration of idea in the character's mind, must have required—again, as it does today—a different approach on the part of the actor. Surely the actor playing the part, in the Globe or in Black-friars, would have been aware of the new demands of the verse. Parts of the rest of the speech are more regular; during the exchange with Camillo, later in the scene, earlier rhythms reappear.

Interestingly, the use of solo speech in *Cymbeline*, while much more frequent, is similar to that in *The Winter's Tale*. Perhaps the reason for this is enlightening. The frequency of such speech may be due to Shakespeare's difficulties in distributing his narrative materials. *Cymbeline* is a very sprawling play, and its slightly higher number of lines of soliloquy or asides may result from an effort to place, at critical junctures in the action, quick summaries of motivation or intention required by the story-line itself. It is worth noting that although there are many more short soliloquies in *Cymbeline* than in *Pericles*, *The Winter's Tale*, or *The Tempest*, most of them are closer to Leontes' in dramatic intention than to any in previous plays. Soliloquies, in the last plays, do not plumb character: they usually set up, quickly—and, in the case of Leontes', with considerable violence—a situation from which the plot will continue or develop, or, indeed, from which it will spring. Whatever may be said of Leontes' overhearing that Polixenes has been his guest for nine months, with Hermione visibly 'spread of late | Into a goodly bulk', the fact remains that in comparison to the deep motivation Greene tried to give his hero in *Pandosto*, Shakespeare has obviously made a special effort to place the impetus for his tale into a single, violently *expressed* episode. He is not concerned, in fact, with Leontes' 'motivation', psychologically; he is concerned now with the extended development of a plot in which moral significance is implicit. In developing such a plot, he would concern himself more with general effect than with details of emotion revealing the depths of one person. He would also become more interested in the theatrical means to express such moral significance as he attached to the plot. In a sense, it is appropriate that the device of earlier drama which brought the audience *into* the play most strongly, should diminish in the context of dramaturgy the purpose of which would be to expand the audience's view in a larger way, to invite them to watch and marvel.

SPECTACLE AND MUSIC

J. M. Nosworthy has set forth in very convenient and useful form, for *Pericles, Cymbeline, The Winter's Tale,* and *The Tempest,* the points at which music is used, what forms it takes, and, where possible, the setting employed.[8] Moreover, he has discussed with great perception the ways in which the use of music in the last plays seems to differ from that in the rest of the canon. It is important to keep in mind, for example, that although there is much music in *As You Like It,* it is not really keyed to the development of plot and theme; and that, as Nosworthy points out, this objection does not apply to *Twelfth Night,* 'where musical and dramatic functions are admirably equated in Feste', whose songs sometimes mirror the 'basic morality' of the play. Music in the last plays, however, plays a much more integral part, serving not only for songs and dances, 'but also for theophanies and for various dramatic functions which may not . . . be dismissed as minor ones'.

It would be superfluous to repeat Nosworthy's list of musical elements in these plays, although one might add the song of Katharine's lady in *Henry VIII* (III. i), the recorders used for background music at Wolsey's banquet, and the 'Sad and solemne Musicke' for Katharine's vision (IV. ii), as well as the six snatches of song sung by the Gaoler's daughter in *Two Noble Kinsmen,* together with various elements of instrumental music connected with the opening masque of that play, the funeral 'Solempnity' (I. v), the Morris dance (III. v), and Venus's altar (V. i). It is more important, however, to suggest how these musical elements—and those which can only be described as 'spectacular'—were meaningfully used.

[8] 'Music and its Function in Shakespeare's Romances', *Shakespeare Survey* 11 (1958), pp. 64–5.

The common view regarding elements of music and dancing in the last plays is that the Blackfriars audience demanded them, and that Shakespeare obligingly included them. I do not think it is to make Shakespeare less 'professional' in his attitude, to suggest that this opinion may be a considerable overstatement. That he was aware of the great popularity of the Court masque during the period of these plays is, of course, true; he could hardly have avoided this awareness. But his use of music and dance in the last plays is, as Nosworthy puts it,

> a progress . . . towards a dramatic action which is surrounded and shaped by music and its companion, the dance, and this is the product of an attitude to life, and not merely of the professional dramatist's desire to utilize the new and fashionable resources of the masque. . . . Had he found the formal masque congenial, he would, no doubt, have made contributions no less distinguished than those of Ben Jonson. But the fact is he did nothing of the kind, and it is legitimate to surmise that he regarded this species of entertainment as something ephemeral which did not, at this late stage, accord with his accumulated dramatic wisdom and the gravity of his thought (*ibid.*, p. 68).

One might qualify this statement by observing that the dance of Satyrs in *The Winter's Tale* (IV. iv) and the visit of the masquers to Wolsey's banquet (*Henry VIII*, I. iv), are elements extraneous to the action, and cater to audience taste more than to dramatic need. But the fact is that a dance of Satyrs is brilliantly appropriate—if also, for Blackfriars, at any rate, theatrically tactful—during the sheep-shearing festivities in the Arcadian setting of this episode. Whether the dance itself was lifted from Jonson's *Masque of Oberon* is immaterial. Similarly, the arrival of the masquers at Wolsey's banquet is also entirely appropriate, dramatically, since it enlarges the character of the King and advances the progress of the plot considerably; it was an episode from Holinshed Shakespeare could hardly have neglected.

There may be some point in reviewing briefly those elements in these plays which might be classified as 'spectacle', including dances on stage, elements of the masque, theophanies, and other special effects. From this sort of general collection, it may be possible to infer specific ways in which Shakespeare used such materials. (I omit purely musical elements collected by Nosworthy.)

Pericles

Two dances in Simonides' court (II. iii), both integral to the action.
Theophany (V. i): Diana appears to Pericles, as in a dream; the
text gives no indication of the method of appearance.
Three dumb shows, as rough paraphrases of action not elaborated
in subsequent scenes (II. Gower, III. Gower, IV. iv. Gower).

Special effects and uses of the stage:

Storm noises (II. i, III. i, neither marked in text).
Off-stage shouts, as in a tournament (II. ii).
Discovery area used (III. i., V. i).

Cymbeline

Theophany (V. iv): '*Solemn music. Enter (as in an apparition*) Scillius
Leonatus, *father to* Posthumus, *an old man, attired like a warrior,
leading in his hand an ancient matron (his wife, & mother to* Posthumus)
*with music before them. Then, after other music, follows the two young
Leonati (Brothers to* Posthumus) *with wounds as they died in the wars.
They circle* Posthumus *round as he lies sleeping.*'

Special effects and uses of the stage:

Battle sounds, probably trumpets (V. ii, not marked in text).
(?) Stage structure: cave.
No evidence of use of discovery area, but see S.D. opening II. ii:
'*Enter* Imogen *in her bed, and a lady*' (cf. *Othello*, V. ii).

Winter's Tale

Two pastoral dances (IV. iv), one of shepherds and shepherdesses,
one 'a Dance of twelve Satyrs'.

Special effects and uses of the stage:

Storm noises (III. iii, not marked in text).
A bear.
Discovery area very likely used for Hermione's 'statute' (V. iii).

The Tempest

A masque of Ceres, interrupted by Prospero before completion
(IV. i).

Special effects and uses of the stage:

A magical banquet, either raised to stage level through trap or lowered (in Blackfriars, more likely) from flies; must disappear in same scene (III. iii).

Storm noises, perhaps practical structure for ships' tackle (I. i).

'a noise of thunder heard' (II. ii. 1 and probably *passim*).

'Thunder and Lightning'; 'He vanishes in thunder' (III. iii).

End of masque of Ceres: 'to a strange hollow and confused noise, they heavily [i.e. sadly] vanish'.

(?) Stage structures: cave, a tree.

Special costuming: magical robes, 'invisible' robe, wings, etc.

Discovery area used (V. i).

Henry VIII

Masquers (I. iv): '*Enter King and others as maskers, habited like shepheards . . . They pass directly before the Cardinal, and gracefully salute him. . . . Music, dance.*'

Special effects and uses of the stage:

Vision (IV. ii): '*Enter solemnly tripping one after another, six personages, clad in white robes, wearing on their heads garlands . . .*' (etc.).

Several state processions; e.g. to the trial of Katharine, for the Coronation of Anne Bullen, for the Christening of Elizabeth.

'*Drum and trumpet, chambers discharged*' (I. iv).

'*Noise and tumult within*' (an off-stage crowd) (V. iii).

A full banquet carried on, served, taken off (I. iv).

Discovery area used (II. iv).

Two Noble Kinsmen

Theseus' wedding masque (I. i).

Morris dance (III. v).

Special effects and uses of the stage:

'Hearses . . . in a funeral Solemnity' (I. v).

Off-stage sounds: 'Noise and hallowing as people a maying' (III.i), howl of a wolf (III. ii), 'a clanging of armour, with a short thunder as the burst of a battle' for Mars' altar (V. i).

Machinery: fluttering doves for Venus' altar; a fired hind in sacrifice.

Structures: a temple (I. i) (?); a bush (III. i and *passim*), three altars (V. i).

It might be well to dispense quickly with any extended discussion of the 'masque elements' in these plays; Nosworthy's statement covers the matter succinctly, and the evidence above would seem to support him.

I Cominius (James Grout) attempts to calm the Roman mob. Act III, Scene i. From the performance at the Roman Baths, Bath Assembly, 1952. Producer: Glynne Wickham. (*Photo: Roger Gilmour*)

I Kathleen Stafford as Volumnia, Barbara Leigh-Hunt as Valeria and Elizabeth

IV Laurence Olivier as Coriolanus. (*Photo: Angus McBean*)

III Anthony Quayle as Coriolanus. (*Photo: Angus McBean*)

There are dances such as those used in Court masques in four of these plays (five, if one supposes that the dancing at Simonides' banquet, in *Pericles*, was in fact 'courtly' enough); each is integral as a dramatic element. The characters in the dream visions of Posthumus and Katharine are costumed emblematically, and no doubt the elaborate directions for this stem from masque usage; but once again the element serves a dramatic purpose in both plays, even if it be said, truly, that these visions may be somewhat extended in duration for spectacular purposes. Neither the masque in *The Tempest* nor that in *Two Noble Kinsmen* is, of course, complete; the latter serves a purely decorative, ceremonial purpose (cf. Emilia's entrance in V. i, with an elaborate direction for order of movement, costumes, and properties), and it is doubtful whether Shakespeare wrote it. The Masque of Ceres, arranged and ordered by Prospero, is a splendid example of Nosworthy's point regarding Shakespeare's use of ideas originating in Court materials; the masque celebrates here the betrothal of Ferdinand and Miranda, and serves, dramaturgically, a function similar to the dances in IV. iv of *The Winter's Tale*, referring as it does to birth and rejuvenation. There is just a possibility that between Acts IV and V (an original act division),[9] something resembling a grotesque anti-masque took place on stage, since we have left Caliban, Stephano, and Trinculo 'hunted soundly' by those spirits '*in Shape of Dogs and Hounds*' set on by Prospero and Ariel; perhaps this pinching and chasing took the form of dance on the cleared stage. If so, it might explain the authority of the Act division which nevertheless ends the previous scene and begins the one following with Prospero; he is to enter in V. i '*in his magic robes*', and has exited at the end of Act IV with a command to Ariel to 'Follow, and do me service'—possibly to help him with the magic robes, as he is later to help him don those of Milan.

On the whole, the use of songs, instrumental music, dance, and ceremonial spectacle in these plays is subordinated to Shakespeare's dramatic goal. Although critics and scholars have made the observation in a number of different ways, there is little disagreement that the form of these plays—again, taken as a whole—was dictated, as Frank Kermode has said,

by the nature of the fables treated . . . [and, furthermore] that these were chosen because they lent themselves to the formulation of

[9] W. W. Greg, *The Shakespeare First Folio* (1955), p. 418, n. 1.

L

poetic propositions concerning the status of human life in relation to nature, and the mercy of a providence which gives new life when the old is scarred by sin or lost in folly (Arden ed., *The Tempest* p. lxi).

Without treating the question in the detail, it is possible to observe that Shakespeare's intentions in this direction are apparent in plays written before the leasing of Blackfriars; the conclusion of *Antony* strikes one without the unutterable sadness of the earlier tragedies, and even carries a sense of the *commedia*, a feeling of affirmation above and beyond the death required by an ordered world. The physical fact of death remains, however, although the observing voice of Reason in Egypt awards it all the awe and solemnity in his great power. Even in *Lear*, one can detect an element which, in another dramatic mould, would find what had been lost and still live, in which the achievement and the wonder could both persist in the real world. That this is what the last romances—including the romantic history, *Henry VIII*—attempt to show, there can be no doubt; that all of these plays (except, perhaps, for *The Tempest*) do so imperfectly may also be true. But the goal of the form, as Shakespeare came to use it, is clear.

Not all the stage effects, spectacle, music, and dance, in these plays are put to absolutely pertinent use; the lists above indicate a number of effects which are peripheral (as many had been in earlier plays) to the main progress of action and idea. The same is true of some of the instrumental music and songs in Mr. Nosworthy's list. If we concentrate our attention, say, upon masque elements, hoping to isolate in them an emphasis corresponding to the moral and dramatic intentions of the plays, we will be disappointed. What *is* apparent in the summary of theatrical effects is that, through a number of different means, Shakespeare used the facilities of the stage to underscore those moments of action in which he wanted to represent the grace which redeems folly and restores life. Except for *The Two Noble Kinsmen*, the planning of which was probably not his responsibility, and for which, after all, he probably wrote very little, there is in each play, from *Pericles* to *Henry VIII*, a moment in which an effect of staging is used to corroborate the hope of the future, a revelation which brings an announcement of forgiveness and promise.

Only two of these moments are literally theophanies—the appearance of Diana in *Pericles* and the vision in *Cymbeline*. In fact, both of these fail to coincide exactly with the moments of greatest joy and promise in the action of the plays, for in *Pericles* this has already taken place in the hero's reunion with Marina (after which the representation of his reunion with Thaisa is a little anti-climactic); and in *Cymbeline* the explanation of the theophany, and the vision itself, are not so powerful as Belarius' narrative in the last scene. Nevertheless, both appear to be experiments towards joining visual and moral wonder, at just the right juncture of plot, in order to crown the effect of the play. In *The Winter's Tale* and *The Tempest*, Shakespeare succeeded absolutely. The lively statue of Hermione, revealed much as a goddess would be, takes the place of one; and Paulina's discovery of the miraculous work is equivalent dramaturgically to theophany. When Hermione comes to life indeed, her descent is accompanied by music, no doubt set to the measured beat of Paulina's verse; and Shakespeare writes into the moment of revelation one of his rare stage pauses, to mark the solemnity of the moment (V. ii. 21). (We should not forget, by the way, the anticipation of this moment given in Antigonus' description of his dream; it is, of course, a reverse image, for Paulina's old husband has seen Hermione in grief.) The corresponding moment in *The Tempest* is another discovery, this time of Ferdinand and Miranda, playing at chess, seen suddenly by the circle of forgiven wrong-doers when Prospero draws the curtain; implicit in the tableau is the hope of the future and the redemption of the past, inspiration for Gonzalo's exclamation that in truth here each character has found himself, 'When no man was his own'. Whatever legitimate use Shakespeare finds for the masque earlier in the play, it is here, in the last scene, that the revelation comes. It should be noted that neither play requires more machinery for these effects than was available at the Globe—although no doubt Ariel's banquet proceeded with more flair in Blackfriars. In *Henry VIII*, spectacle once again coincides with the moment of promise, in this case, again, something close to theophany. In Cranmer's long speech in praise of Elizabeth, the audience would have found, perhaps, emotional response similar to that felt at corresponding times when youth is shown to replace age. Another dimension is added, of course, by an element of nostalgia; the great queen had not been dead for many years. Nevertheless, as an emblematic scene, interpreted as similar in intention to those of Hermione's statue and Ferdinand and Miranda's chess-game, Elizabeth's christening comes near theophany. In this play, too, folly has brought the downfall of the good with the bad, and Shakespeare's use of historical materials should not categorically remove the play from consideration as tragi-comic romance.[10]

Shakespeare's work for the King's Men's use of Blackfriars and the Globe adds to our awareness of him as a mature artist who took commercial considerations in his stride. His own development as a dramatic poet continued, and although some of the theatrical manifestations of his ideas may have been effected with more ease on the private stage now used by his company, there is really no evidence on which to base a suggestion that he altered the natural process of his work to suit the new stage. The techniques of acting style which we can detect in these plays seem on the whole to be those developed by his colleagues (and their competitors) in the previous decades of work in the public theatre. The growing infrequency of soliloquy is an interesting development which was apparently taking place on the public stage as well, and, as was the case with all stage usage evident in the last plays, was a natural concomitant of the development of an art, and not an imposition of one kind of physical plant. The fact that the stage at Blackfriars was shallower than that in the Globe probably did not much affect the basic moves of stage 'blocking'; some of the categories of stage movement had been established too long, and (probably) were too convenient, for much alteration of method on a private stage. No doubt the acoustics in Blackfriars allowed a new range of volume and less full projection than at the Globe; a theatre which seated only one-quarter to one-fifth of a full house at the Globe probably allowed as well for different *uses* of the voice—and here, perhaps, is one way in which staging in a different house may have coincided with the needs of Shakespeare's verse-writing in the last plays. Needless to say, a theatre for which it was not necessary to present as many new plays as the Globe required, may also have allowed for more rehearsal time, and, in turn, for the development of greater nuance in the rendering of this verse. There is, of course, no way to be certain.

Taken as a whole, the acting techniques reviewed above reveal an art conservative in its uses of the past, yet thoroughly capable of a wide range of flexible stage movements, small details of business, modulation of facial expression and address, and stage moves. One suspects that if we could see one of these performances today, we

[10] See discussion by R. A. Foakes, New Arden *Henry VIII*, pp. xxxvii–xlv.

would find some of the moves and expressions much 'larger' than our own, set apart with fewer actual moves on stage than we are accustomed to, and yet intermixed with many details of action rendered in a manner we could consider highly 'realistic'. Frequently scenes would have taken on the appearance of an emblem, the stage 'picture' itself meaningful in terms of the moral content of the action. Always the intention was to represent realistically the motion of the mind and the very shape of nature.

Note

First edition. Coriolanus was entered in the Stationers' Register on 8 November, 1623, as part of the mass entry for the First Folio, in which the play was first published.

Modern editions. Coriolanus was edited by J. Dover Wilson in the New Cambridge Shakespeare (1960); by John Munro, in *The London Shakespeare* (1957), and by Alice Walker (1964). The Arden edition is in preparation.

Scholarship and criticism. Analytical notes on many of the play's characters are in Harley Granville Barker's *Prefaces to Shakespeare, Fifth series, Coriolanus* (1947), reprinted in paperback (1963). For T. S. Eliot's comments on *Coriolanus* see his 'Hamlet' (1919) and a postscript in *The Use of Poetry and the Use of Criticism* (1933).

Laurence Kitchen has an account of Sir Laurence Olivier's performance in the title-role in *Mid-Century Drama* (2nd ed., 1962). The importance of the female characters in this play is stressed, from very different viewpoints, by Una Ellis Fermor, *Shakespeare the Dramatist* (1951), and by J. Middleton Murry, 'A Neglected Heroine of Shakespeare', in *The London Mercury* (1921), pp. 386–94. *Shakespeare Survey* X (1957) contains a retrospect review of criticism in the present century on Shakespeare's Roman plays, by J. C. Maxwell; 'From Plutarch to Shakespeare—a study of *Coriolanus*' by H. Heuer; 'Shakespeare and the Elizabethan Romans' by T. J. B. Spencer; and 'Classical Costumes in Shakespeare Productions' by W. M. Merchant. See also the latter's *Shakespeare and the Artist* (Oxford, 1959), especially Chapter 11.

VII

'Coriolanus': Shakespeare's Tragedy in Rehearsal and Performance

GLYNNE WICKHAM

*

It is tempting for historian, critic, and producer alike, when approaching one of Shakespeare's plays, to suppose that a definitive version of it exists, and that this may be found in his own mind if nowhere else. The only effective counter-weight to such beguiling self-deception is familiarity with the stage-history of the play in question; for in the course of some three hundred years, the swelling list of revivals and editions demonstrates that what one generation regarded as a final answer, the next repudiated as thoroughly misguided.

The producer of the play, since it is his function as an artist to approach it as a work of dramatic art, must convince himself that he *is* possessed of a definitive version: if he fails in this he cannot hope to convince his actors and technical assistants that he can help them to define it for their audiences. On the other hand, if he is wise, he will not overlook what the historian and the critic can tell him about the fortunes of the play when formulating this version: for it is in this way that he may best bring those parts of his production concept which are particular to his own generation, or to himself alone, into harmony with those which governed the writing of the play. Nor has the critic or historian any less to learn from those artistic truths which producer and actors illuminate in performance when it comes to tempering the wilder aspects of their personal theories with the facts of the stage action.

Coriolanus first became public property as a printed text on 8 November, 1623, when it was entered in the Stationers' Register as one of the plays included in the Folio edition of Shakespeare's plays. Most modern editors assign composition and first performance to the years 1609–10. To the literate section of the Jacobean public of those years the story was not new since it was readily available in print in Latin, French, and English versions of Plutarch's *Lives of the Noble Grecians and*

Romans: Thomas North's English translation was published in 1579. To the illiterate it may well have been new; but, as citizens of London, they had at least had first-hand experience in their own streets of personal disaster overtaking a soldier hero turned rabble-rouser in the Essex Rebellion of 1601. To this extent the play treated of a familiar and, maybe, even a topical subject when Richard Burbage and his fellow actors of the King's Company first brought it to life on the stage.

Subsequent generations have held it in varying esteem, seldom bothering to present it on the stage, often debating the political implications of the plot and frequently contradicting one another in their assessments of the hero's virtues and vices. The play was revived in the eighteenth century by James Quin and David Garrick, and in the nineteenth by John Philip Kemble and Henry Irving. Kemble alone, however, added much to his reputation thereby.

Such then, in thumbnail dimensions, is the background against which the intending actor or producer of the play in our own time must order his own thoughts about *Coriolanus*, role and play.

Any theatrical company today, however, must also take account of another factor which cannot fail to obtrude itself upon preparatory thinking—the unprecedented number of Shakespearian revivals of the past two decades. To take England only, large-scale productions of *Coriolanus* have been mounted at Stratford-on-Avon in 1952 and 1959, at the Old Vic in 1954, at the Bath Assembly in the Roman Baths in 1952, and at Nottingham to open the new Playhouse in December 1963: it was broadcast by the B.B.C. in two separate productions in 1950 and 1959 and was served up in 1963 on television in three supposedly painless instalments. No producer who respects his audiences therefore can easily ignore the images which any announcement of a new revival at once recalls; for many people the new production will offer little by way of novelty, while for others it will have to stand comparison with memories prejudiced by nostalgia. Thus he finds himself under strong pressure to adopt an approach where shock-value takes precedence over all other considerations. This pressure exists for both professional and amateur producers, but it is likely to take different forms for each. The professional, in seeking to oblige his management with a box-office attraction or to advance his own career by means of a notable controversy in the press, is inevitably attracted to theatricality or 'gimmick-treatment'. The amateur, in deference to similar pressures of scholarly origin, is just as likely to wander into the quagmire of textual emendation and historicity of representation. Either way the resulting production is certain to depart from the essence of the play and to be carried into the realms of vulgarity or pedantry. If it is easy to obliterate the tragic stature of Coriolanus in a matter of seconds by allowing him to leap to his death in the manner of a trapeze-artist for the sake of the gasp of surprise in the auditorium, it is just as easy to let the whole play evaporate into one great yawn of boredom by refusing to cut a single line of the text. What course then is the producer of today and tomorrow to set his cast if he is to bring his play fresh and revitalized to his audiences without wrecking both on either the Scilla of pedantic historicity or the Charybdis of theatrical banality? My own experience of producing the play at Bath in 1952, together with such knowledge as I possess of the theatre practice of Shakespeare's own day, suggest that the text itself offers more guidance than is often imagined. This chapter endeavours to define the nature of that guidance.

★   ★   ★

There is first the play's title: *The Tragedy of Coriolanus*. This supplies the producer with two clear and important directives. When all else is stripped away—generals, senators, women, citizens, servants—this play is about one man, Caius Martius, surnamed Coriolanus. It is thus in essence a personal tragedy. Moreover, the word tragedy is to be interpreted as it was understood and used by Shakespeare and his fellow actors. The fifteenth-century poet, John Lydgate, had defined tragedy as a particular kind of story which,

> . . . begynneth in prosperite,
> And endeth ever in adversite;
> And it also doth [th]e conquest trete
> Of riche kynges and of lordys grete,
> Of my[gh]ty men and olde conquerou[ri]s
> Whiche by fraude of Fortunys schowris
> Ben overcast & whelmed from her glorie.[1]

Lydgate admits receiving this concept of the word tragedy from his 'master' Chaucer, and in his book *The Fall of Princes* retells most of the stories generally accepted by educated Europeans of his day as 'tragedies'. Among the Princes whose fall he records are Lucifer, Adam, and Julius Caesar. The influence of Christian philosophy thus lies heavy upon a concept of tragedy transmitted by Latin grammarians to the

[1] *Troy Book*, ed. H. Bergen for E.E.T.S. (1906), ii. 168.

vernacular poets of the Middle Ages, and which the fifteenth-century bequeathed to the sixteenth. This concept changed as acquaintance with the surviving texts of plays by Roman and Greek dramatists became more general through translations.[2]

As a result, dramatic tragedy—as opposed to the earlier narrative kind—came into its own again; but even so the growing awareness of pre-Christian, Euripidean and Senecan stage-tragedy was inevitably tempered for Marlowe, Shakespeare, and their contemporaries by familiarity with Christian narrative tragedy in English. Cardinal Wolsey in *King Henry the Eighth* makes this point forcefully on behalf of his author as well as himself:

> . . . he falls like Lucifer
> Never to hope again,

and the reason is said to be because 'his high-blown pride at length broke under him'. His fall is Senecan, but the cause stems from a later, Christian tradition.

It is within this context then that the producer today must approach *The Tragedy of Coriolanus*. Caius Martius is not himself a Prince, but in a republican society he is a prince among patricians. The play is Senecan in that it recounts in dramatic dialogue the fall of a hero from a state of prosperity to one of adversity; but it is also the product of a Christian society in so far as it examines and attaches blame for this fall within the character of the hero. Whatever else the producer may think to do therefore, he contradicts his author's explicit instructions if he places the man Coriolanus anywhere other than at the centre of his production. It is a title-role.

The second signpost that Shakespeare provides to indicate his own intentions resides in the *Dramatis Personae*. Broadly speaking, the cast list of this play divides itself into three distinct groups of people: those concerned with military life, those preoccupied with civil life, and those whose status in the society of the time denied them the right to participate directly in either—a group of women. To some extent therefore this play is concerned with war and also with politics: one of the women, Volumnia, meddles in domestic politics and, together with her two associates, Virgilia and Valeria, erupts surprisingly upon the affairs of war in the final Act. Significantly, two of these women are closer to

[2] See L. Schrade, *La Représentation d'Edipo Tiranno au Teatro Olimpico, Vicence, 1585* (Paris, 1960), pp. 11–32.

Coriolanus himself—Volumnia as mother and Virgilia as wife—than anyone else in the play. The third, Valeria, is something of an enigma since she is given a dominant place in the third scene of the first Act and is then denied any lines of consequence in any of the three scenes in which she subsequently appears (II. i and V. iii and vi). This division of the *Dramatis Personae* is paralleled in the disposition of the stage-action. Roughly half the action is set on or near the battlefield and half of it in the principal arenas of civil politics—senate houses or adjacent streets. Two scenes only are strictly domestic (I. iii and III. ii): both of these are set in Coriolanus' own home, but in neither, significantly, is he presented as the master of his own house.

All this information stems directly from the play's title, the *Dramatis Personae*, and the ordering of the scenes as set out in the first printed edition of the play. No producer (unless, of course, he is so smug or arrogant as to suppose himself more gifted than Shakespeare) can easily afford to ignore it: rather should he follow where it leads. In sum it suffices to wipe out any temptation to regard this play as a dramatic essay on either war and generalship or tyranny and social revolution. Clearly, both of these subjects are treated fully enough to provide the play with a special flavour of its own: both, however, are elements, like the supernatural in *Macbeth*, and not the play's centre or spinal cord. The latter is to be found as the title directs in Caius Martius himself, a man born to privilege and endowed with certain gifts of leadership, who nevertheless so mismanages his own affairs within the course of the stage-action as to be 'overcast and whelmed from (Fortune's) glorie' before its close. This was Essex's case, favourite of the Queen, flamboyant challenger of Irish rebels, at one moment the darling of the London mob, yet destined the next to lose all in the ignominy of a traitor's death on Tower Hill.[3]

Where then does Caius Martius go wrong? Is his fall occasioned by some public folly or by some inner weakness? If we seek answers to this question, Shakespeare again provides guidance—this time within the framework of his plot.

★   ★   ★

The first scene of the play is set in Rome and establishes, in the conflict of patrician and plebeian interests, the background against which

[3] Essex's fall was lamented in such popular ballads as 'Sweet England's pride is gone' and 'Essex' Last Good Night'. He too could not decide for himself whether to seek power in the military or the civil sphere of national affairs.

Caius Martius' bid for the highest office in the state, the consulship, is to unfold: this is the main plot. The last fifty lines of the scene serve to introduce the subplot as well, the rivalry in arms of Caius Martius and the leader of the Volsces, Tullus Aufidius. In this way Shakespeare quickly depicts both the good fortune to which the prince of patricians, Caius Martius, is born and the double test to which his fitness to govern is about to be exposed. Lest there be any misunderstanding, the point is reiterated in the twelfth line of the ensuing scene where Aufidius, addressing the Volscian senate, describes Martius as 'of Rome worse hated than of you'. His powers of leadership are thus to be tested in both military and political conflicts.

With that much defined, Shakespeare then proceeds to introduce us to the third element in his play, his hero's domestic life. After two rough, masculine scenes, one in the hurly-burly of the Roman streets, the other in the Volscian seat of government, we are transported into the calm and privacy of a domestic setting. Moreover, it is worth noticing that this scene is monopolized by women just as the two former scenes are populated exclusively by men. This contrast is so extreme and so unusual in Shakespeare's plays—it is the only scene for women which is neither introduced nor interrupted by a man—as to suggest design rather than accident. The women in question are all closely related to the protagonist: mother, wife, friend, and servants. This is itself significant, and so is the fact that the scene as a whole fails to advance either the main or the secondary action. Why then should Shakespeare have chosen to lavish so much care upon domestic portraiture, and especially at this particular point in the play? To this question should be added another which I have already raised: why should Shakespeare have troubled to invent Valeria, to place her in so attractive a light in this one scene and then dismiss her from any further significant part in the dialogue? Do these problems derive from the lazy working methods complained of by Ben Jonson, or are they important directives to the play's interpreters? In producing the play myself, I accepted the latter view, and in doing so found myself confronted with several unsuspected obligations both to my author and my actors.

The first and most important was in respect of pace. Because the three opening scenes in Act I are uniformly leisured, with only distant rumblings of trouble ahead to give any semblance of movement to the stage-action, a temptation exists to rush through them making heavy cuts in order to plunge as quickly as possible into the more evidently dramatic uproar and violence of the battle before Corioli that spans scenes iv–x. Yet haste at this juncture can well wreck any chance the play may have of reaching its full stature either in Rome or Antium in the last three Acts. Exposition is always a difficult task, and when, as in *Coriolanus*, the scope of the action to be depicted is of so large an order, patience must be exercised if we are to recognize its boundaries and not be overwhelmed by its detail. My point is simply that the producer must respect the play's architecture: for, if he fails to grapple success- fully with its form, his actors have little hope of communicating its meaning. In the three opening scenes, Shakespeare provides him with the code-cypher to the play's form, and this he must endeavour to transmit faithfully to any audience. Rome is the starting point, a city which, notwithstanding its republican constitution, resembles the London of Shakespeare's time in its sense of its own achievement and destiny. The foil is the foreigner, the perpetual threat to tradition, present order, and future achievement. The Volsces therefore must be sharply distinguished from the Romans in all visual aspects of the production and most especially by those contrasts of costume, setting, accessories, manners, stage-position, and general atmosphere that can be conveniently arranged within the compass of scenes i and ii. No- where does Shakespeare suggest that the Volsces are savages. They govern themselves like the Romans in the democratic decency of the Senate House; they entertain their guests both civilly and lavishly; and, in the day of battle, they can raise a formidable army under leaders that even Roman adversaries respect. They are not Romans in that they are foreigners and enemies; but, just as evidently, they are not cave-dwellers. Put another way, if the Roman patricians wear togas,[4] the Volscian lords at least wear robes or gowns. Shakespeare and the audiences before whom the play was first acted had no further to look for the like of Tullus Aufidius and his compatriots than Admiral Medina Sidonia and his captains of the fabled and recently defeated Armada. If objection is raised against this opinion it should be remembered that Aufidius at least is civilized enough to do something that no one in Rome is capable of doing—to put an accurate finger on the particular failings of Caius Martius.[5]

As this background of *welt-politik* is sketched in, so the image of Caius Martius begins to grow. We see him in the first scene misguidedly dispensing the scornful banter that has to be tolerated on the barrack

[4] II. iii. 104.   [5] Act IV, scene vii: see p. 175 below.

square to the citizens of Rome in their own streets. Spectators with eyes to see and ears to hear can hardly fail to recognize for themselves the personal arrogance and political naïveté that informs this attitude. Lest they do, however, Shakespeare spells it out through the mouths of the two tribunes.

SICINIUS: Was ever man so proud as is this Martius?
BRUTUS: He has no equal.

His courage is a byword at home, and, as we are informed in the second scene, knowledge that he is in arms is enough to alarm the Volsces. Moreover, their General Tullus Aufidius knows that none of them may sleep in peace till Martius is struck down, and that this is a task which he has reserved for himself:

If we and Caius Martius chance to meet
'Tis sworn between us, we shall ever strike
Till one can do no more.

It is at this juncture that we are introduced to Martius' wife, a woman as pale and negative as any worshipped in the romantic imagery of Pre-Raphaelite painters and poets. We meet her in company with Volumnia, a mother-in-law as masculine in her sentiments and as domineering in her manner as any ridiculed in music-hall.[6] Both these women, as wife and mother, in their attitudes to Martius and to one another, comment on the image of the man that Shakespeare has sketched in for us in scenes i and ii. If Martius sees himself as indispensable to Rome, that is an image of his mother's making. She even endows him with an imaginary phrase—

Come on you cowards, you were got in fear
Though you were born in Rome.

—which echoes with sinister accuracy the attack which we have already heard him make on the citizens in the first scene.

What would you have, you curs,
That like not peace, nor war? The one affrights you,
The other makes you proud.

His wife, by contrast, is feminine. War is abhorrent to her.

His bloody brow? O Jupiter, no blood!

Yet in her very weakness and gentleness of disposition, she reveals

[6] Before ridiculing Volumnia, however, the producer should read Queen Elizabeth I's speech to her troops at Tilbury on 8th August, 1588. See J. E. Neale, *Queen Elizabeth* (1934), pp. 297-8.

her total incapacity to shift her husband's image of himself or loosen his mother's control over his mind. No wonder she is ignored when Martius returns to Rome as conquering hero (II. i. 160–80). Had he been married to Valeria, things might indeed have been different. She, like Virgilia, is womanly; but she is a woman of spirit, a woman of the calibre of Beatrice in *Much Ado*; and a woman with enough independence of mind to say 'Kill Claudio!' and mean it, is not one whom Volumnia can permit to marry her son. Valeria can only be permitted to remain a friend. Once Shakespeare has made this point (and Act I, scene iii suffices to do that), Valeria can be dismissed from the dialogue. It is enough to present her on the stage as the companion of Volumnia and Virgilia in Rome and Antium, a dumb reminder of what might have been and of why things are as they are.

It is by these means in the three opening scenes that Shakespeare informs us of the fatal immaturity of character that is the particular weakness of this patrician prince and is to occasion his tragic fall. In the world's eyes Caius Martius is every inch a man; married, a father, an experienced soldier and, by the end of Act II when Corioles has fallen, a national hero. Yet for all that, he is also a man who is still so much his mother's pupil as to take Virgilia for his wife instead of someone of Valeria's spirit, and no man where matters of worldly or political judgement are in question. Aufidius, by contrast, both knows his man and picks his moment when, with calculated disdain, he taunts Martius as 'Thou boy of tears' (V. vi. 101).[7] Nor is he any further from the truth when, twenty lines later, he qualifies that description with the words 'unholy braggart'. Aufidius has of course already sized up Martius (IV. viii and V. iii. 190–203) and decided to liquidate him (V. vi. 1–60) before Martius presents himself to the Volscian Senate. All that Aufidius has left to do is to provoke Martius into an outburst of personal feeling sufficiently tactless to serve as his death-warrant. This he accomplishes with considerable finesse. Martius rises to the bait.

> Like an eagle in a dovecote, I
> Flutter'd your Volscians in Corioles;
> Alone I did it. 'Boy'!

[7] Robert Hardy, in the television production, gave substance to this taunt by actually sobbing at the close of the admonition scene (III. ii). Sir Tyrone Guthrie, in his production at the Nottingham Playhouse (1963), carried the matter beyond immaturity and into homosexuality: see *The Times* notice, 12 Dec., 1963.

—a remark which is dazzling in its tragic irony. The squalid murder follows, assuming some gloss of respectability as an act of popular revenge if not of justice. At the same time, while in our horror at the baseness of this deed we acknowledge the stamp of greatness in the murdered man, we also pity the streak of immaturity that put both the consulship outside his grasp and his own person at the mercy of his smaller-minded adversary.

Remote though Coriolanus may be from us by being a Shakespearian character in the first place and a figure of Roman antiquity in the second, his like is still among us in the former captain of games who is deceived into thinking that his prowess on the sports-field endows him with some special right to hold positions of command in any walk of later life. It is excusable if proud parents and schoolmasters encourage a boy in this belief while he is still at school: but the Caius Martius that we are shown by Shakespeare has long left school behind him, and Volumnia, Virgilia, Menenius, and Cominius are all in their several ways to blame for preserving him in the fatal immaturity of this deception. Cominius admires Martius for his professional virtues and eulogizes him before the Senate (II. ii. 80–125): being a professional soldier himself, he fails to see that the qualities which he commends may require some tempering before they can be assets in civilian life. Menenius loves Martius as a favourite son, but to a point where he becomes a bad lover: he recognizes some of Martius' faults, but he prefers to try to excuse them (even to the point of admitting them) rather than to discipline and correct them in Martius himself. Swaddled then as Martius is by all his friends in self-esteem, he cannot but regard himself as indispensable first to Rome and then to Antium. Even banishment from Rome fails to bring any serious awakening; and, when the moment of truth is at last spelt out before the Volsces, it is too late. Aufidius is his superior in political shrewdness if not in arms, and deals out death with truth. The key to the truth is appropriately placed well in advance of both this scene and that of Volumnia's supplication for Rome before her son. In IV. vii, Aufidius discusses Martius with a Lieutenant and advances in lines 35–55 three reasons for his rival's failure to reap the harvest of his own success—pride, defective judgement, and misuse of power. The second and third of these reasons overlap each other in that it is often hard in politics to distinguish between wasted opportunity and lack of diplomatic tact: and where both faults are in evidence it is likely that they have a common origin

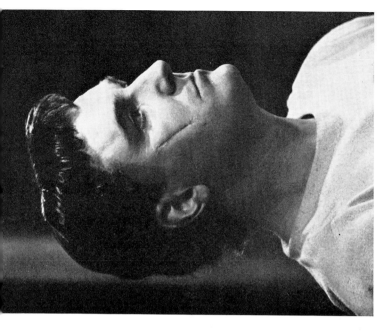

VI Robert Hardy as Coriolanus.
(*Photo: BBC Broadcasting House*)

V Richard Burton as Coriolanus. (*Photo: Angus McBean*)

VII Peter Dews directs some of the cast for the television performance which appeared in 1963. This was Part I of *The Spread of the Eagle* in which Shakespeare's three Roman plays were shown as a nine-part cycle. Robert Hardy played Coriolanus (*Photo: BBC Broadcasting House*)

VIII *Coriolanus* produced at the new Nottingham Playhouse, December 1963. George Selway as Brutus, James Cairncross as Cominius, Leo McKern as Menenius, John Neville as Coriolanus and Kenneth McReddie as an Officer. (*Photo: Nottingham Playhouse*) in exaggerated self-esteem. Too much praise can swiftly translate self-confidence into tyranny: 'thus strengths by strengths do fail'.

If I am correct in my interpretation of the signposts to the play's meaning that Shakespeare bequeathed to us within the form of his text, then the producer's task in assisting his actors to release its meaning in performance is greatly simplified. A quiet and leisured pace in the playing of the first three scenes is a necessary, explanatory preface to what follows. The rest of the play moves swiftly to two climaxes, the one leading inexorably to the other. The battle scenes at Corioles in Act I, scenes iv–x, are so ordered as to present young Martius in the most favourable light possible. His conduct on the field of battle at least is exemplary, and should command the affection of the audience as it commands the loyalty of his hard-pressed soldiers. His physical courage in moments of crisis and his self-effacement afterwards are Shakespeare's means to this end. Important, therefore, though the smoke and noise of battle must be, they must neither of them obscure or drown what Martius has to do or say. His costume must arrest the eye and yet allow him to move with the freedom of an athlete within the limits of the set. And despite this activity, he must occupy positions where his voice can top all other noise. The roar of battle stilled, we may then warm to the man who can remember his debt to a prisoner when fainting himself from loss of blood (I. x. 80–94). Such a commander in the field is worthy of the hero's welcome that he is then accorded in Act II on his return to Rome, and the plotting of the non-combatant Tribunes to feather their own nests at his expense appears as mean as it is small-minded: and in this contrast lies the germ of the play's first climax, the confrontation of headstrong youth, seconded by courage, with cowardice and envy, seconded by political experience and guile. The catalyst is the consulship.

> SICINIUS:　　　　On the sudden
> I warrant him consul.
> BRUTUS:　　　　Then our office may,
> During his power, go sleep.　　(II. i. 203–5)

The result of this struggle is a victory for the patient and cunning exploitation of others by the Tribunes, and banishment for Coriolanus.

Thus the confused clamour of battle gives room to the stately progress into Rome and the formal proceedings of the Senate until this

M

solemn, ceremonial atmosphere itself gives way to the ever-quickening pace of a major political crisis. The storm breaks in Act III, scene iii, where Coriolanus, finding to his uncomprehending astonishment that he *is* dispensable, admits defeat in an agony of subdued rage. Unable to come to terms with the situation, the baited bull rounds on his attackers, reduces the screaming mob to silence by his posture, and launches into an alliterative execration of unparalleled ferocity.

> You common cry of curs, whose breath I hate
> As reek o' the rotten fens: whose loves I prize
> As the dead carcasses of unburied men
> That do corrupt my air: I banish you.   (III. iii. 121–5)

Within this dragon's breath, however, the choice of metaphor betrays the arrogance that brought things to this pass and that will carry the dragon himself in a blind quest for vengeance directly to the second crisis.[8]

On entering Antium, Coriolanus again betrays his own naïveté. He can see that he risks execution, but only admits this possibility in terms of justice (IV. v. 23–5). His experience in Rome has taught him little: that the reward of service given to a former enemy could be murder is as far from his thoughts as that the flattering thanks of his friends and family could lead to his own banishment. To him, dishonour in Aufidius is as unimaginable as ingratitude in the citizens of Rome. This might be taken as evidence of nobility of soul; but, as a measure of political wisdom, it is small. For was it not this same Martius who called his fellow-men 'rats', 'curs', and 'abated captives' to their faces? The author of these sentiments should at least have recognized, as Sicinius does, that these commoners

> Upon their ancient malice will forget
> With the least cause these his new honours.   (II. i. 209–10)

What is there so special or so sacred about Martius that will make men whom he rates as rats behave as if they were angels of virtue to him alone? Failure to ask this question is the fundamental cause both of his banishment and of his violent death.

*   *   *

The play abounds with good acting parts, especially for the junior

---

[8] It is as a dragon that he sees himself once banishment has become inevitable (IV. ii. 27–32).

members of the company. Roman citizens and army messengers, Volscian servants and conspirators all have a chance to impress themselves upon the audience, thanks to their author's skill in characterization and the modulation of mood from scene to scene. Whether it be two officials attending to the seating arrangements in the Roman Senate (II. ii. 1–36) or two Intelligence Officers from the opposing armies at a chance meeting on the highway (IV. iii), young actors are given the invaluable experience of presenting a character that is both an interesting human being and an essential component in the play's design.

The large number of good parts of this kind—I reckon there are nearly twenty of them—presents the producer with three problems which are particular to this play. The first is the casting of these parts. Few professional companies can admit a salary bill that will allow each of these parts to be played by a separate actor: few amateur companies can muster talent enough to fill half of them. Doubling and cutting are the usual answers. Both are dangerous since in cutting there is a risk of damage to the fabric of the play's structure and in doubling there is an equally serious risk of blunting the edges of character delineation. The second problem is one of personal relations in rehearsal: for, if the producer gives these cameos the degree of care in rehearsal that alone will make them worth including, the players of the larger parts begin to suspect that he is neglecting their own needs. To forestall the trouble that can arise on this account, he must not only allocate time with exceptional care in the preparation of his rehearsal schedule, but bring to rehearsal an exceptional sensitivity to the emotional cross-currents flowing through the company from day to day. The third problem is one of vocal balance. Not only have enough actors to be found with a command of two regional dialects distinct enough to contrast Volscians consistently with Romans, but most of these actors are called upon to speak against a background of general tumult and still remain audible. This in my opinion is by far the most difficult technical problem with which the producer is confronted by this particular play.

No producer, professional or amateur, is likely to be so fortunate as to find all these problems solved for him; and clearly each must seek his own solution. What matters is that he should be aware that they exist and that he has found his answers to them *before* he contracts to direct this play. *The Tragedy of Coriolanus* may have affinities with *Hamlet*, *Macbeth*, or *King Lear* in that the title-role is the play's focal centre; but it differs greatly from them all in the style of the text. Poetic soliloquy is rare, and even then the language in which it is cast is extraordinarily condensed.

> O world, thy slippery turns! Friends now fast sworn,
> Whose double bosoms seem to wear one heart,
> Whose hours, whose bed, whose meal and exercise
> Are still together; who twin, as t'were, in love
> Unseparable, shall within this hour,
> On a dissension of a doit, break out
> To bitterest enmity.   (IV. iv. 13–18)

Even the finest imagery is cast in a forbidding form. Volumnia, awaiting Martius' return to Rome, hears trumpets and declares:

> These are the ushers of Martius: before him, he
> Carries noise; and behind him, he leaves tears:
> Death, that dark spirit, in's nervy arm doth lie
> Which, being advanc'd, declines, and then men die.
>   (II. i. 141–4)

Nor is comparison with the other 'Roman' plays or the histories appropriate, since in none of them do crowd scenes outnumber scenes for small groups in the heavy ratio of two to one as is the case in *Coriolanus*. Problems of vocal balance and contrast, therefore, here take on the porportions of an oratorio and even, at times, of opera. I cannot myself see, for example, how Act II, scene i and Act III, scenes ii and iii can be put on to the stage with success unless in terms of opera: another instance is the final uproar in the Volscian Senate. In all these scenes the orchestration of noise both for crowd and soloists must be approached with the same strict attention to clarity of tempo and melodic line as a conductor brings to an operatic score, the actors' moves and positions being determined by considerations of vocal tone and audibility in the first instance and by theatrical effectiveness only in the second.

The Tragedy of Coriolanus then is perhaps the most rewarding of all Shakespeare's plays to produce because of the challenge implicit in the scale of the action compressed into play-form, but only for the company that possesses the technical skill to tackle it: for it is unquestionably the most demanding. I suspect myself that the play was written for an occasion when both halves of 'The King's Men', London and provincial touring company, were available to work together as an ensemble. If this surmise is correct, then Shakespeare was writing with a company of some thirty to forty professional actors in mind instead of the usual sixteen to twenty. In the title-role this plays calls for an actor of quite exceptional physical agility and vocal virtuosity. The major supporting roles, male and female—Aufidius, Menenius, Cominius, Volumnia, and the two Tribunes—are no less varied and rewarding for the actors than those in any other play of Shakespeare's. In addition, the play offers an unequalled range of small speaking parts, each sufficiently exacting to test the strength of the most junior members of the company to the utmost. And even after these demands have been met, there remains a need in several scenes for yet more actors to embellish the stage-action with ceremonial detail—Captains, Heralds, Lictors, Aediles, and the like. The demands on the numerical strength of the company are multiplied proportionately in the technical and financial demands that the play makes upon it—costumes, accessories, properties, and so on. Failure by the producer, particularly in an amateur company, to ensure that the back-stage organization is adequate to cope with the strains this play places upon it, can quickly prejudice whatever success he and his actors may be in sight of before the dress-rehearsals start. And lastly, there is the problem of the text itself, tough, muscular, seldom poetic in an obvious way, yet supercharged by the consistent condensation and economy of its vocabulary. In few of Shakespeare's plays is so much reliance placed on the interior-springing of the lines whether verse or prose. If the rhythms are lost by actors who misplace the accents (or perhaps never find them) much of the dialogue appears nonsensical: this, when allied to the resulting drabness of delivery, serves to alienate an audience's attention. Shouting only makes matters worse, reducing whole scenes or large sections of them to 'inexplicable dumbshow and noise'.

These are some of the traps that lie in wait for the producer whose enthusiasm for the printed version of the play outruns the degree of competence that the play in action demands from him and his actors as artists in the theatre. If, however, the producer can bring himself to trust the guidance and advice that Shakespeare generously provides concerning the direction of the play, his production, for all its particular shortcomings, will yield up a meaning from within the play's form profounder and more striking than any which he may himself invent or presume to impose upon it.

Note

First edition. *The Tempest* was acted at Court on 1 November, 1611, but was not printed until the First Folio of 1623.

Modern editions. The play was edited by Sir A. T. Quiller-Couch and J. Dover Wilson in the New Cambridge Shakespeare (1921), and by J. F. Kermode in the New Arden edition (1954, revised edition).

Sources. William Strachey's *True Repertory of the Wracke, and Redemption of Sir Thomas Gates, Knight* circulated in manuscript in 1610, but was not published until 1625, when it appeared in *Purchas, His Pilgrimes*, Vol. IV, Ch. 6. Morton Luce's old Arden edition (1901) of *The Tempest* contains an appendix on the Bermuda pamphlets; selections are included in the New Arden edition of both Strachey's work and Sylvester Jourdan's *A Discovery of the Bermudas* (1610); fuller selections of both are contained in *The Elizabethans' America*, edited by Louis B. Wright (*Stratford-upon-Avon Library*, 1965). An extract from Florio's translation of Montaigne's essay 'Of the Caniballes' is in Appendix C of the New Arden edition; a convenient reprint of the Montaigne is available in the Everyman Library (Vol. 1).

References. Page references in this chapter to William Strachey's *True Repertory* and *True Declaration* are to the 1906 edition of *Purchas His Pilgrimes*, Vol. XIX. The text of Jourdan's *A Discovery of the Barmudas* is quoted from the 1812 edition of *Hakluyt's Voyages*, Vol. V, but page references are to the more available modernized version in Louis B. Wright, *The Elizabethans' America*. (The STC form 'Jourdan' has been retained in this chapter.)

Scholarship and Criticism. R. R. Cawley wrote on 'Shakespeare's Use of the Voyagers in *The Tempest*', in *P.M.L.A.* XLI (1926). Miss K. M. Lea's *Italian Popular Comedy* (Oxford, 1934) relates the drama to material of the Italian scenari. Among other analogues should be considered *The Rare Triumphs of Love and Fortune* (1589), in the Malone Society Reprints (1931).

Major studies of *The Tempest* include Colin Still, *The Timeless Theme* (1936), and G. Wilson Knight, *The Shakespearian Tempest* (Oxford, 1932). Robert Hapgood's 'Shakespeare and the Ritualists' (*Shakespeare Survey* 15, 1962) is a critical analysis of this aspect of modern interest. C. J. Sisson has written on 'Prospero's Magic' in *Shakespeare Survey* 11 (1959) in relation to contemporary practice.

Biographical note. William Strachey was a member of the Council of the Virginia Company, and a friend of Dudley Digges, brother of Leonard Digges, who contributed commendatory verses to the First Folio. Strachey was also a Sharer in the Revels Company at Blackfriars, before the King's Men took over that theatre.

VIII

'The Tempest':
Conventions of Art and Empire

PHILIP BROCKBANK

★

THERE is enough self-conscious artifice in the last plays to allow us to suspect that Shakespeare is glancing at his own art when Alonso says:

> This is as strange a maze as e'er men trod;
> And there is in this business more than nature
> Was ever conduct of: some oracle
> Must rectify our knowledge.

And it may be that Prospero quietens the fretful oracles in his first audience with a tongue-in-cheek assurance:

> at pick'd leisure
> Which shall be shortly single, I'll resolve you,
> Which to you shall seem probable, of every
> These happen'd accidents; till when, be cheerful,
> And think of each thing well.

The tense marvellings of the play are oddly hospitable to moments of wry mockery. Things are never quite what they seem.

The play's mysteries, however, are authentic not gratuitous; they touch our sense of wonder and they are accessible to thought; and we need no oracle, skilled in the subtleties and audacities of Renaissance speculation, to rectify our knowledge. We must nevertheless seek to attend with the apt kind of attention, to get the perspectives right, and the tone. For, as often in the comedies, the perspectives and the tone are precisely secured, and it is only too easy to upset the balances of convention, of innocence and scepticism, that keep the allegory of the play at an appropriately unobtrusive distance.

There is a multiple, complex allegory. It has to do with the social and moral nature of man, with the natural world, with the ways of providence, and with the nature of art. Yet this very complexity is the source of the play's simplicity—of its power to entertain, to move, and to satisfy our playgoing and contemplative spirits.

The Tempest is about a human mess put right by a make-belief magician. Or, to recast the point in the suggestive neo-platonic phrases of Sidney, it is about a golden world delivered from the brazen by providence and miracle. But there remain more specific ways of saying what it is about. In relation to its immediate sources it touches the colonizing enterprise of Shakespeare's England. In relation to one strain of dramatic tradition it is a morality, about the cure of evil and the forgiveness of sin; in relation to another, it is a pastoral entertainment, fit to celebrate the fertility and order of nature; and it owes to the masque its felicitous handling of illusion, spell, and rite. In relation to Shakespeare's own art, it seems to recollect much that has gone before, and to shadow forth (Sidney's phrase) the playwright's role in the theatres of fantasy and reality.

The several kinds of expressiveness found in the play owe much to the fragmentary source material on the one hand and to the tactful management of stage convention on the other. Theatrical techniques are so used that they illuminate an area of Elizabethan consciousness that was expressing itself also in the activities and in the literature of exploration and empire. Long before we pursue 'meanings' (after the play, brooding upon it) we recognize that the allegory is anchored in the instant realities of human experience. Its aetherial affirmations are hard-won, spun out of substantial material. The truths which offer themselves as perennial are made very specifically out of and for the England and the theatre of Shakespeare's own time. The play is as much about colonization as initiation, as much about the intrigues of men as the tricks of spirits.

The principal documents behind *The Tempest* are well known if not wholly easily accessible; they are William Strachey's *True Repertory of the Wreck*, published in *Purchas his Pilgrimes* together with an extract from the anonymous *True Declaration of Virginia*, and Sylvester Jourdan's *A Discovery of the Barmudas*. The uses to which the play puts these materials would have been very different had it not been for the hospitality of the contemporary theatre (whose tastes Shakespeare himself did most to fashion) to the techniques and interest of the late comedies.

Strachey and Jourdan tell how Sir Thomas Gates and Sir George Summers were driven away from the rest of the fleet, bound for Virginia in June, 1609, by a storm which finally lodged their ship—the *Sea Venture*—between two rocks off the coast of the Bermudas. After many 'rare and remarkable experiences' they built a new boat, *The Deliverance*, and a pinnace, *Patience*, and set sail for Virginia in May, 1610. Their survival (like many another in the pages of Hakluyt) had about it something of the miraculous, and it invited as much comment on the ways of Providence as on the skill and resourcefulness of English sailors.

Shakespeare, with the storms of *Othello*, *The Winter's Tale*, and *Pericles* freshly accomplished for the theatre, would recognize occasion enough for a play in the story of the Bermudas wreck. And the material offers itself most invitingly to a playwright whose interest in the ways of Providence, and in the conversion and salvation of man had matured through long practice in allegoric, romantic comedy. The prose accounts of the wreck are constantly suggestive in ways that would be less noticeable were they read without knowledge of the play. It is often so. The masterpiece illuminates the sources, more than the sources the masterpiece. It is no longer possible to read the collections of Hakluyt and Purchas without recognizing that they offer as much to Shakespeare and to Coleridge as to Captain Cooke.

In the *True Repertory* the storm is both a physical ordeal and a moral:

> a dreadfull storme and hideous began to blow from out the North-east, which swelling, and roaring as it were by fits, some houres with more violence than others, at length did beat all light from heaven; which like an hell of darkenesse turned blacke upon us, so much the more fuller of horror, as in such cases horror and feare use to overrunne the troubled, and overmastered sences of all, which (taken up with amazement) the eares lay so sensible to the terrible cries, and murmurs of the windes, and distraction of our Company, as who was most armed, and best prepared, was not a little shaken. (p. 6)

The 'unmercifull tempest' is a terrible leveller; death at sea comes 'uncapable of particularities of goodnesse and inward comforts', and gives the mind no 'free and quiet time, to use her judgement and Empire'. There are hints enough for the play's opening scene in which hope is confounded by the counterpointed roarings of crew, court, and elements; the dignities of seamanship and of prayer are subdued to 'A confused noise within'. For the dignity of Gonzalo's wit (that alone survives the horror and the test) there is no equivalent in the source. But Strachey has his own way of wondering at man's powers of survival:

> The Lord knoweth, I had as little hope, as desire of life in the storme, & in this, it went beyond my will; because beyond my reason, why we should labour to preserve life; yet we did, either because so deare are a few lingring houres of life in all mankinde, or that our Christian knowledges taught us, how much we owed to the rites of Nature, as bound, not to be false to our selves, or to neglect the meanes of our owne preservation; the most despairefull things amongst men, being matters of no wonder nor moment with him, who is the rich Fountaine and admirable Essence of all mercy.   (p. 9)

And it is easy to see in retrospect how, at a touch, the observations, the marvellings, and the pieties of Strachey might be transformed into the language of *The Tempest* with its capacity for dwelling upon the preservation of life, the rites of nature, and the 'admirable Essence of all mercy'.

The pieties of the prose accounts are more than conventional; they owe their awed intensity to the sequences of catastrophe and miracle that the voyagers endured. We need not hesitate to treat the play as allegory since that is how Shakespeare's contemporaries treated the actual event. After God has delivered the seamen from the 'most dreadfull Tempest' of 'tumultuous and malignant' winds, the authority of the Governor is required to deliver them from what *The True Declaration* calls 'the tempest of Dissention'. Reviewing the mutinies that threatened the survival of the Bermudas party, Strachey writes:

> In these dangers and divellish disquiets (whilest the almighty God wrought for us, and sent us miraculously delivered from the calamities of the Sea, all blessings upon the shoare, to content and binde us to gratefulnesse) thus inraged amongst our selves, to the destruction each of other, into what a mischiefe and misery had wee bin given up, had wee not had a Governour with his authority, to have suppressed the same?   (p. 32)

Reading this passage (and some similar ones) with the poet's eye, we can see how Prospero might have taken shape. From his experience of the theatre Shakespeare's imagination and invention readily made a single figure out of the miraculous deliverer from the sea's calamities, and the 'Governour with his authority' stopping the victims of the wreck from killing one another. It is an apt opportunity to take after *Measure for Measure*, which is about the saving powers of a governor, and *Pericles* with its miraculous deliveries from the sea.

A more specific occasion for the play's rendering of the storm as a feat of providential magic is offered by Strachey's description of the St. Elmo's fire that danced like Ariel about the rigging:

> Onely upon the thursday night Sir George Summers being upon the watch, had an apparition of a little round light, like a faint Starre, trembling, and streaming along with a sparkeling blaze, halfe the height upon the Maine Mast, and shooting sometimes from Shroud to Shroud, tempting to settle as it were upon any of the foure Shrouds: and for three or foure houres together, or rather more, halfe the night it kept with us; running sometimes along the Maine-yard to the very end, and then returning. At which, Sir George Summers called divers about him, and shewed them the same, who observed it with much wonder, and carefulnesse: but upon a sodaine, towards the morning watch, they lost the sight of it, and knew not what way it made. (p. 11)

The elusive, mockingly playful fire and light in the encompassing total darkness, observed with wonder and carefulness by the crew, is poignantly ironic. Strachey leaves the natural phenomenon very ripe for transmutation into stage symbol. 'The superstitious Sea-men', he says, 'make many constructions of this Sea-fire, which neverthelesse is usual in stormes.' The Greeks took it for Castor and Pollux, perhaps, and 'an evill signe of great tempest'. The Italians call it 'Corpo sancto'. The Spaniards call it 'Saint Elmo, and have an authentic and miraculous Legend for it'. The irony is that it could do nothing to help the seamen, but rather quickened their torment:

> Be it what it will, we laid other foundations of safety or ruine, then in the rising or falling of it, could it have served us now miraculously to have taken our height by, it might have strucken amazement, and a reverence in our devotions, according to the due of a miracle. But it did not light us any whit the more to our knowne way, who ran now (as doe hoodwinked men) at all adventures. (p. 11)

It is one of the play's discoveries that this mocking hell is providentially (and indeed playfully) contrived. While allowing Ariel's tale to mimic the lightning, Shakespeare recalls the sonorous miseries described in an earlier passage:

> our clamours dround in the windes, and the windes in thunder. Prayers might well be in the heart and lips, but drowned in the outcries of the Officers: nothing heard that could give comfort, nothing seene that might incourage hope. It is impossible for me, had I the voice of Stentor, and expression of as many tongues, as his throate of voyces, to express the outcries and miseries, not languishing, but wasting his spirits, and art constant to his owne principles, but not prevailing.   (p. 7)

By personalizing, in Prospero, the *natural* processes of the storm and its happy outcome, Shakespeare displays theatrically the exacting cruelties of a providence that works to saving purpose:

> PROSPERO: My brave spirit!
>   Who was so firm, so constant, that this coil
>   Would not infect his reason?
> ARIEL: Not a soul
>   But felt a fever of the mad, and play'd
>   Some tricks of desperation.

Human reason is 'infected' and human skill disarmed in order that all might be brought to shore safely:

> Not a hair perish'd
> On their sustaining garments not a blemish,
> But fresher than before.

This allusion to the shipwreck of St. Paul at Malta (Acts xxvii. 34) reminds us that catastrophic voyages and the ways of Providence are readily considered together. God uses shipwrecks. But the play is more insistent than the New Testament upon the waywardness and apparent arbitrariness of Providence (men hoodwinked, in a maze, amazed) and it has taken its signals from the prose of the voyagers.

At the utmost point of their despair, when skill and energy can do no more, the sailors are ready to surrender passively to the sea. As Jourdan puts it:

> All our men, being utterly spent, tyred, and disabled for longer labour, were even resolved, without any hope of their lives, to shut up the hatches, and to have committed themselves to the mercy of the sea, (which is said to be mercilesse) or rather to the mercy of their mighty God and redeemer.   (p. 195)

That drift from the commonplace 'mercy of the sea' through 'said to be mercilesse' to 'their mighty God and redeemer', is not inertly conventional. It testifies to the quite palpable presence in both stories (but particularly in the opening paragraphs of Jourdan's) of the sequence—storm, fear, death, miraculous renewal of life. While Shakespeare follows Strachey in his treatment of Ariel's description of the last moments of the wreck, he follows Jourdan where he hints at a ceremonious leave-taking on the stricken ship ('Let's all sink wi'th'King . . . Let's take leave of him'):

> So that some of them having some good and comfortable waters in the ship, fetcht them, and drunke the one to the other, taking their last leave one of the other, untill their more ioyfull and happy meeting, in a more blessed world. (p. 195)

The play does not allow too intrusive a ceremonious piety, but rather a wry nostalgia for 'an Acre of barren ground' tempering Gonzalo's patient acquiescence: 'The wills above be done! but I would faine dye a dry death.' The 'more blessed world' is offered nevertheless when all hope is dead, for, as Strachey reports 'Sir George Summers, when no man dreamed of such happinesse, had discovered, and cried Land'.

After the ordeal by sea, the island inheritance. Both Jourdan and Strachey are moved by the paradox that made 'The Devils Ilands' (the name commonly given to the Bermudas) 'both the place of our safetie, and meanes of our deliverance'. Jourdan is particularly eloquent in confronting general, superstitious expectations of the islands with his own ecstatic experience of them. 'But our delivery', he says, 'was not more strange in falling so opportunely and happily upon the land, as our feeding and preservation, was beyond our hopes, and all mens expectations most admirable.' It has the quality of Gonzalo's marvellings. Jourdan tells us that the islands were never inhabited by Christian or heathen but were ever esteemed 'a most prodigious and inchanted place affording nothing but gusts, stormes, and foule weather'. 'No man was ever heard, to make for this place, but as against their wils, they have by stormes and dangerousnesse of the rocks, lying seaven leagues into the sea, suffered shipwrack.'

Jourdan's phrases seem to license the play's magical, paradisial, and mysterious atmosphere, and some may be the germ of the rival versions of Shakespeare's island voiced on the one hand by Gonzalo and Adrian, and on the other by Sebastian and Antonio:

> Yet did we find there the ayre so temperate and the country so abundantly fruitful of all fit necessaries for the sustenation and preservation of man's life . . . Wherefore my opinion sincerely of this Island is, that whereas it hath beene, and is still accounted, the most dangerous, infortunate, and forlorne place of the world, it is in truth the richest, heathfullest, and pleasing land (the quantity and bignesse thereof considered) and merely natural, as ever man set foot upon.   (p. 197)

Shakespeare intervenes to associate the auspicious vision of the island ('The air breathes upon us here most sweetly') with the innocent courtiers, and the inauspicious ('As if it had lungs, and rotten ones') with the culpably sophisticated. But Strachey and Jourdan are equally clear that 'the foule and generall errour' of the world distorts the truths about the islands which are in time revealed to those who experience it.

In the sources, as in the play, the island deliverance is a beginning and not an end. Once saved from the wreck, the survivors have still to be saved from each other. Strachey tells how Sir Thomas Gates dispatched a longboat (duly modified) to Virginia, moved by 'the care which he took for the estate of the Colony in this his inforced absence' and 'by a long practised experience, foreseeing and fearing what innovation and tumult might happily arise, amongst the younger and ambitious spirits of the new companies'. The Governor's authority, however, proves equally essential to the prosperity of both the communities, of the Bermudas and of Virginia. Strachey writes of the onset of the island mutinies:

> And sure it was happy for us, who had now runne this fortune, and were fallen into the bottome of this misery, that we both had our Governour with us, and one so solicitous and carefull, whose both example (as I said) and authority, could lay shame and command upon our people: else, I am perswaded, we had most of us finished our dayes there, so willing were the major part of the common sort (especially when they found such a plenty of victuals) to settle a foundation of ever inhabiting there . . . some dangerous and secret discontents nourished amongst us, had like to have been the parents of bloudy issues and mischiefs.   (p. 28)

And the *True Declaration* discloses the analogous issues and mischiefs in Virginia:

> The ground of all those miseries, was the permissive Providence of God, who, in the fore-mentioned violent storme, seperated the head from the bodie, all the vitall powers of Regiment being exiled with Sir Thomas Gates in those infortunate (yet fortunate) Ilands. The broken remainder of those supplyes made a greater shipwracke in the Continent of Virginia, by the tempest of Dissention: every man over-valuing his owne worth, would be a Commander: every man underprizing anothers value, denied to be commanded.   (p. 67)

The play's second act does most to explore the mutinous disaffections that attend upon and threaten 'the vitall powers of Regiment'. Its Neapolitan courtiers fittingly convey the temper of Virginia's 'younger and ambitious spirits':

> There be that can rule Naples
> As well as he that sleeps; lords that can prate
> As amply and unnecessarily
> As this Gonzalo; I myself could make
> A chough of as deep chat.

'Every man underprizing anothers value, denied to be commanded.' And the drunken, anarchistic landsmen represent the discontents of the 'common sort' on the Island. By extending the powers of Ariel and Prospero over both groups of conspirators, moreover, Shakespeare allows a fuller expression to the moral ideas that issue in the *True Declaration's* reflection on 'the permissive Providence of God'. The conspiracies are at once permitted and constrained.

It is altogether appropriate that the Governor's authority should be represented as a care for 'the state of the Colony' and not as a bent for empire and sovereignty. The *True Declaration* finds for the word 'colony' its richest meaning and fullest resonance: 'A Colony is therefore denominated, because they should be Coloni, the Tillers of the Earth, and Stewards of fertilitie.' 'Should be'; but are not, for:

> our mutinous Loyterers would not sow with providence, and therefore they reaped the fruits of too deere bought Repentance. An incredible example of their idlenesse, is the report of Sir Thomas Gates, who affirmeth, that after his first comming thither, he hath seen some of them eat their fish raw, rather then they would go a stones cast to fetch wood and dresse it.   (p. 68)

The tillers of the earth and the fetchers of wood, runs the argument, are the heirs to God's plenty: 'Dei laboribus omnia vendunt, God sels us all things for our labour, when Adam himselfe might not live in Paradise without dressing the Garden.' It is this thought that seems to hover mockingly behind the log-bearing labours of Ferdinand. Prospero, imposing the task, does not do as Sir Thomas Gates and set his own hand 'to every meane labour' dispensing 'with no travaile of his body'. He rather exercises over the Prince (himself a potential governor) the rule of Providence's dominant law; he sells Miranda (the richest of the island's bounties) only in return for work.

Once the recalcitrant passions of the Virginian colonizers have been tamed, once they have ceased to 'shark for present booty' out of idleness and lawlessness, they may hope to enjoy the bounty of nature. This idea is in itself almost enough to suggest the invention of Caliban. Strachey speaks of the 'liberty and fulness of sensuality' that drew the 'idle, untoward and wretched' to murmuring discontent, and 'disunion of hearts and hands' from labour (p. 28). The grotesque, spectacular figure of Caliban, and his conspiracy with the butler and the jester, enable Shakespeare to make Strachey's point within the conventions of masque and comedy.

Caliban, however, seems like Prospero to be doubly fashioned from the travel literature. Not only is he a theatrical epitome of the animal, anarchic qualities of the colonizers, he is also the epitome of the primitive and uncivilized condition of the native American. Strachey tells how the Virginian Indians severely tested the magnanimity of the Governor 'who since his first landing in the Countrey (how justly soever provoked) would not by any meanes be wrought to a violent proceeding against them'. But, like Caliban, they have natures on which nurture cannot stick; pains humanely taken are quite lost. One of the Governor's men—alas for tractable courses—is carried off into the woods and sacrificed; and the Governor 'well perceived, how little a faire and noble intreatie workes upon a barbarous disposition, and therefore in some measure purpose to be revenged' (p. 62).

But when Caliban consorts with Trinculo and Stephano the play expresses, with joyous irony, both the common appetites and the distinctive attributes of man primitive and man degenerate. Caliban's scorn of Trinculo's tipsy acquisitiveness, 'Let it alone, thou fool; it is but trash', measures the distance between them. Fittingly, the strictures of the *True Declaration* fall most heavily upon those delinquent colonizers who 'for their private lucre partly imbezeled the provisions', spoiling the market by leaving the Virginians 'glutted with our Trifles' (p. 70).

As witnesses both to the fine energies of Caliban and to his truculence, the first audiences of *The Tempest* might well have asked for themselves the questions that Purchas sets in the margin of *The True Repertory*:

> Can a Savage remayning a Savage be civill? Were not wee our selves made and not borne civill in our Progenitors dayes? and were not Caesar's Britaines as brutish as Virginians? (p. 62)

To this last question *Cymbeline* had already supplied something resembling Purchas's own answer, 'The Romane swords were best teachers of civilitie to this & other Countries neere us.' *The Tempest* leaves us to wonder at a range of possible answers to the first. For Shakespeare's understanding of Caliban is not co-extensive with Prospero's. 'Liberty' and 'fulness of sensuality' (to recall Strachey's terms) are auspicious when opposed, not to temperance, but to constraint and frigidity. Hence Caliban's virtue and dignity, and the quickness of his senses accords with his love of music—an Indian and a Carib characteristic remarked by the voyagers.

As his name may be meant to remind us,[1] Caliban is conceived as much out of the reports of the Caribana as of those of the Bermudas and Virginia. *Purchas his Pilgrimage*[2] tells of the *Caraibes*, the priests of the Cannibal territory in the north of Brazil, to whom 'sometimes (but seldome) the Divell appears', and of their witches 'called *Carayba*, or holiness'. There is here just enough pretext for associating Caliban with the blacker kind of sorcery that Shakespeare allows to Sycorax.

Sycorax represents a natural malignancy ('with age and envy . . . grown into a hoop') consonant with her negative and confining skills. Unlike the *Carayba* of Purchas's account, however, she does not embody a native devilry and priestcraft, but is a disreputable exile from Argier with only a casual claim to dominion over the island. Thus the play qualified the righteousness of Caliban's resentment and complicates the relationships between native and colonial endowments.

---

[1] Gustav H. Blanke, *Amerika im Englischen Schrifttum des 16. und 17. Jahrhunderts* (1962), points out that one Bodley atlas has the version 'Caliban' for 'Cariban'. The genesis of names is always elusive. It is noticeable that Strachey (p. 14) names the historian of the West Indies, Gonzalus Ferdinandus Oviedus, which might have supplied Gonzalo and Ferdinand.

[2] *Op. cit.* 3rd ed. (1617), Book IX, Chap. 5, p. 1039

N

We are left to wonder about the ultimate sources of the moral virus that has infected what might have been a golden world, and Prospero's account of Caliban's genesis ('got by the devil himself Upon thy wicked dam') may be taken either as imprecation or as a fragment of bizarre biography.

When Shakespeare confronts Prospero with Caliban he does not restrict the range of his implications in the theatre to the command that a colonial governor might seek by kindness and by torment to secure over a native. That relationship itself is only one expression of what Montaigne, in a passage familiar to Shakespeare from the 'Essay On Cannibals', called the bastardizing of original naturality by human wit. Shakespeare's scepticism, like Montaigne's, recoils upon authority itself. Prospero's malice ('tonight thou shalt have cramps') is a comic instance of the barbarism of civilization that Montaigne finds more shocking than cannibalism; we mangle, torture, and mammock our living neighbours not from natural perversity but 'under pretence of piety and religion'.

The secret dialogue that, metaphorically speaking, Shakespeare conducts with Florio's Montaigne is an intricate one. Gonzalo's Utopian vision is at its centre. Much of Florio's prose is assimilated into the routine of the verse, but the quiet climax of Gonzalo's musings—to do with the fecundity of the anarchic paradise—is intensely in the mode of the last plays:

> Nature should bring forth,
> Of it own kind, all foison, all abundance,
> To feed my innocent people.

Florio says that his admirable savages have no need to gain new lands, 'for to this day they yet enjoy that naturall ubertie and fruitfulnesse, which without labouring toyle, doth in such plenteous abundance furnish them with all necessary things, that they need not enlarge their limits'. Gonzalo is mocked by the sophisticated conspirators for, as it were, his reading of Florio. Shakespeare contrives to vindicate Montaigne's contempt for the 'unnatural opinion' that excuses the 'ordinary faults' of 'treason, treacherie, disloyaltie, tyrannie, crueltie, and suchlike'; for however apt and amusing the taunts of Antonio and Sebastian, their persistent malice is seen for what it is, and Gonzalo's words are never quite out of key with the mood that the island scenes have created in the theatre. At the same time, Montaigne's sanguine vision of uncultivated innocence is exquisitely, and critically, related to the dreams that a benign but vulnerable ageing courtier might have of sovereignty. Where Montaigne believes (or pretends to believe) that the wild nations in reality 'exceed all the pictures wherewith licentious Poesie hath proudly imbellished the golden age', Shakespeare leaves the notion to an old man's fantasy. But a significant fantasy, properly entertained by 'Holy Gonzalo, honourable man'.

When 'foison and abundance' are again at the centre of attention we are contemplating the betrothal masque. The masque has several kinds of appropriateness in a play about colonization. It accords with Strachey's concern with bounty and the proper regulation of passion, and it reminds us of the indivisible integrity of the laws of nature and government. Miranda's presence on the island has some occasion, perhaps, in the story of Virginia Dare, grand-daughter of Captain John White, born in 1587 in the first English colony of Virginia and left there in a small party.[3] But it matters more that Purchas comments in his marginal note to Strachey's account of the marriage of one of Sir George Summers's men: *The most holy civill and most naturall possession taken of the Bermudas by exercise of Sacraments Marriage, Childbirth, &c.* (p. 38). The sacrament of marriage is looked upon as the perfection of the island's sovereignty. Prospero's admonition that Ferdinand should not break Miranda's 'virgin-knot before | All sanctimonious ceremonies may | With full and holy rite be minister'd', is not only in character (the officiously solicitous father), it is also a full recognition that heaven rains down blessings only upon those who honour the sanctities of its order:

> No sweet aspersion shall the heavens let fall
> To make this contract grow; but barren hate,
> Sour-ey'd disdain and discord shall bestrew
> The union of your bed with weeds so loathly
> That you shall hate it both.

The metaphors take life from the island truths about 'the tillers of the earth and the stewards of fertility'; life flourishes best by cultivation and restraint.

The masque decoratively, but with a quick pulse, endorses the sustaining idea; the 'sweet aspersion' that the heavens let fall is recalled by Ceres' 'upon my flowers | Diffusest honey-drops, refreshing showers'. There is much to remind us of the continuity of the play with pastoral

[3] See Wright, *The Elizabethans' America*, p. 133.

comedy—with *As You Like It* and *The Winter's Tale*. 'So rare a wondered father and a wise', says Miranda, 'Makes this place Paradise.'

Purchas almost immediately follows his note on the marriage sacrament with another on a camp atrocity—'*Saylers misorder*'. The effect in the narrative is a paler version of that in the play when Prospero suddenly remembers 'that foul conspiracy|Of the beast Caliban and his confederates'. Strachey tells how a sailor murdered one of his fellows with a shovel, and how others conspired to rescue him from the gallows 'in despight and disdaine that Justice should be shewed upon a Sayler'. The 'mischiefs of mariners' reported by Strachey are intensified by the activities of 'savage spies' from among the disaffected Indians (p. 50). The Governor's nerves and moral resolution are, like Prospero's, severely tested.

The Tempest does not, however, return to the moral antinomies of pastoral comedy—opposing the seasonal, fecund processes of nature to human sophistication. Its most memorable nature has little to do with that which fills the garners and brings shepherds and sheep-shearing into *The Winter's Tale*. It is not the 'great creating nature' that Perdita honours in her festive ceremonies. It is an elemental nature, made of the air, earth, and water that meet on a tempestuous coast, and in listening to the play's many mysterious and subtle evocations of the ways of the elements we may be aware still of the poet's transfigurations of the sailors' experience.

Shakespeare is sensitive to the narrative sequence (already noticed) of storm, fear, death, and the miraculous renewal of life in the island's 'temperate air'. Shakespeare's tact sustains the sequence without surrender to superstition (*pace* Gonzalo's marvellings) and without inviting moral exegesis. In Ariel's opening songs and in Ferdinand's exquisitely mannered reception of them, the truth of the sequence becomes lyrical and musical:

> Sitting on a bank,
> Weeping again the King my father's wreck,
> This music crept by me upon the waters,
> Allaying both their fury and my passion
> With its sweet air.

The quieting of storm and sorrow have in the theatre become the same process. Grief is transposed into melody. The word 'air',

like Ariel's song itself, hovers elusively between atmosphere and
melody:

> This is no mortal business, nor no sound
> That the earth owes. I hear it now above me.

The island's airs are themselves melodious, and when Ferdinand finds
Miranda 'the goddess | On whom these airs attend' the suggestions of
aetherial harmony are perfected.

Ariel's second song offers what is perhaps the play's most eloquent
and characteristic symbol:

> Those are pearls that were his eyes:
>   Nothing of him that doth fade,
> But doth suffer a sea-change
>   Into something rich and strange.

The sea-change metaphors are a more searching expression of moral
change as *The Tempest* presents it than the overtly pastoral convention
could supply, and can touch more closely the mysteries of death.

Its beginnings in Shakespeare are familiar in Clarence's dream in
Richard III—significantly a *dream*, and a reaching-forward to the mood
and tenor of the last plays:

> O Lord, methought what pain it was to drown,
> What dreadful noise of waters in my ears.

The pain and noise of drowning were still 'beating' in Shakespeare's
mind when he wrote *The Tempest*, and the consolatory transformations
are remembered too:

>   and in the holes
> Where eyes did once inhabit there were crept,
> As 'twere in scorn of eyes, reflecting gems,
> That woo'd the slimy bottom of the deep
> And mock'd the dead bones that lay scatter'd by.

It is (as A. P. Rossiter once said) 'submarine Seneca'; but it is ready to
become 'Those are pearls that were his eyes'. The marine fantasy seems
to owe nothing to seaman's lore (Hakluyt and Purchas collect mostly
matter-of-fact accounts of the genesis of pearls) although the travel
books have much to say about the 'great store of pearl' to be found in
Bermuda seas. It suffices that Shakespeare's early experience in the
mode enabled him to refine and to amplify his distinctly surrealist

vision of death by water. But Clarence expresses too the continuing physical ordeal:

> but still the envious flood
> Stopp'd in my soul and would not let it forth
> To find the empty, vast, and wand'ring air;
> But smother'd it within my panting bulk,
> Who almost burst to belch it in the sea.

The sentiments and images are soon quite subdued to the English Senecal conventions—the 'melancholy flood With that sour ferryman which poets write of'; but not before Shakespeare had written:

> O, then began the tempest to my soul.

The sequence, storm, fear, death, is in Clarence's experience uncommsummated by the liberation that the strange word 'belch' seems to promise.

It is otherwise in *Pericles*, another play in which marine nature is more poignantly mysterious, more eternal and more consolatory than pastoral nature:

> Th'unfriendly elements
> Forgot thee utterly; nor have I time
> To give thee hallow'd to thy grave, but straight
> Must cast thee, scarcely coffin'd, in the ooze;
> Where, for a monument upon thy bones,
> The aye-remaining lamps, the belching whale
> And humming water must o'erwhelm thy corpse,
> Lying with simple shells.

In *Timon of Athens* too, the sea retains its cleansing sanctity when the pasture that lards the rother's sides and the sun that breeds roots in the corrupt earth are forgotten:

> Timon hath made his everlasting mansion
> Upon the beached verge of the salt flood,
> Who once a day with his embossed froth
> The turbulent surge shall cover.

The sea 'whose liquid surge resolves | The moon into salt tears' is symbol too of a perpetual compassion:

> rich conceit
> Taught thee to make vast Neptune weep for aye
> On thy low grave, on faults forgiven.

The prose accounts behind *The Tempest* offer Shakespeare new opportunities for this morally expressive sea-eloquence.[4] Ariel admonishes
the courtiers as if their survival from the wreck were owed to their
destined unfitness for the sea's digestion:

> You are three men of sin, whom Destiny,—
> That hath to instrument this lower world
> And what is in't,—the never-surfeited sea
> Hath caus'd to belch you up.

But the sea-swell of the rhythm subdues the joke to the solemnity of the
occasion. Prospero, in a slow movement of the play (the still figures and
the leisured speech) that makes it remarkably fitting, uses the figure of
the cleansing, clarifying sea:

> Their understanding
> Begins to swell, and the approaching tide
> Will shortly fill the reasonable shore
> That now lies foul and muddy.

The sea is an almost constant presence in the play's verbal music;
both the dancing kind:

> And ye that on the sands with printless foot
> Do chase the ebbing Neptune,

and the more sombre:

> Methought the billows spoke, and told me of it;
> The winds did sing it to me; and the thunder
> That deep and dreadful organ pipe, pronounc'd
> The name of Prosper; it did bass my trespass.
> Therefore my son i'th'ooze is bedded; and
> I'll seek him deeper than e'er plummet sounded,
> And with him there lie mudded.

The moral sonorities are the sonorities of the sea. The apprehension of
final judgement is expressed by way of sea, wind, and thunder; but
'deep and dreadful' and 'bass' are as apt for the sea as they are for the
thunder; while the thunder lingers upon the next lines stirring the
words 'deeper' and 'sounded' as they are used of the plumb-line, and
coming to rest in 'mudded'.

[4] See for example *Purchas his Pilgrimage* (1617), p. 654.

Elsewhere, language used about music and about haunting noises is not directly about the sea, but might well have been:

> Even now we heard a hollow burst of bellowing.

It might be a breaking wave. Recalling the 'humming water' of *Pericles*, it is apt that Caliban should speak of instruments that 'hum' about his ears. Humming is a common spell of the play's language:

> The noontide sun, called forth the mutinous winds.

What is manifest in the detail of the play's accomplishment is manifest still in its large design—which owes more to the literature of sea-survival. The suggestion that the action of *The Tempest* takes place under the sea is witty and illuminating. The first scene is about men drowning, and its conventions are decisively naturalistic—there at least the storm is not merely symbolic. But the second scene changes the mood and the convention; the perspectives shift; time and place lose meaning, and characters and events shed a measure of their routine actuality. The play becomes a masque; and not improbably a masque resembling a masque of Neptune, with Ariel and Caliban seen as mutations of triton and sea-nymph. If contemporary productions, however, had looked for hints for figures and décor in the literature of Virginian colonization, they would have found them in John White's 'True Pictures and Fashions'.[5]

To dwell upon the 'sea-sorrow' and 'sea-change' processes of the play is to recognize the difference from the more usual changes associated with pastoral in other comedies and late plays. Only *Pericles* resembles *The Tempest*. In *The Winter's Tale* moral growth is presented as a seasonal process, enabling Leontes to greet Perdita, when innocence returns to Sicilia in the last act, with the words: 'Welcome hither as is the spring to earth', and 'the blessed gods | Purge all infection from our air | Whilst you do climate here'. But conversion and repentance are not in *The Tempest*, simple processes of growth. They are elusive mysteries, requiring strange mutations and interventions; occurring within dream states, under spells, conditionally ruled by laws that Shakespeare is content to offer as 'magical'. But it is the sea, as the

---

[5] *The Trve Pictvres and Fashions of the People in . . . Virginia . . . draowne by Iohn White*, appended to *A briefe and true report of the new found land of Virginia* (Frankfurt, 1590). See particularly the figure of *The Coniuerer* or *The Flyer*.

Elizabethan imagination dwelt upon it, that supplied the language of moral discovery.

Shakespeare's gift, it might be said of this and other plays, was to allegorize the actual; to conjoin his responsiveness to the moral order with his sense of turbulent, intractable realities. In lesser degree that was Strachey's gift too, and Jourdan's. But to the reconciliations accomplished in this play, Shakespeare's theatrical art brings a severe qualification—one that might be expected at this mature and resourceful phase of English drama. It is brought home to us that harmony is achieved in the human world only by allowing to Prospero and to Providence the powers of a playwright; particularly of a playwright skilled in masque—for the cloud-capped towers and all the things that vanish when the magician forfeits his power are recognizably the paraphernalia of masque. In this sense Prospero is indeed Shakespeare, but not Shakespeare the private man (whether retired or exhausted) but Shakespeare the professional playwright and masque-maker, perceiving that the order he seems to reveal in the world that the voyagers disclose to us is a feat of theatrical illusion. The magic does not work everywhere and for ever. From the poetic world there is the return to Milan where Sebastian and Antonio will keep their hard identities. Prospero returns himself and the audience to vulnerable humanity.

The end of the play, however, does not wholly determine its final impression. The climax of the moral magic discovers Ferdinand and Miranda playing at chess. We may remember that a world chess master, Giacchino Greco (il Calabrese), was much about that time visiting England from Italy. Or we may take it that the game is a proper symbol of comedy—of conflict transposed into play. As T. E. Hulme once said—'Many necessary conditions must be fulfilled before the chess-board can be poised elegantly on the cinders'. Life is only provisionally, for the span of a play which obeys all the unities, a perfectly coherent moral order; and where there is no art—no play— we have leave to doubt that there can be order. Unless it is to be found among Montaigne's savages.

Note

First editions. Cymbeline was first printed in the First Folio of 1623. Simon Forman saw it performed at the Globe, probably in the spring of 1611; it was played at court on 1 January, 1634. *Henry VIII* was also first printed in the First Folio; it is generally accepted that the Globe Theatre was burned during a performance of this play on 29 June, 1613.

Modern editions. Cymbeline has been edited by J. M. Nosworthy in the New Arden Shakespeare (1955), and by J. C. Maxwell in the Cambridge New Shakespeare (1960); *Henry VIII* is edited by R. A. Foakes in the New Arden series (1957), and by J. C. Maxwell in the Cambridge series (1962).

Scholarship and criticism. The main source material of both plays is well represented and discussed in their modern editions, to which reference is made in this chapter by editors' names; the following articles are also referred to by their authors' names: J. P. Brockbank, 'History and Histrionics in *Cymbeline*', *Shakespeare Survey*, 11 (1958); Emrys Jones, 'Stuart Cymbeline', *Essays in Criticism*, 11 (1961); Robin Moffet, '*Cymbeline* and the Nativity', *Shakespeare Quarterly*, XIII (1962). Studies of standard importance, treated to like abbreviation in reference, include G. Wilson Knight, *The Crown of Life* (1958 edition), *The Sovereign Flower* (1958); Bertrand Evans, *Shakespeare's Comedies* (1960); J. R. Brown, *Shakespeare and his Comedies* (1962 edition). F. R. Leavis's essay on 'The Criticism of Shakespeare's Late Plays' is reprinted in *Shakespeare Criticism 1935–1960*, ed. Anne Ridler (1963). Incidental use has been made of Edgar Wind, *Pagan Mysteries of the Renaissance* (1958), and of W. F. Staton and W. E. Simeone, *A Critical Edition of Sir Richard Fanshawe's 1647 Translation of Giovanni Battista Guarini's Il Pastor Fido* (1964); their discussion of pastoral tragi-comedy is useful for the dramatic art of the English stage in Shakespeare's day. Quotations from *Cymbeline* and *Henry VIII* are given with reference to the New Arden editions; other references are to *Il pastor fido* (Venice, 1602), Fairfax's *Godfrey of Bulloigne* (1600), and Dekker's *The Whore of Babylon* (*Dramatic Works*, ed. F. Bowers, Vol. 11, 1955).

IX

'What's past is prologue':
'Cymbeline' and 'Henry VIII'

BERNARD HARRIS

★

THE title comes, of course, from *The Tempest*, at the moment when Antonio tries to understand the nature of the events in which he and his companions are caught up:

> We all were sea-swallow'd, though some cast again,
> And by that destiny to perform an act
> Whereof what's past is prologue, what to come
> In yours and my discharge.   (II. i. 251)

Here the dependence of the present upon the past and the posited freedom of future actions are related in stage-terms expressly fitting for that play. Antonio's words, as editors note, draw on theatrical vocabulary; 'cast', 'perform', 'act', 'prologue', and 'discharge' ('taking a part'). But though the imagery is of acting the total metaphor remains elusive, even submerged; a tempest was the prologue of this play, a shipwreck its initial event, recovery its essential action, and for that final outcome, that salvaging of the moral self, a word is found, 'discharge', which involves acting, implies obligation, and also means the unlading of a ship.

The felicity of the utterance is not admired, nor its drift perceived: 'What stuff is this!' says Sebastian, claiming that

> I myself could make
> A chough of as deep chat.

Yet he is as much mistaken in this as Antonio; for it is part of the intricate economy of *The Tempest* that the narration of past events and the control of their consequences are kept within the province of Prospero.

Equally, *The Winter's Tale*, though complex in its development of a double-plot, offers us the initial terms for approaching this drama of intertwined family destiny through the appropriate device of personal human reminiscence charged with impersonal menace, whereby we learn of the shared childhood of Leontes and Polixenes,

> Two lads that thought there was no more behind
> But such a day tomorrow as today.

This problem of the shaping or misshaping destiny of the past is natural to those themes of the late plays which treat of loss and restoration, disjunction and pattern. But in *Cymbeline*, more than perhaps in any of Shakespeare's plays, the problem of structure and utterance are complicated by the necessary attention to the past as history. For *Cymbeline* derives its past from disparate sources and its time goes by many clocks. The consequences of diverse actions are only brought fully into relationship in an extended final denouement unparalleled for its provision of multiple judgements. Criticism has often found the play incoherent, and though recent commentary has provided us with fresh understanding of the kind of knowledge of the past which its first audience shared, to some extent it remains true that *Cymbeline* appears as one of the more difficult of Shakespeare's plays about which to obtain any general consensus of opinion. It seems worth asking, therefore, whether its dramatic mode is really so preposterous as so much criticism finds it to be, and whether enforced comparison with the late romances, usually in terms of wholly literary analysis, restrict the recognition of its tragi-comic form.

It seems possible, without too much crude simplification, to discern two differing and fundamentally irreconcilable attitudes towards *Cymbeline*; that which J. C. Maxwell calls 'an older and more hardheaded tradition, whose classic expression is Johnson's comment', and another, presumably soft-headed tradition, which has reverenced certain elements in the play, especially those claimed as qualities of an absolute truth fulfilled in the character of Imogen.

Johnson's view, shared by Mrs. Charlotte Lennox, was particularly dismissive of 'the folly of the fiction, the absurdity of the conduct, the confusion of the names and manners of different times, and the impossibility of the events in any system of life'. In this statement common sense resists the irrational, the iconoclast of artificial unities rejects the wilful artifice of a new unity, and the moralist appeals to 'life' unreflected in art. Yet Schlegel, believing *Cymbeline* to be 'one of Shakespeare's most wonderful compositions', observed that he had 'connected a novel of Boccaccio with traditionary tales of the ancient Britons', and was content to accept that the dramatist

> has contrived, by the most gentle transitions, to blend together into one harmonious whole, the social manners of the latest time with heroic deeds, and even with the appearance of the gods.

The changing preoccupations of thought which exercise themselves in the ephemeral tasks of criticism have continued to be as markedly opposed in the present century. Masefield is representative of many critics who have seen in the play a subject 'only partly extricated', and in its romance an obscurely personal motive; thus his final comment on the 'strange, touching, very Shakespearean romance, of the thing long lost beautifully recovered before the end' is that 'Shakespeare had lost a child'. And even in criticism which avoids biographical facts as irrelevant the consolations afforded by the play have been seen as relying upon other evidence than the conduct of dramatic action. John Bailey, while convinced that 'there is no play in which Shakespeare shows more of his own kind of truth', believed that what mattered to Shakespeare was not 'the consequences of his story as a whole but the truth of each separate action, the vitality and humanity of each separate person'. Hence while remaining a work by 'a master of the secrets of the human heart', enshrining the special truth of Imogen, 'As the work of a dramatist *Cymbeline* is nothing.' Even Granville-Barker's account of *Cymbeline*, which contains one of the few treatments of the dramatic nature of Shakespeare's 'sophisticated artlessness', also reveals a near-Johnsonian impatience with the 'futile suffering' of Imogen, and makes a moral objection that 'surely it is a vicious art that can so make sport of its creatures'. The art itself is tragi-comedy, Granville-Barker concedes,

> But tragi-comedy—in this phase of its development, at least—is a bastard form of art; better not judge it by too strict aesthetic law.

By what law, then, is *Cymbeline* to be judged? To what is its significance, when admitted, related? Certain literary approaches to both topics gave occasion for F. R. Leavis to issue a caution that

> we must be on our guard against approaching any play with inappropriate preconceptions as to what we have in front of us. By assuming that the organization is of a given kind we may incapacitate ourselves for seeing what it actually is, and so miss, or misread the significance.

The fullest account of the play is undoubtedly that of G. Wilson Knight, who dates the play after *The Winter's Tale* and *Pericles* and finds the dramatist not feeling his way but incorporating in *Cymbeline* 'a re-working of themes ... into a more comprehensive design.' Among these recurrent themes, referred backwards and forwards throughout the range of Shakespeare's work, are those of Shakespeare's 'two primary historical interests, the Roman and the British, which meet here for the first time'; they meet in terms of both national and personal interest, and there is in the relationship of Imogen ('not merely a single lady, but Britain's soul-integrity'), of Posthumus ('imaginatively at least a composite of the British and the Roman'), and of Iachimo ('a Renaissance Italian', 'typically foreign'), a whole framework of historical thinking which justifies 'the close reference of the sexual to the national in *Cymbeline*'. In Knight's reading of the play 'the heritage of ancient Rome falls on Britain', a tutelage acknowledged by Cymbeline in personal terms becomes representative of a national destiny betrayed by its natural inheritor, the Italy of the Renaissance. It is a transaction approved by the gods:

> Jupiter's blessing on Posthumous' marriage and the Soothsayer's vision thus make similar statements. Both symbolize a certain transference of virtue from Rome to Britain.

And fittingly, the unity of the personal and national themes, are sought in an image, offered by the play, which incorporates the dramatist's personal testament:

> Shakespeare's two national faiths are here married; his creative faith in ancient Rome, felt in the Roman dramas from *Titus Andronicus* to *Coriolanus*, and his faith in England.

This deeply considered account has not won acceptance from the play's most recent editors, and it is notable that they concur most in rejecting the centrality of the national, British matter. Thus Nosworthy found it 'futile to object that the Cymbeline narrative element does not harmonize with the other plots, for romance can accommodate such anomalies'; and in this case 'Cymbeline, dull though he may have been, would have served, had it not been for what it entailed—namely a retreat to some of the least romantic pages of Holinshed'; hence, there is 'this initial error in plot selection'. Maxwell supports the wager story as 'the central theme of the plot', but with a hesitancy prompted by the power of the play's comic exploitation, so that 'here, too, we are conscious of a reluctance on Shakespeare's part to commit himself wholly to the claims of his material'.

Since so much criticism of *Cymbeline* returns to this puzzle of the discrepant claims of Shakespeare's material it is worth trying to determine what claims that material originally possessed for the dramatist's contemporaries, how far Shakespeare's decision to cast so much diverse metal into one mould was unprecedented, and whether we can use further inspections of the play's tragi-comic art to understand better how much its 'experimental' form serves its theatrical experience.

*   *   *

Understanding begins with Cymbeline. Coleridge, writing of the relationship established between the names of Shakespeare's plays and their transmitted ideas, declared that '*Cymbeline* is the only exception'; and then sought to prove the rule by claiming that even *Cymbeline* has advantages 'in preparing the audience for the chaos of time, place, and costume, by throwing the date back into a fabulous king's reign'. This is an initial 'inappropriate preconception' that Shakespeare's use of the past has the same connotations for us as it had for his audience. Even Wilson Knight, working with the preconception that *Cymbeline* is 'to be regarded mainly as an historical play', dismisses Cymbeline as a man, and finds him important as a king; but as king in role, rather than in history.

Several commentators have noted, however, that the importance of Cymbeline's reign for historians lay in events outside Britain. Studying the detailed way in which *Cymbeline*'s historical sources possess 'dramatic and poetic potential' J. P. Brockbank suggests that

> Holinshed's (or Fabyan's) brevities noticing the birth of Christ and the rule of Augustus may have stimulated in Shakespeare's imagination a comparable range of thought.

Comparable that is, to the range displayed in John Speed's *History* (1611), which elsewhere offers material for dramatic concerns arguably nourished within the play. It is perhaps interesting (in view of criticism which has connected *Cymbeline* with King James) that the speculative connection between Christ and Augustus was not made only by historians, but received royal recognition: in 'A Meditation vpon the 27.28.29. Verses of the XXVII Chapter of Saint Matthew' King James observed that it had not beene fitting that the Saviour of the World ... should haue beene borne but vnder a King of peace, as was *Augustus*, and in a time of peace, when as the Temple of Janus was shut, and whenas all the World did pay him an vniuersall contribution as is said in the second of Saint *Lukes Gospel*. Of which happy and peaceful time the Sibyls (though Ethnickes) made notable predictions, painting forth very viuely the blessed Child that then was to bee borne.[1]

And it may be worth adding that at least one contemporary of Shakespeare, writing summary accounts of the significant facts of the reigns of English kings found one supreme event to honour Cymbeline: in 'ohn Reynolds's *Epigrammata* (1611) there is a set of inscriptions upon JReges' of which number 20 reads

Cymbelinus Christi tempore

> Cymbeline tuo rex Christus nascitur aevo,
> Historias ornat res ea summa tuas.[2]

R. Moffet, admitting that 'the customes that the Britaines paie the Romans' (Holinshed's phrase for the tribute theme) have 'a considerable part in Shakespeare's play', emphasizes that it is 'the birth of Jesus Christ which made the reign unique', and finds this 'central fact ... reflected in the form and details of the play'. As instances, Moffet indicates changes which Shakespeare made in the wager plot, enabling him to stress in Iachimo 'a variant of the pattern of false values', and in Imogen and Posthumus qualities of 'ideal excellence', thus bringing the wager theme into a redemptive context. Similarly, Moffet brings out the Christian element of the prophesying, establishing a Christian scriptural and sacred poetical tradition for the final augury, whereby that eagle's flight into the sun, while retaining its emblematic significance of virtue migrating from Rome to Britain, has also 'a traditional meaning which gives it even more universal scope'. The legendary meaning, attested by the bestiaries, by Spenser, and by the psalms, is that of 'general rejuvenation and renewal of life and vision, applicable

---

[1] 'A Paterne for a Kings inauguration', in *A Collection of His Maiesties Workes* (1616), p. 609.

[2] Nos. 21 and 22 are on 'Guiderius' and 'Arviragus frater'; No. 10 is tersely unsympathetic on 'Leir':

> Leirus erat, quando Leircestria tecta locavit,
> Delirus, quando Regna reliquit, erat.

to all the surviving persons of the play and to the whole world in which its action takes place'.

This final peace, related by Nosworthy to 'the peace which passeth understanding', and here set in the specific context of 'the unique moment' of Cymbeline's reign, has been given additional, topical context in Emrys Jones's remarkable study of the relationship of the historical material of *Cymbeline* to contemporary history. Thus the play's concluding 'peace-tableau'

> presents dramatically the stillness of the world awaiting the appearance of the Christ-child, but it also pays tribute to James's strenuous peace-making policy.

Jones's discussion of the topical references in the play are both convincing and speculatively enticing. Most important, perhaps, is the connection established between the use of the Tudor dynastic myth to establish James's succession in the line of Brutan kings, monarchs of the west. The landing of Henry, Earl of Richmond, at Milford Haven began the process which resulted in the Tudor rule, and consequently the Stuart. The insistence upon Milford as the meeting place of Imogen, Cloten, and the princes, together with the Roman ambassador, is thus explained, and in the play's own terms; for 'Shakespeare's geography in this play is not a literal but a symbolic one'. Around this central discovery accrete certain relationships which take us outside the action of the play to its implications for Stuart times. Thus, the reign of Cymbeline, offering only peaceful happenings, had to be supplemented dramatically by the wars of Guiderius, but the character of Cymbeline himself, at the end of the play, 'has a direct reference to James I', drawing upon that western monarch's motto of 'Beata pacifici', his chosen role as peace-maker, the parallel between Cymbeline's submission to Rome and James's attempted negotiations with the papacy, and perhaps, most tangentially, supported further by the fact that Shakespeare provides Cymbeline (unhistorically) with a daughter and two sons, which James had.

These three critical enquiries, into the dramatic potential of the historical source material, into a tradition of historical Christian thought, and into the relationships which Cymbeline effects between past and present history, help to restore to us some of the possible preconceptions of the dramatist and his audience. Moreover, such enquiries establish unappreciated interests and pressures both sustained within the play and exerted by it. Yet in redressing the balance of these concerns all three critics restrain full justification of the dramatic art of *Cymbeline*. Indeed, they all make specific reference to Leavis's contention that, unlike *The Winter's Tale*, *Cymbeline* is not 'organized from "a deep centre"'. As a consequence, Brockbank concludes

> We are haunted by intimations of a profound significance, but it is constantly clear that the apocalyptic destiny of Britain cannot be reconciled with the form of pastoral-romance on any but the terms which Shakespeare's offers.

On this same point Moffet suggests that

> we have here for once a play whose 'centre' is something not stated or presented and an action whose climax and justifying event is not shown but assumed as shortly to take place, and that it is for this reason that we find in it a striving after union, disparate pieces artificially yoked, rather than unity itself.

Similarly, Jones derives the weakness of *Cymbeline* from elements within it which 'we usually associate with the Jacobean masque'; by contrast with *Macbeth*, where the royal compliments lie 'at the perimeter', the association of Cymbeline with James provides a central embarrassment, not least the problem of the wicked Queen. In short:

> The whole play suffers, as *Macbeth* does not, from being too close to its royal audience, and despite some brilliant things there is, imaginatively, a central fumbling, a betrayal of logic.

Such concurrence of qualified approval is notable. But do not these elements of a pervasive, romantic historical myth, sacred reference and political relevance also demonstrate that *Cymbeline* fulfils the demands of the art of pastoral tragi-comedy? The 'centre' of that dramatic mode is not 'given', but something sought through sequence and contrast and achieved only in a final dramatic revelation.

To argue this is to take account, however briefly, both of dramatic theory and theatrical fact; and both seem necessary. For to dismiss tragicomedy as 'a bastard form of art—in this phase of its development', is simply to call on canon law to prohibit a natural union, and so far from determining the issue merely repeats the objections made against *Il pastor fido* before it reached print. The stock response merits no more than the standard answer of Guarini:

> Art observes that tragedy and comedy are composed of hetero-

geneous parts, and that therefore if an entire tragedy and an entire comedy should be mixed, they would not be able to function properly together as a natural mixture, because they do not have a single intrinsic natural principle, and it would then follow that in a single subject two forms contrary to each other would be included. But art, a most prudent imitator of nature, plays the part of the intrinsic principle, and while nature alters the parts after they are united, art alters them before they are joined in order that they may be able to exist together and, though mixed, produce a single form.

(ed. cit., p. 3)

The theory is no more satisfying than those we possess for tragedy or comedy, but the principles are those by which Guarini established a version of the dramatic mode which was popular for two centuries. It is worth setting *Cymbeline* against that mode, as much as against its sources and analogue in inferior Elizabethan historical romances, or a related but less ambitious work like *Philaster*. For the achievement of *Cymbeline* on the stage, though uniquely rendered, is of a kind which challenges comparison with the work that made a like ambitious use of its dramatic conventions. Such comparison is usually prohibited. Jonson both entices us to seek for Guarini's influence while sneering at his popularity:

> All our English writers,
> I mean such as are happy in the Italian,
> Will deign to steal out of this author, mainly:
> Almost as much as from Montagnié:
> He has so modern and facile a vein,
> Fitting the time, and catching the court ear!
>
> *(Volpone*, III, ii)

And J. M. Nosworthy has contended that much in *Cymbeline* that is 'Elizabethan, and pastoral, and decorative, and even conventional'

> does not mean that Shakespeare, in 1608 or thereabouts, went to school with Guarini or with Beaumont and Fletcher, but simply that he returned to his own earlier practices.[3]

Whether or not Shakespeare knew Italian is unimportant; he certainly knew the play which his company performed as *The Faithful Sheperdess*; and whether or not Shakespeare went to school with Guarini

---

[3] 'The Integrity of Shakespeare: illustrated from *Cymbeline*', *Shakespeare Survey* 8 (1955).

is equally unimportant; but we may need to if we are to find the fullest theatrical context and contemporary tradition for *Cymbeline*.

The world of *Il pastor fido* is that of Arcadia, a state under the tyranny of what Guarini calls 'the horrible tribute' of human sacrifice demanded by the gods; a land ravaged by the wild boar, and a people awaiting the return of the peaceful past, their hope sustained and tantalized by the prophecy that the marriage of two of divine origin, and the voluntary sacrifice of a self-denying victim, will achieve redemption for the state. A complex double-plot generates the maximum misunderstandings between lovers, by jealousy, disguise, and separation; love is ridiculed by sophisticated lust; the heroine is tricked into appearing guilty of adultery; yet the faithful shepherd, Mirtillo, survives the scorn of Amarillis and gratuitously takes her place as the necessary victim for outrage. The play has many themes and is expansive both in its treatment of them and its hospitality to other matters, competing with the *Aminta* in literary competition, parody, and parallel. The great central episode of the boar-hunt is raised to the status of symbolism involving destruction and renewal, and the theme of tyranny and freedom is acted out in the related subplot of the love of Dorinda and Silvio. The fifth Act is devoted to the prolonged denouement of the knotted plots, turning eventually upon the identification of Mirtillo as the child, lost twenty years before, of the chief priest Montano, and hence of race divine. Thus the edict of the gods, formerly seen as ominous, is freshly interpreted, and Mirtillo, about to suffer under one law, is seen as the means of accomplishing the double terms of the prophecy. The denouement leads to a double conclusion; when the reported adultery is shown to be false the blood-sacrifice is transformed to a bloodless rededication of the state in the temple; and on finding that the pardon of the gods is being universally repeated even the malicious agent Corisca asks 'Ma che badi Corisca? | Commodo tempo e di trouar perdono' (Gg4^r).[4] Corisca, the calumniator believed, asks forgiveness and receives it from Mirtillo and Amarillis, with whose marriage the play concludes.

The play gathered into a dramatic unity themes familiar in classical poetry and situations recurrent in the long tradition of romance novels, and offered them in a political context provided by the prologue intended for performance at the celebrations for the marriage of Charles

----

[4] 'What stick'st thou at Corisca? 'tis a day | Of Pardons this', Fanshawe, *ed. cit.*, l. 5497.

Emmanuel, Duke of Savoy, to Catherine of Austria, daughter of Philip II of Spain. More than half a century later, in offering his translation of this 'famous Dramatick Poem' to Prince Charles in 1647, Fanshawe recalled the significance which Arcadia was intended to have for Savoy, and declared that Guarini had attempted

> to make *a Dernier effort* (as the French call it) or generall muster of the whole forces of his Wit before his Princely Master (the then *Duke of Savoy*) and withall to insinuate and bring into that awfull presence, in their masking clothes (as I may say) such principles of Vertue, and knowledge *Morall, Politicall, and Theologicall*, as (per-adventure) in their own grave habits, out of the mouthes of severer Instructers, would not have found so easie admittance to a Prince in the heat of his youth, and with the glorious triumphs and felici-ties of his royall Nuptials then celebrating.

There is no need to trace out those principles, and kinds of know-ledge, which Fanshawe found disseminated by the choruses of *Il pastor fido*, and still capable of furnishing 'a *Lantskip* of these Kingdoms' in the times of civil war. But the example of *Il pastor fido* might make us less dependent, in trying to experience the special theatrical art of *Cymbeline*, upon solutions owed to biographical speculation of a private nature.

To appreciate *Cymbeline* to the full there seems no doubt that we should endeavour to see it with proper regard for its Stuart mode, as a *dernier effort*, a general muster of the whole forces of Shakespeare's wits, drawing upon the past resources of themes in his poems, comedies, histories, and tragedies, to provide an offering for its sophisticated audiences at the Globe, at Court, and its author's royal patron. Only then perhaps could we adequately recognize the manner and extent in which the play's virtuous principles, and its moral, political, and theological knowledge, are insinuated in their masking clothes.

The world of *Cymbeline* is both wide-ranging and deep-focused, its action is doubly set in Britain and Italy, and its span of time moves from legendary antiquity, to the Renaissance, and on into the present.

> Its affairs are political, nationalistic, heroic, pastoral, connubial, religious, and amatory; dangers and disguises multiply freely. The characters know separation, deceit, love, hate, hopelessness, pain and death; they hope beyond reason and beyond true report.
>
> (Brown, p. 237)

The play's beginning offers us national and private dissensions. A king, though privately grieving, has banished his daughter because she has married a commoner rather than a prince, her stepmother's son. The act has brought discord between the king and his courtiers, though the disharmony is dangerously concealed. For the prince is a boor, 'a thing' says the first gentleman, 'Too bad for bad report'; whereas the commoner is a non-pareil, and though the same spokesman 'cannot delve him to the root', yet that root is meant to have magically virtuous properties, and regard for it is reverent rather than ignorant. Posthumus is of British stock, his father honoured in battle against the Romans and his qualities designated in Roman-style; thus 'Posthumus Leonatus' contrives to unite a heroic origin with a folk-hero appeal stemming from the special circumstances of his birth. Cymbeline himself has suffered, twenty years before, the loss of two sons, and we are alerted by the conventions of romance to expect their reappearance, and for Cymbeline's care of Posthumus to be rewarded eventually by reunion after trial. Similarly, the fairy-tale relationship of stepmother and heroine, developed sharply in the second scene, is already pointed in the first.

The several pasts of family and national history, and the many kinds of treatment of experience made available by the conventions of historical legend, romance, and fairy-tale, are displayed in this prologue-like first scene. Art is playing the role of the intrinsic principle, manifestly adapting the parts selected before they are joined so that they may be able to exist together. But it is the special theatrical characteristic of *Cymbeline* that even while the conduct of its action makes plots converge, themes intertwine, and character relationships become more extensively involved, other aspects of its stage presentation insist upon our observing necessarily distinct responses until the full and sustained unity of the denouement is comprehensively plotted. Shakespeare is reluctant, perhaps, not so much about engaging too closely with his material as about forsaking any of the possible means of offering it. Hence, although we are unlikely now to say that 'As the work of a dramatist *Cymbeline* is nothing', we are capable of stating, as J. F. Kermode does, that in *Cymbeline* Shakespeare set himself 'masterproblems in dramaturgy almost entirely for the sake of solving them'.[5] And even the most appreciative and detailed analysis of that dramaturgy emphasizes Shakespeare's scarcely human control; thus Bertrand

[5] *Stratford-upon-Avon Studies* 3: *Early Shakespeare* (1961), p. 227.

Evans, attending to the most conspicuous element of the play's dramatic technique, declares that what makes *Cymbeline* extraordinary

> is at once the fantastic complexity of its uses of discrepant awareness and the consummate skill with which its intricacies are managed: with greater finality than does any other play, it evinces Shakespeare's mastery of infinitely complex art. . . . From the point of view of the creation, maintenance, and exploitation of discrepant awareness—considered both quantitatively and qualitatively—*Cymbeline* is Shakespeare's greatest achievement. (p. 248)

Nor does this mastery of an infinitely complex art attempt to transmute the necessarily dramatic crudities required to preserve the barbaric elements of some of its themes. As J. R. Brown comments, the art of *Cymbeline*

> is complex as well as primitive, and these two qualities are interdependent. The dramatic idiom is entirely suitable for establishing a wide view of the stage and for exploiting contrasts and relationships. (p. 238)

It is an idiom drawing heavily, as does *Il pastor fido*, upon soliloquy, both for character revelation, and amplification of theme (such as the praise of sleeping beauty and the stylized attack upon women), upon a poetic lyricism which 'dilates' its themes as well as developing them, and upon the manifold possibilities of intrigue drama, with its properties of handkerchiefs, letters, rings, potions, and proofs, of magic, whether poison, incantation, prophecy, miraculous descent of a god, or family ghosts, and of the occasion and technique of masque and pageant.

To a considerable extent criticism and stage-experience alike can familiarize us still with the powerful relationships between past dramatic modes and their continuing potency. There is no need to dwell, for instance, on the uses to which the Shakespearian theatre put its costumes; it is enough to note their prodigal employment in *Cymbeline*, whether in the literal disguises of Imogen as a page in service, of Cloten as an erotic-fetichistic wooer, the lost princes as wild hunters, or in that preoccupation with the outward and inward man associated with Posthumus and governing his change of dress in accordance with the dictates of a reassumed loyalty. More interesting are verbal devices, less explored, which are designed to effect similar relationships of image and stage situation. Consider those running references to hunting, distinct but not wholly detached from the episode of the slaying of Cloten, which arise in different contexts and are touched afresh each time with varying significance. Thus Cloten, seeking admittance to Imogen's presence, thinks in terms of bribery and sacrilege not unknown even in the royal sport:

> 'Tis gold
> Which buys admittance (oft it doth) yea, and makes
> Diana's rangers false themselves, yield up
> Their deer to th'stand o'th'stealer.   (II. iii. 68)

Imogen, struggling to penetrate the treachery of Posthumus's murderous orders and Pisanio's possibly treacherous complicity, sees herself as a destined victim in a cruelly selective game:

> Why hast thou gone so far,
> To be unbent when thou hast ta'en thy stand,
> Th'elected deer before thee?   (III. iv. 108)

Bellarius, ironically unaware of what barbarity will be unleashed later and what human sacrifice will be celebrated, encourages his charges to the chase with natural joy and domestic comfort:

> he that strikes
> The venison first shall be lord o' th' feast,
> To him the other two shall minister.
> (III. iii. 74)

This 'hunters' language' is easily modulated in Posthumus' mouth to serve a patriotic note when he recalls how Bellarius rallied the British forces with the cry

> 'Our Britain's harts die flying, not our men:
> To darkness fleet souls that fly backwards; stand,
> Or we are Romans, and will give you that
> Like beasts which you shun beastly, and may save
> But to look back in frown: stand, stand!'

and how in consequence some warriors rejoined the heroic trio,

> 'gan to look
> The way that they did, and to grin like lions
> Upon the pikes o' th' hunters.   (V. iii. 24)

Such multiple cross-references are figures in the play's intricately knit verbal texture, like the 'valuation' imagery of commerce, and of rarity and artistic worth; all draw widely and technically upon the audience's knowledge and interest. Other verbal devices reach out of the dramatic convention to establish contact with other literary modes. J. M. Nosworthy has shown in the play a 'kind of double signification that belongs to animal fable of the Aesop kind' in the moral and emblematic associations which connect birds and character's qualities, relating the practice to Jonson's usage in *Volpone*, though distinguishing the particular purpose to which the device is put in *Cymbeline*. Comparison might also be made with Guarini's recourse to a similar means of stabilizing his play's decorum by bestowing upon his characters an 'informing trait' conforming to an 'ethical principle'.

Such devices of the dramatic use of language remain available to a modern audience, but others, more specifically attuned to the taste of a Stuart audience, present difficulty.

Jones is surely right to demonstrate our lost understanding of those elements in *Cymbeline* which assumed familiarity with Jacobean panegyric, pageant, and masque occasions. It is not a matter only of unrecognized royal eulogy, and dramatic presentation of Tudor myth. But if we are to claim that the masque had strengths as well as weaknesses of structure we shall need to show that *Cymbeline* assimilated into its highly complex dramatic mode not only conventions of pastoral tragi-comedy, but methods offered by masque conventions for altering tone and tension. *Cymbeline*, in the theatre, remakes with dramatic purpose those masque conventions of handling characters, sometimes humanly direct, sometimes typified and representational; its plot proceeds by revelations not only of tragi-comic character discrepancy and false identity, but by establishing moments calling for enlarged responses, sometimes 'out of character' on naturalistic terms. One instance of this may suffice to show the relationship between 'character' and topical historical and patriotic reference. Criticism often makes an undue fuss about the alleged incongruity of the behaviour of Cloten and the Queen in face of the Roman demand (III. i). Here the disreputable Cloten and the malevolent Queen suddenly find patriotic defiance and wifely loyalty. Cloten's vaunt

> Britain's a world by itself, and we will nothing pay for wearing our own noses

and the Queen's reminder to Cymbeline that his isle stands

> As Neptune's park, ribb'd and pal'd in
> With rocks unscaleable and roaring waters

are properly traced by editors to thoughts first provided in Holinshed, the first to that Virgilian text 'Et penitus toto divisos orbe Britannos' (*Eclogues* I., 66), the second to Caesar's discovery of another world not compassed by the sea but encompassing it. To relate these utterances only to the chronicles is scarcely to show their literary currency; to note that they are common ideas is to make their dramatic point vaguer than need be. And since Imogen's related phrases

> I'th'world's volume
> Our Britain seems as of it, but not in't:
> In a great pool, a swan's nest . . .
> (III. iv. 138)

have occasioned some ingenious glossing,[6] it is worth noting that ideas of volume, isolation, Neptune's domain and that evocative nest are all brought together in Giles Fletcher's *Christ's Victorie and Triumphs In Heaven, and Earth, over and after Death* (1610):[7]

> And if great things by smaller may be ghuest,
> So, in the mid'st of Neptunes angrie tide,
> Our Britain Island, like the weedie nest
> Of true Halcyon, on the waves doth ride,
> And softly sayling, skornes the waters pride:
>   While all the rest, drown'd on the continent,
>   And tost in bloodie waves, their wounds lament,
>   And stand, to see our peace, as struck with woonderment.
>   (*Christs Triumph after Death*, stanza 21)

Fletcher's marginal note to this stanza reads, 'Shadowed by the peace we enjoy under our Soveraigne'; the following stanza compares the ruinous state of France, Greece, Spain, and the Netherlands, and succeeding stanzas refer again to James explicitly as a 'Picture of peace', and the continuing prospect held out by Prince Henry.

Similarly, in Jonson's masque *Love freed from Ignorance and Folly* (1611) the first riddle of the Sphinx concerns the paradox of finding 'a world the world without': demonstrating that the whole series of

---

[6] Dowden bookishly offered 'a page of the world's great volume, but, as it were, a page torn from it' (see New Cambridge edition, p. 178*n*.)

[7] The connection, if accepted, may support the latest accepted date for *Cymbeline*.

riddles are propounded 'according to the mystical arguments of Cusanus'. Edgar Wind locates the theme of 'the world outside the world' in Bruno's *Eroici furori*, where it is already 'interpreted as a compliment to England': the riddle is quickly read, and like the rest deftly applied to Albion under James. Shakespeare did not necessarily share Jonson's reading, though he could have made a chough of as deep chat if he wanted, but he certainly shared his audience. And to them the whole theme of the sacred destiny of Britain had a poetic force and immediacy to which the crudely physical Cloten and the mythologically fey Queen here make appropriate, where we find incongruous, response: nor is Imogen's willingness to venture into foreign lands so naïvely whimsical as we may think.

The motto which all these characters play with was a Stuart conceit which Wind pursues as far as the seal of Charles II, which showed the British king as ruler of the seas with the 'altered legend':

> Et penitus toto regnantes orbe Britannos.

And if we choose to follow the theatre history of *Cymbeline* into that era we shall find no less radical an adjustment of the play's historical emphasis; one permitting us to understand, by perspective, both the context which its original audience possessed for it, and the contrivance of adjustment needed in a period of steadily deteriorating comprehension.

By the time of Thomas D'Urfey's *The Injured Princess, or, The Fatal Wager* (1682)—head-titled 'The Unequal Match'—the past of Britain is no longer able to elicit sure interest: hence Posthumus and Imogen are provided with names from heroic romance, Ursaces and Eugenia; France is restored as the scene of the wager and the proper source of corruption, thus Shatillion replaces Iachimo, though the usefulness of that villainous name is secured by giving it to a new minor figure, the unpleasant Jachimo. The abiding theme of the wars of the British and Romans as exemplified in the ever-popular Fletcher's *Bonduca* take a stranger turn in George Granville's semi-opera *The British Enchanters, or No Magic Like Love*,[8] and the adapter of *The Merchant of Venice* may have been influenced by *Cymbeline*. But now the peace between Britain and Rome takes the more familiar fantasy of the transference from Rome to Britain of effective imperial power. Some old strains are

---

[8] Published in his *Poems on Several Occasions* (1721), but acted in part-version in the victorious year of 1706.

struck when King Celius admonishes the Emperor Constantine and his
fellow prisoner, Lucius, in these terms:

> Roman, consider well what Course you run,
> Resolve to be my prisoner, or my Son.
>   If this sound Rude, then know, we *Britons* slight
> The supple Arts that Foreigners delight
> Nor stand on Forms to vindicate our Right.
>
>   (III. ii)

The vindication is formidably completed by military victory, and the
typically heroic suicide of Constantius at Oriana's feet; the play's
universal peace is ushered in by a speech of 'Prophetic Fury' by the
enchantress Urganda, who unveils a pageant ('Here a Scene represents
the Queen and all the Triumphs of her Majesty's Reign'), and offers us
an immediate and explicit answer to the play's historical meaning:

> Discord and War and Tyranny shall cease,
> And jarring Nations be compell'd to Peace;
> If curious to inspect the Book of Fate,
> You'd further learn the destin'd Time and Date
> Of *Britain's* Glory, know, this Royal Dame
> From *Stuart's* Race shall rise, ANNA shall be her Name.

This tribute to the last Stuart is no more extravagant than those paid
to the dynasty a century earlier, whether in pageant, drama, or such a
collection as *The Triumphs of King James The First* (1610). But the
sentiments which finally break out from the precarious framework of
The British Enchanters only confirm the indulgent nature of its art.
Equally, that fatal reductive facility of D'Urfey (who also perpetrated
Bussy D'Ambois, or The Husband's Revenge), caused the unrestrained
substitution of contemporary nationalistic topicality along with a
general trivializing of *Cymbeline*'s domestic and dynastic issues.

These failures to distinguish between the decorums of art and life, or
between meaningful and negligent anachronisms (which so confused
Mrs. Lennox), might make us cautious enough to ask whether *Cymbeline* was indeed muddled in execution because of the proximity of its
royal audience, and whether our distance from the latter is an un-
bridgeable gap in the theatre.

But though the patriotism of *Cymbeline* may well be more direct
than we have recognized, it is scarcely of the overt kind flaunted by

the author of *Rapta Tatio*[9] (1604), when he signed his dedicatory epistle 'Enter at your commaunde, Your Country-man and a BRITTAINE', and Shakespeare would have been equally aware of the same author's comment

> some haue sayd *Procul a Ioue et a fulmine*; the conuersations of Kinges haue euer beene helde like the nature of the Flames, warme further of, and burning neerer.   (B4ʳ)

There seems nothing esoteric about *Cymbeline*, and Shakespeare did not need to be privy to the conversation of a king who would declare at his own table that 'the civil law of the Roman emperors ought to be substituted in room of the common law of England'. James's policy was publicly expounded. Shakespeare is likely to have shared in the poetic excitements of the new thinking about royalty and rule made possible by the peaceful accession, but he is also as likely as Fletcher[10] to have been critical about specific aspects of political policy.

The topical appeal of the play has gone so long undetected that we are entitled to suppose that they were never of a disproportionately disruptive nature, and our recovery of this further relevance need not make us lose either critical proportion or theatrical context.

The patriotism of the play, like all its other elements, is exploited not only for topicality but for permanent dramatic effect, along with heroic material of more than national consequence contributing to the play's concern with the moral nature of loyalty (Imogen's 'What is it to be false?'), self-sacrifice, and virtue of more than personal significance. As illustration of the ways in which *Cymbeline* employs and discards its nationalism in the process of developing its own imaginative culture we may consider the relationship of Posthumus to Imogen and of Imogen to the play's larger demands upon her.

To Cymbeline Imogen is 'the great part of my comfort', but to Posthumus she is love itself, something he has failed and that failed him, a wife who, he thinks, betrayed him, and whom he thinks he has murdered. Yet when Posthumus opens the last Act of the play he makes an inventory of his misfortunes in a significant order of moral recovery. After a commonplace warning to husbands that they might

[9] Full title, *The Mirrour of his Maiesties present Gouernment, tending to the Vision of his whole Iland of Brittonie.*

[10] See P. Davison, 'The Serious Concerns of *Philaster*', *English Literary History*, 30, 1 (1963).

find themselves similarly obliged to 'murder wives much better than themselves', and an expression of regret that a good servant should have obeyed an unjust order, Posthumus struggles with the more complex problem of the gods' justice. He wishes they had punished him for his own greater faults before he could kill Imogen for her lesser. But he concedes that some privileged creatures die 'for little faults' ('That's love | To have them fall no more'), while others are allowed to go on punishing themselves until they learn 'thrift' from indulgence. Now that Imogen belongs to the gods he recognizes a double obligation, to person and to duty: having killed Britain's mistress he will not fight against her country. Leaving the ranks of the 'Italian gentry' he becomes a 'Briton peasant', in preparation for what he expects to be military defeat and death, to be offered as a triple atonement, to country, family, and wife.

Yet Posthumus' recovery lies neither within his own power nor on his own terms. When, in the second scene, he defeats and spares Iachimo, the latter does not recognize a disguised nobility more effective than his own and attributes his disgrace to having 'belied' Imogen, an act which 'Takes off my manhood' and provoked such power that even the air of her country 'Revengingly enfeebles me'. In the third scene, after Posthumus has recounted the unexpected British victory he is forced to acknowledge that his patriotism has failed him, and has to take back his Italian identity in an effort to secure that destruction he seeks 'by some means for Imogen'. In the fourth scene of his 'welcome bondage' this seems promised; but, while he sleeps, the 'poor ghosts' of the Leonati avert his death; drawing upon human grief, the force of 'Great nature', pride of ancestry, and the love of Imogen, their appeals, culminating in a demand for recognition by the gods of his service to Cymbeline, addressed to Jupiter:

> Thy crystal windows ope; look out;
> no longer exercise
> Upon a valiant race thy harsh
> and potent injuries.

Where Posthumus' own endeavoured offering is insufficient, these supplications of the already dead are restorative. The descent of Jupiter is doubly effective, in the sense of stage spectacle and dramatic purpose. He sets at rest the 'Poor shadows of Elysium', justifies his own 'potent injuries' to Posthumus as trials well spent, honours by his protection the love of Imogen and Posthumus who were married in his temple.

Yet it is wholly characteristic of the self-sufficient art of *Cymbeline* that
having raised its own god it requires him to condescend in the humblest
task of its stage-business, donating to Posthumus that tablet of cryptic
prophecy.

The descent of Jupiter is an astonishing means of reconciling the
play's insistent demands for some external judgement upon those events
which have caused division and seeming loss in all the spheres the
drama has encompassed. Those critics who dispute the authenticity of
the vision simply rebel against the claims of the dramatic art to accom-
plish its own judgement. We are forced to see in Jupiter's appearance
the introduction of an apparent poetic justice which assimilates to itself
other manifestations of omnipotence. Thus, at the heart of Jupiter's
speech his phrasing borrows terms of Christian revelation:

> Whom best I love I cross; to make my gift,
> The more delay'd, delighted.

We may be entitled to see in this a suggestion of that complete Christian
fulfilment which some critics hold that the play approaches. But the
language is also that used by the Chorus of *Il pastor fido* to make precisely the same point about the connection between that play's pattern
of misfortune and the purposes of destiny:

> forse quella,
> che pare inevitabile sciagura,
> Sarà lieta ventura.   (E1ᵛ)[11]

But where Guarini places the comment early in his play, establishing a
continuous relationship between the nature of his art and the workings
of destiny, Shakespeare not only withholds it ('the more delay'd,
delighted'), but shows us a god content to submit those who have
succeeded in summoning him to the total arbitrament of that long
succeeding final scene, so yielding to the demand of a more powerful
tragi-comic art.

To earn his place in that court of judgement Posthumus is forced to
play with his patriotism, and exchange his heroism for humiliation.
And to an even greater extent Imogen, the injured princess, is made a
victim of the play's devices. She is wooed by a song whose beauty is
ridiculed by the buffoon who has commissioned it; she is courted by
false sophisticated flattery, and her reward for rejecting it is to be spied

[11]   what we imagine is
          Our greatest crosse, may prove our greatest blisse,
                                        (Fanshawe, *ed. cit.*, l. 1151)

upon while sleeping and robbed of her emblem of plighted troth to
furnish the stage-property for a lie. Imogen is no more capable, however, than Posthumus of proving her integrity by her own means,
until she too makes a total submission of self.

Her search for justification is brought to ridicule. She sets off, on
Pisanio's counsel, like a heroine of epic romance, crying 'O, for a horse
with wings!', longing to haste as

> Erminia fled, scantly the tender grass
>   Her Pegasus with his light footsteps bent,
> Her maiden's beast for speed did likewise pass.
>   (Bk. VI, canto cxi)

Commentators long ago pointed to resemblances between the conduct
of Imogen and Erminia,[12] who goes searching for her knight, hides
among shepherds in a pastoral interlude, and comes upon Tancred
apparently dead; and there are further hints which the first audience of
Cymbeline might be expected to catch from Fairfax's popular rendering
of Tasso's pseudo-history, with its far-flung world of clashing civilizations, its insistent and unabashed nobility ('The royal eagles upon high
mountains fly'), to whose hero God grants a solemn vision, sent stream-
ing through a 'crystal port', demanding pardon for the banished
Rinaldo and promising an empire ruled by Christian arms and at peace.
Tasso's world is not only a skilled mingling of past and contemporary
heroism; its chivalry is bedevilled by potent magic, and its battle scenes
sometimes possess a dreamlike horror, in which a headless ghost is
conjured by witchcraft, another headless warrior continues to ride into
action, and in which Rinaldo's trunk is falsely identified by his armour:

> A warrior tumbled in his blood we saw;
>   His arms, though lusty, bloody, hack'd and rent,
>   Yet well we knew when near the corse we draw,
> To which (to view his face) in vain I started,
>   For from his body his fair head was parted . . .
>   (Bk. VIII, canto li)

Cymbeline exploits the lurking incongruities of such material and
travesties the chivalric mood for its own ends. But these lie well

---

[12] Shakespeare might be expected to know, perhaps poignantly, that King
James valued Edward Fairfax's translation of the *Gerusalemme Liberata* 'above
all other English poetry'; or so said Brian Fairfax. See C. P. Brand, *Torquato
Tasso* (1965), p. 241.

beyond the burlesque by which they are accomplished. When Imogen played the faithful shepherdess, offering herself as a sacrifice to Post-humus and entreating Pisanio to butcher her, the false heroics were patent, not least to her. Now her decision to venture ('though peril to my modesty') into masculine disguise and conduct is equally vulnerable, and is thwarted by a magic potion. The play whose primary action turns upon one lie reaches its first climax with a stage spectacle in which Imogen seems about to be buried beneath a whole garland of inter-woven deceits. That famous mock funeral and its dirge have been called by Bertrand Evans 'the richest context that Shakespeare ever constructed in our minds to embellish one moment':

> for these lads are not Cadwal and Polydore, mountain rustics, but Arviragus and Guiderius, princes royal; Euriphile, whose funeral they remember and whose dirge they repeat, was not their mother, but their nurse; the youth Fidele is not a boy, but a girl; not only a girl, but a princess; not only a princess, but their sister; and, on top of all, not dead. (p. 274)

Moreover, the moment is not ended. A topless man lies beside Imogen whom she will wake to mourn as Posthumus and so embrace in ignorance that 'harsh, noble, simple nothing' Cloten. Nor is that act atonement enough; Imogen only begins upon that when she recog-nizes that she cannot answer the questions of Lucius because she has falsified her own past:

> I am nothing; or if not,
> Nothing to be were better. (IV. ii. 367)

She gives a fictitious name to her supposed dead master, and the name in which she resumes refuge and offers fresh service is itself sufficient mockery, 'Fidele'.

The comic menace and near-demented ingenuity of this scene force Imogen out of her true identity as an injured princess as surely as Post-humus is ejected from that patriotism which Dr. Johnson called the last refuge of a scoundrel. Is the art which contrives this entertainment so surely 'inhuman' as Granville-Barker claimed? Certainly the play remains conscious of what is implied in some lines of its opening scene, that any account of a human being may

> Crush him together, rather than unfold
> His measure duly. (I. i. 26)

Yet it torments its characters not only to reduce them beneath their humanity but to let them move beyond it. And it manipulates its history of the past to extract from it some principle of tribute owed to a more than national sovereignty. The diverse meanings of one of Shakespeare's longest plays are not to be crushed together where the dramatic action is devoted to unfolding them in due measure.[13] But as the play gathers towards its conclusions it is possible to see certain congruities established between its themes of personal and national destiny.

One of the simpler ways in which present contents are found inadequate to meet the demands inherent in the past is shown when the royal princes revolt against the protective and artificial naturalness of the life afforded them by Bellarius:

> GUIDERIUS: Haply this life is best
> (If quiet life be best) sweeter to you
> That have a sharper known . . . but unto us it is
> A cell of ignorance, travelling a-bed,
> A prison, or a debtor that not dares
> To stride a limit.   (III. iii. 29)

When the war intrudes upon their sanctuary they see it as a chance to change that valour which has been 'to chase what flies' for service in the army:

> ARVIRAGUS: By this sun that shines
> I'll thither: what thing is't that I never
> Did see man die, scarce ever look'd on blood,
> But that of coward hares, hot goats, and venison!
>   (IV. iv. 34)

And Bellarius goes with them from a necessity that it is more than his own:

> Lead, lead. The time seems long, their blood thinks scorn
> Till it fly out and show them princes born.

Bellarius' confidence that past truth will out is one which we share as an audience; but the denouement is far from a steady progress towards related proofs. In some ways it is a series of re-trials in which the main

---

[13] 'To an American who was complaining that a certain performance of *Cymbeline* was too long, [Poel] had replied, "That is because they've cut so much"', R. Speaight, *William Poel and the Elizabethan Revival* (1954), p. 263.

characters all have to expose themselves again to unknown fears. Cymbeline himself learns that his past life was a lie; and the Queen's death, however much required by tact, is also required in terms of the play's final concerns; for, quite simply, the fairy-tale element cannot be allowed to survive into that last scene of determined inquisition; and, more complexedly, Cymbeline learns from his wife's betrayal a magnanimity which he will need to exercise more largely:

> Mine eyes
> Were not in fault, for she was beautiful:
> Mine ears that heard her flattery, nor my heart
> That thought her like her seeming. It had been vicious
> To have mistrusted her.   (V. v. 62)

It is in the expression of sentiments of such persevering trust that the final scene can be said to protect itself against the critical charge that it diminishes its human characters. For as they struggle, comically, melodramatically, and heroically, to make their contributions to a general truth, they one by one are caught by the past they acknowledge and risk its fresh contrivance. Thus Bellarius puts himself in jeopardy to prove to Cymbeline that the princes are his sons, when Guiderius is about to suffer for Cloten's death, freely confessed. And perhaps the toughest lesson that the last scene yields is that to be fully human it is necessary to be more than merely human. For none of this truth would have been revealed or its human risks justified if Imogen, granted a wish by Cymbeline, had used it as we, Lucius, and common custom expect. But she does not use the chance to free Lucius, her protector, from punishment; intuitively, she uses it to nail the essential lie of Iachimo's right to wear Posthumus' ring, and so makes it possible for everyone else to free themselves from a false past.

In the community of trust which the last scene creates it becomes possible for Cymbeline to honour the past of Britain itself and freely render tribute to the civilization which tutored it in law, teaching, by the widest implication, Posthumus to recognize that the power he has over Iachimo is to spare him.

It seems certain that the Stuart audience would be capable of reading into that final peace and pardon a testimonial to King James's larger desires, even if those have scarcely been directly represented in the play's conduct: and it is possible that the early audience was able to move beyond the temporal framework of the play's references to the event of promise which glorified Cymbeline's reign. What seems equally certain is that our tentativeness in experiencing the play in the theatre is not removed by fresh knowledge of the material it works with, valuable though that fuller realization is: nor is that tentativeness a theatrical weakness, due to something only partly 'extricated'; it is rather a valid experience of tragi-comedy, which does not possess the finality of tragedy or the confidence of comedy. The Soothsayer may assure us that

> The fingers of the powers above do tune
> The harmony of this peace.

But the solemnity of the utterance cannot prevent our eyes from straying to the musicians' gallery; is he not, in his own way, coming in on cue to correct, however radiantly, his own earlier comic misreading of augury? Cymbeline's final speech, controlling what Granville-Barker aptly visualizes as the play's pageant close, gathers in authority, civil ('publish we this peace') and military ('so through Lud's town march') and closes on a heroic note:

> Never was a war did cease
> (Ere bloody hands were wash'd) with such a peace.

No doubt this would catch at James's ear, for it harmonizes with that victorious conclusion in Tasso, where Godfrey ('His bloody coat he put not off') runs to the temple to rededicate himself and his forces in peace (Bk. XX, canto cxliv). Yet the lines which seem to hang above this triumph-ending in the theatre are those with which Cymbeline sets forward to the temple of 'great Jupiter', retaining 'a touch of that "pagane rite and custome" which opens the *Brut*' (Brockbank, p. 48):

> Laud we the gods,
> And let our crooked smokes climb to their nostrils
> From our blest altars.

Wherefore 'crooked'? Should not the smoke of an acceptable sacrifice rise undeviously to the heavens? It seems a final image of that tragi-comic recognition of the tortuous indirectness by which human beings contrive to approach the truths possessed by the gods. Even so Carino hesitantly contemplates his offering:

> Eterni Numi: o come son diuersi
> Quegli alti inace Sibili sentieri,

Onde scendono a noi le vostre grazie:
Da que fallaci, e torti,
Onde i nostri pensier salgono al cielo.   (Ee3^v)[14]

★   ★   ★

The end of *Cymbeline* exhibits 'a reticence appropriate to a play that has shown such discords before such peace' (Brown, p. 245). It is a reticence the more remarkable if we accept Wilson Knight's claim that 'you can feel, in *Cymbeline*, through the often fanciful plot, a sense of national destiny pushing through' (*S.F.*, p. 80). But since there will scarcely be any need to point out that recent criticism of *Cymbeline* provides fresh testimony to his perceptions of relationship between its concluding augury and the close of *Henry VIII*, a footnote may be permitted on the artistic reticence not always demonstrated in that scene.

Henry VIII is a play in which Shakespeare shows himself more at ease in the court of King James than we might wish him to have been, whether or not in the company of Fletcher; as the result there is a long-standing critical and scholarly division about authorship, date, tone, intention, and characterization, and rather more solutions than the play offers problems. Some are real, and the whole complex matter of structure is not perhaps to be so confidently dipsosed of as Wilson Knight accomplishes by observing:

> At first sight the plan of *Henry VIII* seems unco-ordinated and loose, but it obeys the same law as Shakespeare's earlier national play, *King John*.   (*S.F.*, p. 81)

But if our repeated sight of the play is in the theatre it can be seen more properly to obey its devised laws. And this is not to fall back on the plea that the play makes good theatre—it is very far from being actor-proof —but simply to acknowledge that the play is supremely conscious of its first audience in a way so explicit that a modern audience can still grasp at its proffered guidance. The play protects itself with a defensive pro-logue not only against vulgar versions of its theme, like Rowley's *When You See Me, You Know Me*, but against our supercilious incredu-lity that the story should be attempted. The prologue appeals to our

[14]   O eternall Gods,
Between our pray'rs slow-winding paths, what odds
There is (by which we climb to Heav'n) and those
Directer lines by which to us Heav'n bowes!
                              (Fanshawe, *ed. cit.*, l. 5221)

sense of dignity and attributes to its audience a capacity for pity; it thus establishes a contract between its 'gentle hearers', including that 'understanding friend' beneath the platform,[15] and the good intentions of a company unwilling to forfeit

> Our own brains and the opinion that we bring
> To make that only true we now intend . . .
>   (Prologue, 20)

In such a context of self-consciousness the play's 'chosen truth' is something less than Wilson Knight's 'choice and real thing, which to reduce to "fool and fight" would be sacrilege' (C.L., p. 272); but it is certainly not cynically less than it simply states. The play is an historical romance, in which 'All is True' in the sense that all has been derived from chronicle record; but it remains a chosen truth that it expects its audience to find humanly sympathetic, dramatically entertaining, and politically instructive. Probably most of our difficulties in reaching a balanced critical view of the play derive from the play's determination to balance the potentially irreconcilable issues then so partisan and perhaps permanent.

Hence, as J. C. Maxwell justly comments, 'most of the really explosive Reformation themes have been tactfully omitted' (ed. cit., p. xxxii); but those that remain are skilfully manipulated to justify the play's concentration upon the misery which mightiness meets and introspectively meditates upon, and the pageant-ceremony which both sustains its human ambition, tempts it, and subdues it. The cross-rhythms of pride and submission, rise and fall, are episodically treated obviously enough by matters of pageant marshalling which juxtapose with no less deftly arranged analyses of the interior life. The play scrupulously attempts no less dexterous adjustments of historical biography, atoning for its difficulties over Katharine's treatment by granting her a private vision of final justice, presenting a double case for Wolsey while maintaining its own verdict, and humanizing Henry's more obsessive traits by treating his lust as love and so directly rehabilitating both Anne Boleyn and helping to set aside that distasteful problem of Elizabeth's bastardy. The play in the theatre makes heavy demands upon sentiment, but it does so in a sophisticated manner, for it contrives to mock the common mob ('what a fry of fornication is

---

[15] See new Arden edition, p. 6n.

at door!'), and allows us to be conscious of our separation from those unpleasant youths

> that no audience but the tribulation of Tower-hill, or the limbs of Limehouse their dear brothers, are able to endure.   (V. iii. 60)

And at the same time the play extracts the utmost theatrical appeal from its audience's melancholy acquaintance with scaffold-speeches, breaking into elegies which rival the sententious excitations to virtue made popular in the heroic dramas of political ambition. Yet if the language of the play sometimes comes near to strangling itself in tears, it is only a further extension of that relationship which the play constantly effects between human actions and those unwearying and impersonal events which the play's muted imagery of sun, sea, and rocks steadily reinforces. The pathos, misery, and fears of the play are its strongest theatrical effects, and the epilogue expresses a doubt whether we shall take away more from the play than a legend of a good woman; and it is so doubtful of even this that it concludes in a self-dismissive bawdy jest. Yet the play's final prophecy survives not only the final rather gauche presentation of Henry as a doting father, and any special application it might well have had to the marriage of the Princess Elizabeth.[16] And it is certainly a vision powerful enough to warrant Wilson Knight's interpretation of its panegyric qualities as reaching beyond the play's immediate themes to their continuity and persistent appeal in some continuing concept of Britain's destiny.

But in the context of the play as experienced in the theatre it seems arguable that we are conscious of a more explicit Shakespearian concern. For as editors have shown, the terms of the prophecy are scrupulously derived from contemporary handling of scriptural utterance applied to homiletic understanding of the reigns of Elizabeth and James. There is no room here for the kind of humorous word-play and dubious etymological interpretation shown in Shakespeare's treatment of Philharmonius' prophecy and knowingly ridiculed by Fletcher (or by Shakespeare):

> help me, thy poor well-willer,
> And, with thy twinkling eyes, look right and straight
> Upon this mighty *morr*—of mickle weight—
> *Is*—now comes in, which being glu'd together
> Makes *morris*, and the cause that we came hither . . .
>   (*Two Noble Kinsmen*, III. v. 119)

[16] R. A. Foakes establishes the connection, New Arden edition, xxxi–ii.

The propriety of Cranmer's prophecy is not that of something glued together to flatter James, but nor is it necessarily an ecstatic promise of a new golden age. We may grant that

> The 'stately cedar' of Cymbeline is transferred to a contemporary monarch, James I, under whom England's destiny is to expand.
>
> (*S.F.*, p. 86)

But to a contemporary audience, asked to listen with particular care to a serious and considered account of their past destiny and future security, the prophecy also contains a patient rebuke to those popular and tendentiously violent interpretations of the nature of England's destiny in the continuing struggle with Rome. Consider Dekker's way of presenting prophecy, in his fantasy of pseudo-Spenserian nomenclature and pseudo-Shakespearian vocabulary *The Whore of Babylon* (1607), when Elizabeth receives her counsellors:

> FLORIMELL: She that was held a down-cast, by Fates doome,
>   Sits now aboue their hopes: her maiden hand,
>   Shall with a silken thred guide Fairie land.
> OMNES: And may shee guide it—
> FIDELI: Euen till stooping time
>   Cut for her (downe) long yeeres that she may climbe
>   (With ease) the highest hill old age goes o're,
>   Or till her Fairie subiects (that adore
>   Her birth-day as their beeing) shall complaine,
>   They are weary of a peaceful, golden raigne.
> TITANIA: Which, that they never shall, your stately towers
>   Shall keepe their ancient beauty: and your bowers
>   (Which late like prophan'd Temples empty stood,
>   The tops defac'd by fire, the floores by blood,)
>   Shall be fill'd full of *Choristers* to sing
>   Sweet heavenly songs, like birds before the Spring:
>   The flowers we set, and the fruits by us sowne,
>   Shall cheere as well the stranger as our owne.
>   We may to strange shores once our selves be driven,
>   For who can tell under what point of heaven
>   His grave shall open? neither shall our oakes,
>   Trophies of reverend Age, fall by our stroaks,
>   Nor shall the brier, or hawthorne (growing under)
>   Feare then, but flie to them, to get from thunder,
>   And to be safe from forraine wild-fire balles,

Weele build about our waters wooden walles.
OMNES: On which weele spend for you our latest lives.
(I. ii. 40)

Later, one of Dekker's stock Cardinals displays the kind of fear Dekker
intended his audience to share:

I CARDINAL: Say that *Titania* were now drawing short breath,
(As that's the Cone and Button that together
Claspes all our hopes) out of her ashes may
A second† Phoenix rise, of larger wing,   † *King Iames*
Of strong talent, of more dreadfull beake,
Who swooping through the ayre, may with his beating
So well commaund the winds, that all those trees
Where sit birds of our hatching (now fled thither)
Will tremble, and (through feare strucke dead) to earth,
Throw those that sit and sing there, or in flockes
Drive them from thence, yea and perhaps his talent
May be so bonie and so large of gripe,
That it may shake all *Babilon*.   (III. iii. 232)

There seems no doubt, as C. V. Wedgwood writes, that the advantages of James's policy of neutrality towards Spain

> were not at all so obvious to a people who, quite apart from a sin-
> cere desire to assist their Protestant co-religionists in the struggle
> with the Whore of Babylon, were concerned to break down Spanish
> sea-power, still dominant in the West Indies and threatening in
> the English Channel, and to make way for their own expansion.[17]

The occasion of the marriage of Princess Elizabeth with the Protestant
hero might have been a highly suitable one for a revival of sentiments
which had their courtly counterpart in Drummond of Hawthornden's
wish that Prince Henry had died in the act of conquering Rome.

But just as Shakespeare was more concerned in poetically reconciling
his private phoenix and the imperial and sacred eagle on the cedar of
Cymbeline, so he persists, in the determined quietism of *Henry VIII*, in
equating the expansion of England with the spreading cedar branches,
and sees that they might flourish just as generously if they are free from
predators. What's past is not forgotten in *Henry VIII*, but it goes on
being a prologue of promise to its first or any audience only so long as
it chooses to make new truth.

[17] *Poetry and Politics under the Stuarts* (1960), pp. 16–17.

Note

First edition. The Two Noble Kinsmen was first printed in a Quarto edition of 1634, and was reprinted in the Second Folio of John Fletcher's works in 1679.

Modern editions. H. Littledale edited the play (1876–85) in an edition which remains important both for its text and collection of early critical opinions. C. H. Herford's 1909 edition is available in the Temple Dramatists series. Quotations in the following chapter from *The Two Noble Kinsmen* are given with line references to the edition by C. F. T. Brooke in *The Shakespeare Apocrypha* (1908). In other quotations line references are to P. Alexander's *Tudor Shakespeare* (1951), F. L. Lucas's *The Complete Works of John Webster* (1927), and *The Works of Ben Jonson*, ed. C. H. Herford, P. and E. Simpson (1925–52). References to the plays of Beaumont and Fletcher are by volume and page to the edition by A. Glover and A. R. Waller (Cambridge, 1905–12).

Scholarship and Criticism. Of importance for the general question of collaboration between Shakespeare and Fletcher are E. K. Chambers, *William Shakespeare*, 2 vols. (Oxford, 1930); Theodore Spencer's 'The Two Noble Kinsmen', *Modern Philology*, XXXVI (1939); Marco Mincoff's 'The Authorship of *The Two Noble Kinsmen*', *English Studies*, XXXIII (1952); and K. Muir, *Shakespeare as Collaborator* (1960), which includes mention of *Cardenio* and *The Two Noble Kinsmen*. Further discussions are in editions of *Henry VIII*, by R. A. Foakes, New Arden (1957), and J. C. Maxwell, New Cambridge (1962). Clifford Leech has written on *The John Fletcher Plays* (1962). Among older studies whose arguments are still important are A. H. Thorndike's *The Influence of Beaumont and Fletcher on Shakespeare* (Worcester, Massachusetts, 1901), and C. M. Gayley's *Francis Beaumont, Dramatist* (1914). M. Eccles wrote on 'Francis Beaumont's *Grammar Lecture*' in *Review of English Studies*, XVI (1940).

Studies in the taste and critical principles of the time include G. F. Reynolds's '*Mucedorus*, Most Popular Elizabethan Play?' in *Studies in the English Renaissance Drama* (New York, 1959); E. M. Waith, *The Pattern of Tragicomedy in Beaumont and Fletcher* (1952).

P. Bertram has written on 'The Date of *The Two Noble Kinsmen*' in *Shakespeare Quarterly*, XII (1961); F. O. Waller on 'The Printer's Copy for *The Two Noble Kinsmen*' in *Studies in Bibliography*, XI (1958); and Cyrus Hoy on 'The Shares of Fletcher and his Collaborators in the Beaumont and Fletcher Canon', in *Studies in Bibliography* (1956–62).

Several new contributions to the discussion of *The Two Noble Kinsmen* have been published since this chapter was written. Image clusters characteristic of Shakespeare are analysed by E. Armstrong in *Shakespeare's Imagination* (revised 1963), Appendix B, and by C. H. Hobday in 'Why the Sweets Melted: A Study in Shakespeare's Imagery', *Shakespeare Quarterly* XVI (1965). A. C. Partridge in *Orthography in Shakespeare and Elizabethan Drama* (1964), Appendix vii, has some new suggestions on the mode of collaboration. P. Bertram has argued in favour of Shakespeare's authorship of the whole play.

P. Edwards, 'On the Design of "The Two Noble Kinsmen"', *Review of English Literature* V (1964), is an important critical reassessment of the play.

X

Shakespeare and the New Dramatists of the King's Men, 1606–1613

RICHARD PROUDFOOT

★

WE have no complete record of the repertory of the King's Men between 1606 and 1613 but there is good evidence for their performance or ownership of thirty-five extant plays and five lost plays in this period. No less than sixteen of the surviving plays were written, wholly or in part, by Shakespeare. These include old plays revived, namely *Henry IV*, both parts, *Much Ado About Nothing*, *Julius Caesar*, *Othello*, and *Macbeth*; new plays by Shakespeare alone, *Antony and Cleopatra*, *Timon of Athens*, *Coriolanus*, *Cymbeline*, *The Winter's Tale*, and *The Tempest*; and new plays written in part by him, *Pericles*, *Henry VIII*, *Cardenio*, and *The Two Noble Kinsmen*. Shakespeare's works clearly formed the backbone of the repertory until about 1610, but by then Fletcher was beginning to assume the position of leading playwright for the King's Men in which he continued after Shakespeare's retirement about 1613 until his own death in 1625. Fletcher had a hand in at least nine plays performed by the company before 1613, his three collaborations with Shakespeare; four plays written with Beaumont, *Philaster*, *The Maid's Tragedy*, *A King and No King*, and *The Captain*; and two unaided plays, *Bonduca* and *Valentinian*.

By this stage in his career Shakespeare must have begun to feel some of the inconveniences of success. It was during these years that stationers most blatantly attributed to him plays which he did not write: *A Yorkshire Tragedy*, 'Written by W. Shakespeare' and the second edition of *The Troublesome Reign of King John*, 'Written by W. Sh.', appeared in 1608 and 1611; *The London Prodigal*, 'By William Shakespeare', had already been printed in 1605. The attribution of *The Troublesome Reign* was clearly fraudulent, the other two might have been mistakenly assumed from the fact that the plays concerned were performed by the

King's Men. Thomas Heywood records that Shakespeare was 'much offended' with William Jaggard over his 1612 edition of *The Passionate Pilgrim* (quoted in Chambers, II. 218): the misattribution to him of plays must likewise have given offence.

A new problem was the emergence of a generation of playwrights young enough to have been brought up on a theatrical diet in which Shakespeare's own works were prominent. Before Tourneur, Webster (a new dramatist though possibly not a young man), Beaumont and Fletcher, we hardly find dramatists whose whole work shows an awareness of Shakespeare, expressed not only in conscious imitations but in a frequent tendency to echo the plays which had taught them much of what they knew about writing for the stage. These men all wrote for the King's Men during Shakespeare's later years and ten of their plays are known to have been acted by them by 1613: Webster's *The Duchess of Malfi*; Tourneur's *The Revenger's Tragedy*, and a play, now lost, called *The Nobleman*; and the plays of Beaumont and Fletcher already listed.

The only other prominent contributor to the repertory of the King's Men that we know of at this time was Ben Jonson, who wrote for them *Volpone*, *The Alchemist*, and *Catiline*. These were also the years in which Jonson began his long and distinguished series of Court masques in which members of the King's Men took part when an anti-masque was required.

Our list of the extant plays in the repertory is completed if we add Barnabe Barnes's *The Devil's Charter*, George Wilkins's *The Miseries of Enforced Marriage*, and a group of plays of unknown authorship, *The Fair Maid of Bristow*, *The Second Maiden's Tragedy*, *The Merry Devil of Edmonton*, and the revised version of *Mucedorus*, as printed in 1610. The later attribution of *The Merry Devil* and *Mucedorus* to Shakespeare may have been due to the known connection between the plays and his company.

It is the purpose of this chapter to suggest some of the ways in which Shakespeare's plays influenced those of his colleagues and how their work, in turn, may have influenced him.

*   *   *

John Webster and Cyril Tourneur went on writing revenge tragedy after Shakespeare had written *King Lear* and *Macbeth*, in which he relegated revenge to a subordinate position as a motive of tragic action.

He went on in *Coriolanus* and *The Tempest* to show the limitations of the revenge ethic, as Tourneur was also to do in *The Atheist's Tragedy*, but in the meantime Webster and Tourneur continued, in the tradition of *Hamlet*, to write the plays which set them beside Shakespeare as tragic writers: *The White Devil*, *The Duchess of Malfi*, and *The Revenger's Tragedy*.

Of the two Webster shows less direct influence of Shakespeare: lacking some of his skill in the portrayal of character and the significant shaping of plot, he nevertheless reaches moments of intensity parallelled only in Shakespeare's works. It is in scenes of passionate or disturbed emotion that Webster most readily slips into reminiscence of Shakespeare. The last act of *The White Devil* contains the most striking echoes, first in the passionate outburst of Cornelia when her son Flamineo kills his brother Marcello, and again when she re-enters, mad. On the first occasion she echoes Lear's words over the dead Cordelia:

> Fetch a looking glass, see if his breath will not stain it; or pull out some feathers from my pillow, and lay them to his lips.
>
> (V. ii. 38)

on the second, she echoes Ophelia's mad scene:

> You're very welcome.
There's Rosemary for you, and Rue for you,
Hearts-ease for you.   (V. iv. 70)

Webster rarely echoes Shakespeare so clearly as this, it almost seems as if he is trying to impart something of the pathos of Lear and Ophelia directly to Cornelia, who has not played a prominent part in the earlier action and who is suddenly called upon to evoke a sympathy which the audience might not be very ready to extend to the sententious beldame of the earlier acts. Apart from rare verbal echoes, of which these are the most remarkable, Webster seems to have assimilated whatever he may have learnt from Shakespeare to the point where specific indebtedness is hard to indicate.

Shakespeare's influence on Tourneur is more widespread and more apparent. *The Revenger's Tragedy* is like *Hamlet* not only in being a play of revenge: its hero, Vindice, is a full-length portrait drawn from a few aspects of the complex character of Hamlet, the graveyard philosopher of the gravediggers' scene, the malcontent courtier of the exchanges with Rosencrantz and Guildenstern and, above all, the man obsessed with sexuality as a physical symbol of evil and corruption. This last quality in Vindice leads Tourneur to echo not only *Hamlet* but also *King Lear*. Lear's mad scenes contain much of the material of Vindice's disgust. The limits of Tourneur's characterization, announced by the 'humours' names which his characters bear—Vindice, Castiza, Ambitioso, and the like—show as active an influence of Jonson and Marston as of Shakespeare.

The Atheist's Tragedy draws more heavily and less creatively on Shakespeare, as Robert Ornstein has demonstrated in his chapter on Tourneur in *The Moral Vision of Jacobean Tragedy*. Here, again, Shakespearian reference seems to be used to produce an immediate emotional response in the simplest way. Webster and Tourneur were already in danger from the influence of Shakespeare, but they rarely fell into the trap of writing mere Shakespearian pastiche.

A glance at the minor works in the repertory again shows the pervasive influence of Shakespeare. Leaving aside mere verbal echoes, we find that both *The Fair Maid of Bristow* and *The Merry Devil of Edmonton* show evidence of Shakespearian imitation. *The Fair Maid* is a tragicomedy whose climax clearly recalls that of *Measure for Measure*, not only in lines like 'Intents are nothing till they come to acts' (Q. 1603, D4^v), but in the actions of Sentloe, who is believed to have been murdered and who visits his supposed murderers in prison, disguised as a friar, confesses them and waits until he is sure of their repentance before revealing himself. The Shakespearian touches in *The Merry Devil* are restricted to the character of Blague, host of the George Inn at Waltham, who seems to be imitated from the host in *The Merry Wives of Windsor*. Barnes may be showing knowledge of *Antony and Cleopatra* when he refers to the asps used by a murderer in *The Devil's Charter* as 'Cleopatra's birds', but his style and dramatic technique are very old-fashioned for the date of his play (1607) and his most noticeable debt is to Marlowe, especially to *Dr. Faustus*.

The only other play in this group that demands mention is *Mucedorus*. It is hard to perform the feat of historical imagination demanded by this play and to see what qualities made it one of the most popular plays of its age. George F. Reynolds has recently tried to date its popularity from the revival by the King's Men at Court on 3 February, 1610; but, although the revival may have increased its appeal, it was not forgotten in the years between its first printing in 1598 and 1610. A second edition would not have been printed in 1606 if there had been no demand for the play. It is very likely that Shakespeare introduced the bear in *The Winter's Tale* after observing the mixed effect, first frightening, then comic, produced by the bear in *Mucedorus*.

Turning next to the plays which Ben Jonson wrote for the King's Men we are at once confronted with a problem. There is no evidence to suggest that Webster, Tourneur, or Barnes ever came into close personal or professional contact with Shakespeare, and George Wilkins has come to be canvassed as a possible collaborator with him in *Pericles* mainly because his novel *The Painful Adventures of Pericles Prince of Tyre* is based on the play. Jonson, on the other hand, is known to have been a close friend of Shakespeare's and to have shown great interest in his work. Surely the clash of personalities and differences of opinion between these two men about how a play should be written must have had an effect on the practice of both?

Jonson reached the height of his powers in *Volpone* and *The Alchemist*, the comedies he wrote for the King's Men in these years; but they illustrate as clearly as his unsuccessful tragedy, *Catiline*, how little he had in common with Shakespeare in aims or methods. There is no point in these plays where we can say with confidence that Jonson has learnt from Shakespeare. Nevertheless it is essential to remember that Jonson's well-known strictures on his friend were usually no more than qualifications tempering high praise for the man and his work. Even if Jonson was prepared to tell William Drummond in 1619 'That Shakespeare wanted Art', when he came to write his memorial verses for the first Folio he expressed a more balanced opinion:

> Yet must I not give Nature all: Thy Art,
>   My gentle Shakespeare, must enjoy a part.
> For though the Poet's matter, Nature be,
>   His Art doth give the fashion. And, that he,
> Who casts to write a living line, must sweat,
>   (Such as thine are) and strike the second heat
> Upon the Muses' anvil: turn the same,
>   (And himself with it) that he thinks to frame;
> Or for the laurel, he may gain a scorn,
>   For a good Poet's made, as well as born.
> And such wert thou.

No comment of Jonson's on the later Roman plays of Shakespeare is extant, unless a general disapproval can be deduced from his satirical allusion, at the very end of *The Silent Woman*, to a line from *Coriolanus*:

'He lurched all swords of the garland' (II. ii. 99). On the other hand he left ample evidence of his contemptuous attitude to *Pericles*, *The Winter's Tale*, and *The Tempest*. His criticisms are directed at two points: the plays are old-fashioned and they contain unnatural and improbable characters and events. *Pericles* is the epitome of 'some mouldy tale' ('Ode to Himself') and yet it is the kind of play that still succeeds in 1629 with the sort of audience that Jonson himself had laughed at in 1614 for tolerating the view that '*Jeronymo*, or *Andronicus* are the best plays yet' (*Bartholomew Fair*, Induction). His irritation with 'Tales, Tempests and such like Drolleries' clearly refers to Shakespeare and seems to be a mixture of scholarly disapproval of the type of popular drama that Sidney had deprecated so justly and so long ago, and of irritation that such nonsense still was popular in a way that his own plays were not.

It is unlikely that we shall ever know what effect Jonson's criticisms had on Shakespeare. Perhaps a line in *Julius Caesar* did originally read 'Caesar did never wrong, but with just cause' as Jonson says it did in his *Timber*: if so the Folio reading, 'Know, Caesar doth not wrong, nor without cause | Will he be satisfied' (III. i. 47–8), may show Shakespeare's readiness to learn from his critics. The unwonted concern about the unity of time discernible in the choric apology spoken by Time in *The Winter's Tale* (IV. i), might possibly have had its origin in critical argument between Shakespeare and Jonson, perhaps about *Pericles*. This is, of course, the merest speculation, but when Shakespeare, in *The Tempest*, takes pains to point out in the dialogue that the duration of the action is only four hours we can hardly avoid supposing that he is setting out to prove to someone that he can observe the strictest unity of time when he chooses to.

If the plays of Shakespeare and Jonson give little indication of influence either way, the same cannot be said of Jonson's masques. The great series of masques which he wrote for Christmas entertainments at the courts of James I and Charles I began in 1605 with *The Masque of Blackness*. The association of the King's Men with these masques may have begun with the need for professional actors to present the anti-masque of witches in *The Masque of Queens* (February, 1609) and the anti-masque of satyrs in *Oberon* (January, 1611). Prince Henry's masque, *Love Restored*, which was presented in January, 1612, opens with a long scene of prose dialogue performed by 'Gentlemen the King's Servants', presumably the King's Men.

The most immediate effect of the masques on Shakespeare is in the sheep-shearing scene in *The Winter's Tale*. In the middle of the scene 'three carters, three shepherds, three neat-herds, three swine-herds, that have made themselves all men of hair' and 'call themselves Saltiers' (IV. iv. 318–21), dance for the amusement of the company at the feast. The additional detail that 'one three . . ., by their own report, . . ., hath danced before the king' suggests that Shakespeare here made use of a dance and dancers from *Oberon*. A clearer debt to Jonson is apparent in the masque in *The Tempest* (IV. i) which recalls in several particulars Jonson's *Hymenaei* (January, 1606). The most striking similarities are the appearance in both of Juno and Iris (perhaps the *Hymenaei* costumes were still available), and the use in both of clouds as machinery for a descent.

If there is something slightly patronizing in the tone of Jonson's references to Shakespeare—notoriously the allusion to his 'small Latin, and less Greek'—it can be attributed to Jonson's awareness that he was a scholar and that Shakespeare was not. We find a similar tone in references to Shakespeare by some other dramatists. Webster, in the epistle prefaced to the 1612 edition of *The White Devil*, classes Shakespeare's 'right happy and copious industry' with that of Dekker and Heywood, and the three find their place at the end of his list of dramatists, after Chapman, Jonson, Beaumont and Fletcher. Although Webster apologizes for naming them last it is clear that he ranks Shakespeare among the popular writers and does not quite class him either with the scholars, Chapman and Jonson, or with those 'worthily excellent' gentlemen, Beaumont and Fletcher. Beaumont too, as his only direct allusion to Shakespeare shows, was not impressed by his learning:

> . . . here I would let slip
> (If I had any in me) scholarship,
> And from all learning keep these lines as clear
> As Shakespeare's best are, which our heirs shall hear,
> Preachers apt to their auditors to show
> How far sometimes a mortal man may go
> By the dim light of Nature, . . .
>
> (quoted in Chambers, II, 224)

Few poets have acquired such fame in their own time for so small a poetical output as Beaumont. In the ten years of his active literary career he produced two plays and one masque on his own, at least six

more plays in collaboration with Fletcher and a small body of non-
dramatic verse, mainly occasional. There is a characteristic note of
irritation in Jonson's remark to Drummond: 'Francis Beaumont loved
too much himself and his own verses.' He might have been more
charitable if his young friend and disciple had achieved less fame less
quickly.

Beaumont was more acutely aware of Shakespeare's work than any
of his colleagues. In his earliest work, a humorous Grammar Lecture
written for the Christmas festivities at the Inner Temple some time
between 1601 and 1605, Beaumont already displays an active interest
in the theatre. He shows his contempt for the popular approval of
'some pretty play with a fool and a devil in it' and offers advice about
theatre-going to the younger students:

> for your young student that doth desire plays, believe it most faith-
> fully, let him bring me his groat or sixpence and I will teach him to
> see a play at the Bank side with Templerian credit enough, only
> invading some sufficiently obscured sculler at some unacquainted
> watergate as I shall direct him.

Mark Eccles, commenting on this passage (R.E.S. (1940), p. 412),
points out that if Beaumont frequented the Bankside playhouses during
his years at the Inner Temple he must have gone mainly to see the
Chamberlain's, later King's, Men at the Globe as they were the only
company playing there between 1601 and 1605, apart from Worcester's Men who played at the Rose in the winter of 1602–3.

Beaumont was well acquainted with Shakespeare's work by the
time that he became a dramatist himself. His two unaided plays, *The
Woman-Hater* and *The Knight of the Burning Pestle*, echo Shakespeare
in a way that suggests both fascination and irritation with his style.
When Beaumont imitates Shakespeare directly it is often with the
intention of parody. His most frequent use of the technique is in the
subplot of *The Woman-Hater*, which presents the adventures of Lazarillo, 'a voluptuous smell-feast', in pursuit of a rare delicacy, the head
of a fish called umbrana. The mock-heroic use of Shakespearian echoes
is frequent and may be illustrated by this parody of Othello's 'Farewell'
speech.

> Farewell Millain, farewell Noble Duke,
> Farewell my fellow Courtiers all, with whom

> I have of yore made many a scrambling meal
> In corners, behind Arrases, on stairs;
>
> . . . .
> Farewell you lusty Archers of the Guard,
> To whom I now do give the bucklers up,
> And never more with any of your coat
> Will eat for wagers, . . .   (x. 109)

The parody is crude but the central contrast between Othello's military prowess and Lazarillo's feats of eating is clearly and amusingly presented.

The echoes of *Hamlet* in the main plot of the play are less clearly parodic. When Gondarino, the woman-hater, addresses Oriana, a lady who pursues him in order to ridicule his 'humour', in terms such as:

> It comes again; new apparitions,
> And tempting spirits: stand and reveal thyself,
> Tell why thou follow'st me? I fear thee
> As I fear the place thou camest from: Hell.
>
> (x. 96)

and

> . . . that pleasing piece of frailty, that we call woman . . .
>
> (x. 100)

we sense rather Beaumont's inability to write passionate speeches without echoing Shakespeare than specific attempts at parody.

That Beaumont shared Jonson's impatience with what he found bombastic in Shakespeare is made even clearer in *The Knight of the Burning Pestle*. When Ralph, the grocer's apprentice, is called on to demonstrate his ability to 'speak a huffing part' he chooses Hotspur's hyperbolical lines on honour.

The share of Beaumont in the plays which he wrote for the King's Men in collaboration with Fletcher remains unclear, for the good reason that, unlike Fletcher, he did not write a large number of unaided plays which would provide clear evidence of his style. His two plays certainly do not show that frequent imitation of Shakespearian characters and situations which is found in their joint work, but we know so little of the method of their collaboration that it would be dangerous to allocate verbal echoes of Shakespeare in their plays to Beaumont and imitations of his characters and situations to Fletcher, as the evidence of their independent works might suggest.

Certainly Fletcher's debt to Shakespeare differs strikingly from Beaumont's. His first comedy, *The Woman's Prize or, the Tamer Tamed*, is a satirical sequel to *The Taming of the Shrew*. Petruchio has remarried after the death of his first wife and his new wife, Maria, tames him as effectively as he had tamed Katharina in Shakespeare's play. A few more details correspond to *The Taming of the Shrew*: Fletcher uses the name Tranio and he provides Maria, like Katharina, with a younger sister wooed by two suitors, one young and one old. These details, however, are insignificant beside the central impulse to reverse Shakespeare's moral of wifely subjection by borrowing and inverting his central situation. Fletcher's considerable borrowing and reversal of situations from Shakespeare in later plays has recently been examined by Clifford Leech in *The John Fletcher Plays*, Chapter VI. What he added was usually an awareness of the sensational possibilities of the situation. In *The Woman's Prize*, Maria refuses to sleep with her husband until he will concede her equality and the whole tone of the play consequently acquires a slightly prurient sophistication quite foreign to *The Shrew*.

Bonduca, written by Fletcher for the King's Men between 1609 and 1614, shows a pervasive influence of Shakespeare. Its striking similarity to *Cymbeline*, particularly in the treatment of the wars between the Britons and the Romans, has been discussed by Leech. But Fletcher's debt is not only to *Cymbeline*: like Shakespeare's Cleopatra, Bonduca is more of a hindrance than a help in battle, and this parallel is confirmed when the British general curses her, after she has contributed to his defeat, in a scene (vi. 123) clearly modelled on *Antony and Cleopatra*, IV. xii. Another leading character is the Roman general Penius, who refuses to obey an order to bring his troops to battle from his newly appointed commander-in-chief, Suetonius. It is clear from the way in which Fletcher introduces Penius that he is modelling him on Coriolanus. The clue is given in his opening line, 'I must come?' (vi. 94), a retort to Suetonius's order, whose peremptory tone he will not accept. He continues through some twenty lines of dialogue to play on the word 'must'.

> But did he say, I must come?
>
> ... Are all my actions
> So poor and lost, my services so barren,

> That I'm remembered in no nobler language
> But Must come up?
>
> ... Must come up;
> Am I turn'd bare Centurion? Must, and shall,
> Fit embassies to court my honour?   (vi. 94)

Fletcher clearly has in mind Coriolanus's retort to the tribune Sicinius,

> Shall remain!
> Hear you this Triton of the minnows? mark you
> His absolute 'shall'?   (III. i. 88)

The similarity is reinforced when Penius leaves the stage and Drusus, one of his officers, describes him:

> He's a brave fellow;
> And but a little hide his haughtiness,
> (Which is but sometimes neither, on some causes)
> He shows the worthiest Roman this day living.
>   (vi. 98)

Penius is a reduction of Coriolanus to a formula of pride and repentance: he is wholly predictable. The Romans win a victory without him and his remorse and suicide follow as a matter of course. Fletcher achieves suspense and surprise only by a typically ingenious twist of the plot which delays his suicide for a few lines.

The influence of Shakespeare on the collaborative works of Beaumont and Fletcher is well illustrated by *Philaster*. Shakespearian situations and characters are borrowed and simplified, and verbal echoes, especially of the tragedies, are very frequent. The central resemblance is between Philaster's situation and that of Hamlet: both are rightful heirs to thrones occupied by usurpers. The similarity extends to the King in *Philaster* whose resemblance to Claudius includes a soliloquy of remorse recalling *Hamlet*, III. iii. 36–72, especially in its closing lines,

> but how can I,
> Look to be heard of gods, that must be just,
> Praying upon the ground I hold by wrong?
>   (i. 99)

Philaster himself is an unsatisfactory character mainly because he is more often called upon for passion than for action, and because his passion too frequently has Shakespearian overtones, drawn not only from *Hamlet* but also from *King Lear* and *Othello*. The greatest successes of Beaumont and Fletcher, *The Maid's Tragedy* and *A King and No King*, are triumphs of ingenious contrivance; the comparative failure of *Philaster* is that the contrivance is not yet ingenious enough, and this failure is clearly reflected in the extent to which the play draws upon Shakespeare.

The echoes in *The Maid's Tragedy* are less pervasive. Again *Hamlet* is most frequently echoed, and again the closest link is between the King and Claudius. Amintor, tricked into marriage with the King's mistress, Evadne, is restrained from revenge by his loyalty and addresses the King in words that echo a speech of Claudius to Laertes (IV. v. 119–22):

> but there is
> Divinity about you, that strikes dead
> My rising passions, as you are my King,
> I fall before you, and present my Sword
> To cut mine own flesh, if it be your will.
>
> (i. 33)

The central action of the following scene is also Shakespearian in inspiration: it is the celebrated quarrel of Amintor and Melantius which borrows its pattern of alternating attack and counter-attack from the quarrel of Brutus and Cassius in *Julius Caesar* (IV. iii). By the time they wrote *A King and No King*, Beaumont and Fletcher were shaking off the influence of Shakespeare. There is nothing in this play that is explicable only in terms of his influence. Even the cowardly captain, Bessus, is their own peculiar version of the *miles gloriosus* and shows no signs of being imitated from Falstaff or Parolles. What is most noticeable about this play or about their comedy, *The Scornful Lady*, which the King's Men had acted by 1616, is how completely the two young dramatists had developed a manner of their own. If any influence is still perceptible it is rather that of Jonson's comedies than Shakespeare's tragedies.

★   ★   ★

If there are features of the plays of Beaumont and Fletcher, writing both separately and in collaboration, which can only be explained as borrowings from Shakespeare, the opposite case, that there are features of *Cymbeline*, *The Winter's Tale*, and *The Tempest* which point without doubt to the influence of Beaumont and Fletcher's plays, is much more difficult to maintain. There is no proof that *Philaster* was written before *Cymbeline* and yet the weight of the argument has always rested on the similarities between these two plays. The contention that Beaumont and Fletcher initiated a new vogue of tragi-comedy about 1609 will not stand up to close scrutiny either: their first successful tragi-comedy was *Philaster* and it was written later than *Pericles*, at least, if not after *Cymbeline*.

What is really new in their plays is their polite tone: their characters, with few and insignificant exceptions, are ladies and gentlemen. Dryden thought that 'they understood and imitated the conversation of gentlemen much better'[1] than Shakespeare. If their success had a perceptible influence on him it is perhaps to be seen in the anonymous courtly gentlemen who appear so much more frequently in his last plays than in any that he wrote before 1609. The most striking example is the relation of the recognition scene between Leontes and Perdita by three gentlemen in *The Winter's Tale*, V. ii. It is possible that in the same play the influence of Beaumont and Fletcher accounts for Shakespeare's unique withholding of material information from his audience, allowing them to believe that Hermione is dead until the last scene. The effect, however, is not merely the relief that follows our discovery, for instance, that the love of Arbaces and Panthea in *A King and No King* is not after all incestuous; as F. P. Wilson pointed out,

> The resurrection of . . . Hermione is not the surprise-packet of Beaumont and Fletcher, not a mere device to stimulate or unravel plot, but that motive of forgiveness and reconciliation which lies at the heart of the play.[2]

Why did Shakespeare end his career by writing a group of plays in collaboration with Fletcher? The question is, of course, unanswerable, but that is no reason for leaving it unasked. A great deal of the reluctance which has been shown in accepting the evidence for this partnership presumably results from a tacit assumption that Shakespeare was too great a poet to condescend to collaborate with so manifestly inferior an artist as Fletcher. To make this assumption is to close our eyes to certain facts about the relationship between Shakespeare and his colleagues to which I have already alluded. Socially Shakespeare could

---

[1] *Essays*, ed. W. P. Ker (1926), i. 81.
[2] *Elizabethan and Jacobean* (1945), p. 128.

never quite attain to the status of Beaumont and Fletcher: in spite of his prosperity and his coat of arms he had, like the Clown in *The Winter's Tale*, become a 'gentleman born' fairly late in life. In addition, his standing as principal playwright for the King's Men seems to have been equalled by Beaumont and Fletcher during the brief period of their collaboration. It is likely that in Fletcher Shakespeare recognized his natural successor and that their collaboration represents his gradual withdrawal in favour of the younger dramatist. Fletcher's reputation has suffered since the seventeenth century, but to Dryden 'he was a limb of Shakespeare' and no overwhelming disparity of achievement between the two was yet apparent.

Three plays are involved; *Cardenio*, acted at Court during the Christmas revels of 1612–13 and again on 8 June, 1613; *Henry VIII*, acted at the Globe in 1613, at least on 29 June when the theatre burnt down during the performance; and *The Two Noble Kinsmen*, written later than February, 1613, and probably performed before the end of the year, although it was not printed until 1634. It will not do to suppose that Beaumont's marriage had anything to do with Fletcher's finding a new partner. Beaumont was not married until 1613 and in that year he wrote his *Masque of the Inner Temple and Gray's Inn*, which was presented at court on 20 February, and probably also wrote, with Fletcher, *The Scornful Lady*. By this time Shakespeare and Fletcher had written at least *Cardenio*. It seems on the whole more likely that the collaboration had something to do with Shakespeare's gradual retirement from the affairs of the company, which is generally thought to have taken place after 1610.

The study of this partnership is complicated at the outset by difficulties relating to two of the three plays involved. *Cardenio*, which we have good external grounds for accepting as a play by Shakespeare and Fletcher, survives, if at all, only in an adaptation by Lewis Theobald called *Double Falsehood*, which was acted at Drury Lane in 1727 and published in 1728. The question whether *Double Falsehood* was or was not based on a manuscript or manuscripts of *Cardenio* is likely to remain unanswered, and even those scholars who are inclined to believe that it was must hesitate before trying to sort out the broken fragments of original Shakespeare and Fletcher from Theobald's avowedly thorough adaptation.

Henry VIII is more helpful, but here there is no external evidence that Fletcher had a hand in the play and the attribution of certain scenes to him on internal evidence alone is likely to remain a subject of dispute and disagreement. The presence of two hands in the play is, at least, not immediately suggested by unequivocal changes of style from scene to scene, such as are found in *The Two Noble Kinsmen*. This lack of blatant inconsistency has led the most recent editors of the play to argue for its unity of conception, even though R. A. Foakes would like to see the play as Shakespeare's work with, at most, touching up by Fletcher, while J. C. Maxwell prefers to regard the play as 'a work of collaboration in the ordinary sense of the term' even if 'there was no such close everyday collaboration as we may suppose between Beaumont and Fletcher'.

The strongest link in the chain connecting the names of Shakespeare and Fletcher is *The Two Noble Kinsmen*. Recent studies of the play suggest a growing acceptance of the claim made on the title-page of the quarto of 1634 that the play was

Written by the memorable Worthies of their time;

{Mr. John Fletcher, and } Gent.
{Mr. William Shakespeare.}

Naturally most attention has been devoted to the question of Shakespeare's share in the play. The evidence on which at least Act I and Act V, scenes i, iii, and iv can be attributed to him is admirably summarized and strengthened by Kenneth Muir in *Shakespeare as Collaborator*. The cumulative weight of evidence drawn from the examination of metre, vocabulary, imagery, and style, is sufficient to warrant Muir's conclusion that 'The play has as much right to be included in editions of Shakespeare as *Sir Thomas More* or *The Passionate Pilgrim*, and perhaps as much as *Titus Andronicus*, *1 Henry VI*, and *Pericles*.' Less attention has been directed to the consideration of the play's achievement as a whole and there has been a very understandable tendency to concentrate on what is identified as Shakespeare's work at the expense of Fletcher's.

The Two Noble Kinsmen, as its prologue announces, is based on Chaucer, on one of his most extended and ambitious poems, *The Knight's Tale*. The way in which the tale is dramatized is most unusual and different parts of the play bear strikingly different relations to it. This may be seen clearly by dividing the play into four parts. The first is Act I, in which the opening situation of the tale is presented in greatly extended form and with the introduction of much new material but

R

with no signs of close verbal correspondence. The second comprises the main-plot scenes of the succeeding Acts: II. ii, iii, and v; III. i, iii, and vi; IV. ii, and V. i, iii, and iv. In these scenes, mainly by Fletcher, except for Act V, the tale is followed closely and particular passages in it are identifiable as the immediate sources of scenes or speeches in the play. The main exceptions to this general account result from the enlargement of the role of Emilia, who is much more prominent than Chaucer's Emelye. Other additions are the use of victory in the games to establish Arcite in disguise at the court of Theseus (II. iii, v) which seems to have been borrowed from *Pericles* (II. i, ii), and the un-Chaucerian encounter of Palamon and Arcite in III. iii, in which Fletcher most fully exploits the conflict in them between love of each other and love of Emilia. The third part is the smallest, including only the central section of II. iii and III. v, the scenes which present the preparations for the May-day morris dance before Theseus and its performance. The celebration of May is alluded to by Chaucer but the entertainment itself comes from the second anti-masque of Beaumont's *Masque of the Inner Temple and Gray's Inn* and the surrounding business carries faint echoes of *A Midsummer Night's Dream* and *Love's Labour's Lost*.

The fourth part is entirely un-Chaucerian and tells of the love of the Jailor's daughter for Palamon, her resulting madness and its cure: it comprises II. i, iv, and vi; III. ii, iv, and v; IV. i and iii, and V. ii. This subplot is remarkable because its omission (and the deletion of some twenty lines of V. iv) would leave the play coherent and complete, except that Palamon's escape from prison would be unexplained. Whoever wrote this subplot was clearly embarrassed by its separateness from the main action. The Jailor's daughter is usually presented in soliloquy until she goes mad and her meeting with the disconsolate morris dancers in III. v is a desperate contrivance to involve her in the action. Although they welcome her as a substitute for a missing girl there is no indication that she is to perform in the dance before Theseus, and indeed her madness almost precludes the possibility of her doing so.

There are some grounds for regarding this plot as an afterthought, written to separate the scenes of the main plot without in any way interfering with it. Two points in particular seem consistent with this view. II. ii opens with the stage-direction '*Enter Palamon and Arcite in prison*', and yet some ten lines earlier, near the end of II. i, we find the direction '*Enter Palamon and Arcite above*'. The action is continuous,

Palamon and Arcite must appear in II. i and they must be 'above' in II. ii. At the end of II. ii a 'Keeper' removes first Arcite then Palamon from the prison: the same character is called 'Jailor' in II. i and in all the other scenes in which he appears. The unnecessary stage-direction and scene division at the beginning of II. ii and the anomalous use of 'Keeper' for 'Jailor' later in the scene are explicable if we suppose that II. i and the remaining subplot scenes were written after II. ii or at least independently of the main plot and perhaps by a third collaborator who was neither Shakespeare nor Fletcher. The second point which suggests the separate composition of the subplot occurs in V. iv. F. O. Waller has pointed out that the reference to the Jailor's daughter in this scene, the only main plot reference to the subplot, is possibly an interpolation. The clue is provided by line 48, where the quarto reads: '1.2.K. Wee'l follow cheerefully.' Dr. Waller has shown that this line, spoken immediately after a line by the first Knight alone and breaking the metre where it stands, completes both sense and metre if it is read as the second half of line 26 where it exactly answers a speech by Palamon.

> PAL. Ev'n he that led you to this Banket shall
>   Taste to you all.
> 1.2.K.   Wee'l follow cheerefully.

The twenty-two intervening lines of dialogue can be omitted without loss and with them the Jailor, whose presence, although not inappropriate at an execution, is not otherwise required by the action of the scene. The style of the lines differs markedly from the rest of the scene and the suspicion that they are only a botched expedient to make the two plots meet is heightened by the fact that they are used to repeat a point already made earlier in the play (IV. i. 25-8), and involve Palamon in the provision of two separate presents to swell the dowry of the Jailor's daughter. This is not the place to indulge in hypothesis about the authorship of these scenes. The point that needs to be made is that they exist apart from the rest of the play and so give some indication of the way in which the play was written, by suggesting that the collaboration of Shakespeare and Fletcher in the main plot may have been supplemented by the work of a third author who provided the subplot of the Jailor's daughter and may have had something to do with the morris dance scenes.

Some such attempt to clarify the problem of authorship must precede criticism. What we have is a play which Shakespeare may or may not have plotted in its entirety but of which he only wrote Act I and the bulk of Act V, although traces of his work may be present in the intervening Acts, notably in the opening speech of Arcite in III. i. The critical problem may be imagined by supposing that *The Tempest* survived in a similar state, Acts I and V of Shakespeare's play having been joined by three acts written in collaboration by other writers with, at most, a speech or two from Shakespeare's own pen, perhaps Ferdinand's soliloquy from the opening of III. i, to maintain the parallel. All that would remain would be the outline of the main plot, presented mainly in two scenes (I. ii; V. i) whose poetic power goes hand in hand with a most undramatic formalism in exposition and resolution of themes. So far the parallel with *The Two Noble Kinsmen* would hold, but there is nothing in it like the opening scene of *The Tempest*: none of its comic scenes and little of its prose carry any suggestion of Shakespearian authorship.

In *The Two Noble Kinsmen* there is a complete disparity of style, theme, and characterization between Act I and the rest of the play which is only in part reconciled in the Shakespearian scenes of Act V. The contrast of styles is between what Theodore Spencer called the 'clotted rhetoric' of the Shakespearian scenes and 'Fletcher's easy liquescence': other critics, though wishing to qualify the force of his terms, have found the same contrast. In theme and character the contrast is at least as great.

Act I is a very free reworking of lines 1–174 of *The Knight's Tale*, in which Chaucer recounts how Theseus, returning to Athens with his bride, Ypolita, and her sister Emelye, meets a band of widows, headed by the widow of King Capaneus, by whom he is persuaded to attack Creon in Thebes and recover from him their husbands' remains for burial. After the battle, in which Theseus kills Creon, two young knights are found in the carnage 'Nat fully quike, ne fully dede'! Their identical 'cote-armures' reveal that they are cousins and of the blood royal of Thebes; they are Palamon and Arcite. They are taken to Athens and imprisoned there.

The changes that Shakespeare made in dramatizing this incident can mostly be attributed to his desire to introduce a series of conflicting values into the play. The Act was clearly written with a recent memory of the whole of the tale in mind and we can see in it approaches to the main problems involved in the dramatizing.

The first conflict is in the mind of Theseus and arises because in the play he is not yet married to Hippolita. In I. i he is intercepted by three Queens, dressed in black, on his way to the temple where his marriage is about to be solemnized: love contends with honour until Hippolita herself, Emilia, and his friend Pirithous all join the Queens in persuading Theseus to postpone his wedding until he has avenged the dead Kings on Creon. The moral is drawn at the end of the scene:

> As we are men
> Thus should we do, being sensually subdued
> We lose our human title;   (I. i. 257)

I. ii introduces Palamon and Arcite before the battle. Once again honour is in danger, this time because of the corruption of Theban society.

> ARCITE: I spake of Thebes
>   How dangerous if we will keep our Honours,
>   It is for our residing, where every evil
>   Hath a good colour; where every seeming good's
>   A certain evil,   (I. ii. 40)

Just as they conclude their diatribe against the vices of Thebes, and in particular of their uncle Creon 'A most unbounded Tyrant, whose successes | Makes heaven unfear'd' (I. ii. 70), news arrives of the war with Athens. Honour, which prompted their desire to leave Thebes, now requires that they defend their city against the invader.

> PALAMON: Our services stand now for Thebes, not Creon,
>   Yet to be neutral to him, were dishonour;
>   Rebellious to oppose: (I. ii. 111)

The conflicting demands of honour in this scene are paralleled in I. iii, where the conflict is one of love. The first point at issue is whether Theseus loves Hippolita better than his friend Pirithous, with whom he has shared many dangers.

> HIPPOLITA: I think
>   Theseus cannot be umpire to himself
>   Cleaving his conscience into twain, and doing
>   Each side like Justice, which he loves best.
> EMILIA: Doubtless
>   There is a best, and reason has no manners
>   To say it is not you.   (I. iii. 51)

Emilia's courtesy is not borne out by the rest of her speech in which she describes her own love for a dead friend of her childhood, 'the maid Flavina', and concludes

> That the true love tween maid and maid, may be
> More than in sex dividual.   (I. iii. 91)

When Hippolita presses her she further maintains that she will never love a man, although she allows Hippolita's confidence in Theseus' love and her

> great assurance,
> That we, more than his Pirithous, possess
> The high throne in his heart.   (I. iii. 106)

Of course, this theme of conflict is not the only point of the scene. Dramatization of *The Knight's Tale* must involve considerable enlargement of the role of Emilia and must give her a closer involvement in the action. Chaucer's Emelye is a chaste Amazon, almost an emblem of her patroness Diana, and the question of her marriage to Palamon does not arise until the very end of the tale, many years after the death of Arcite. In Act I of the play, Emilia's reiterated reluctance to think of marriage suggests that Shakespeare intended to retain the Chaucerian conflict between virginity and the idea of marriage and it is certainly this conflict which she expresses in her prayer to Diana in V.i. Fletcher, however, presents her in an agony of attempted choice between Palamon and Arcite, particularly in IV. ii, and it is inevitably this conflict which Shakespeare has to portray in V. iii to maintain suspense while Emilia awaits the result of the tournament.

The introduction of Pirithous in Act I anticipates Chaucer's first mention of him and has two motives. The first is to avoid the need to introduce him as a new character once the main action has begun; the second is to provide, in his friendship with Theseus, an ideal standard beside which to set the friendship of Palamon and Arcite. The second purpose is never clearly apparent after Act I.

The Act ends with two short plot scenes: in scene iv, Theseus receives the thanks of the three Queens and orders the removal of Palamon and Arcite from the battlefield, with a brief tribute to their exceptional bravery in the battle; in scene v, the three Queens bring the Act to a close as formal as its opening, with a dirge after which each goes her own way to bury her dead husband. The scene ends with a couplet that has caught the ear of many critics,

This world's a City full of straying streets,
And Death's the market place, where each one meets.
                                    (I. v. 15)

This was surely suggested by some lines near the end of the tale,

> This world nis but a thurghfare ful of wo,
> And we been pilgrimes, passinge to and fro;
> Deeth is an ende of every worldes soore.
>   (1989)

It is the only striking verbal echo of Chaucer in Act I, and it comes from a distant part of the tale.

The remainder of the main plot is far less free in its handling of Chaucer, indeed all but three of its scenes contain passages adapted directly from the tale. The three scenes, II. v, III. iii, and V. iii, all contain incidents invented by the playwrights which have no parallel in the tale. If Act I elaborates on Chaucer, the later Acts usually simplify, reducing the lapse of time, eliminating minor characters and relegating the gods to a merely decorative function in the background of the story. Only two incidents are altered, the manner of Arcite's return from exile and the final tournament, which carries no death penalty for the losers in Chaucer; but the portrayal of the three leading characters, Palamon, Arcite, and Emilia, differs greatly both from Chaucer and from our expectations at the end of Act I.

Kenneth Muir, in describing Palamon and Arcite as 'the twin heroes' and as 'indistinguishable as Tweedledum and Tweedledee', has put his finger on the central problem of characterization facing any playwright dramatizing *The Knight's Tale*. If he decides, as Fletcher decided, to make dramatic capital out of suspense and to tantalize his audience with doubt as to which will win Emilia in the end, it will be necessary to begin by presenting the cousins as precisely identical 'Twins of honour' (II. ii. 21). They are distinguished by Shakespeare as little in the climactic scene of prayer to the gods (V. i) as they were in I. ii, but here it is enough that Arcite is praying to Mars and Palamon to Venus; the true conflict is between the powers of war and love more than between Arcite and Palamon, and the final triumph of love is far from being a personal triumph of Palamon over Arcite.

To distinguish the two heroes was Fletcher's job, as author of the central Acts, but it was also his job to maintain suspense about the final outcome while subtly preparing the audience for it. The initial quarrel is close to Chaucer. Palamon, seeing Emilia from the prison window, is overwhelmed by love: 'By heaven, she is a Goddess' (II. ii. 156). Arcite, seeing her after Palamon, loves her too, but 'as a woman, to enjoy her' (II. ii. 201). Palamon starts the quarrel and in every encounter between them in Acts II and III it is Palamon who takes the offensive while Arcite refuses to admit that his grievance is just and maintains an irritating calm in face of his accusations. If there is something ludicrous in Palamon's ranting, there is also something sinister in Arcite's self-possession. A further distinction is built up during Acts II and III, reaching a climax in III. vi when the two confront each other before Theseus. As they wait for Emilia to make her choice of one of them, each resigns himself to the death promised to the loser:

> PALAMON: If I fall from that mouth, I fall with favour,
>   And Lovers yet unborn shall bless my ashes.
> ARCITE: If she refuse me, yet my grave will wed me,
>   And Soldiers sing my Epitaph.   (III. vi. 339)

From this point it is clear that Palamon is 'the Lover' and Arcite 'the Soldier', indeed the identification is merely anticipated from their later choice of gods to invoke before the final trial.

The distinction is deliberately prevented from becoming more than superficial in order that suspense may be kept up until the end. The best instance of the manipulation of character to create suspense is in IV. ii. The scene opens with a long soliloquy by Emilia in which she weighs the rival merits of her suitors while she studies their portraits. Arcite is mentioned first, with much emphasis on his beauty and the alacrity which fits him alike for 'Loves and Fights'; then follows Palamon, whose 'bold gravity' is seen to excel Arcite's 'sprightly sharpness' as an incitement to love. Emilia's confusion is finally expressed when she calls on Theseus and Hippolita, each of whom is both soldier and lover, to help her to decide;

> For if my brother but even now had ask'd me
> Whether I lov'd, I had run mad for Arcite,
> Now if my sister; more for Palamon.
> Stand both together: now, come ask me, brother.
> Alas, I know not: Ask me now, sweet sister,
> I may go look.   (IV. ii. 47)

This levelling of the odds continues in the second half of the scene where Theseus hears descriptions of the knights who have come to second Palamon and Arcite in the tournament. First a Messenger describes Arcite's first knight, a soldier, like his principal, then Pirithous, whose approval perhaps counts for more than that of an unnamed Messenger, gives an account of Palamon's first knight, as we expect by now, a lover:

> he has felt
> Without doubt what he fights for, and so apter
> To make this cause his own.   (IV. ii. 108)

When the Messenger comes to describe a third knight, whom Pirithous has noticed too, we are surprised that neither of them tells us whose side he is on, and indeed Fletcher seems to have intended this minor mystification to reinforce our sense of the equality of the opposed parties, because this knight would be equally at home on either side:

> when he smiles
> He shows a Lover, when he frowns, a Soldier:
> About his head he wears the winner's oak,
> And in it stuck the favour of his Lady.
>   (IV. ii. 152)

If the handling of Palamon and Arcite in the central Acts of the play suggests manipulation for the maximum of immediate effect on an audience, the case of Emilia is even clearer. Here the effect desired is not only suspense but pathos. Just as the melodramatic potentialities of the heroes' conflict between love of each other and love of Emilia induced Fletcher to invent an extra episode (III. iii) in which to exploit them, so he invented a useful pathetic situation by giving Emilia the power of life and death over Palamon and Arcite and then showing her inability to exercise it. Indeed it is hard to see what part Emilia could have played in Acts II–IV if her choice had been between virginity and marriage, as Shakespeare apparently intended, rather than between her two suitors. At this point caution is needed because the last scene in which Emilia's dilemma is exploited is V. iii, probably a Shakespearian scene. What is quite clear is the inconsistency between Shakespeare's portrayal of her in I. iii and V. i and Fletcher's in, for instance, II. ii

and IV. ii; the girl whose inability to prefer one lover to the other
leads her to say

> I am sotted,
> Utterly lost: my Virgin's faith has fled me.
> (IV. ii. 45)

is not the same as the Emilia who prays to Diana, saying

> This is my last
> Of vestal office, I am bride habited,
> But maiden hearted.   (V. i. 155)

The discrepancy is as remarkable as that between Fletcher's Palamon
in III. iii, joking about his past love affairs, and Shakespeare's virgin
knight in V. i.

The opposing powers of love and war, which Fletcher juggles so
skilfully throughout the central Acts, are brought face to face in V. i.
The good humour with which Chaucer presented the conflict between
Venus, Diana, and Mars and the sinister ingenuity with which Saturn
resolved it are alike absent from the play. Mars the destroyer and
Venus the restorer are both monstrous in the exercise of their power
over men. The effect of the great set speeches in V. i is to dwarf the
speakers of them, and divert our interest towards the powerful but
capricious gods. Our interest in the human actors is not restored in
the later scenes, but the theme of the all-powerful gods is not developed
either; in particular Saturn, who contrives the poetically just ending of
Chaucer's tale, is relegated by Shakespeare to a brief simile (V. iv. 75)
and the accident which kills the victorious Arcite is presented as the
last, ironic action of a Fortune whose power over events is loosely
equated with that of the gods; Arcite himself had recognized the
supremacy of Fortune as he departed to the war against Theseus:

> Let th'event,
> That never erring Arbitrator, tell us
> When we know all our selves, and let us follow
> The becking of our chance.   (I. ii. 129)

The mood of the last two scenes is predominantly gloomy. When
Emilia learns of Arcite's victory in the tournament, all she can think
of is the consequence, that Palamon must die. Her unhappy question,
'Is this winning?' (V. iii. 156), evokes a sympathetic response from
Hippolita:

> Infinite pity
> That four such eyes should be so fixed on one
> That two must needs be blind for't.
>
> (V. iii. 164)

The subsequent death of Arcite hardly improves the situation and his death-bed renunciation of Emilia passes almost unnoticed by Palamon, with the result that the final speech of Theseus can hardly be accepted as a true summing-up of the action, at least in its emphasis on the justice and equality of the gods. Only the note of human impotence in face of divine inscrutability fully expresses the sadness of Palamon's success. Theseus had spoken, after his victory over Creon, of

> Th'impartial Gods, who from the mounted heavens
> View us their mortal Herd, behold who err,
> And in their time chastise: (I. iv. 6)

and it is on the same note that he closes the play.

> O you heavenly Charmers,
> What things you make of us! For what we lack
> We laugh, for what we have, are sorry: still
> Are children in some kind. Let us be thankful
> For that which is, and with you leave dispute
> That are above our question.   (V. iv. 149)

If the comment lacks final conviction it is because we don't know why Arcite deserved punishment and can only see the divine solution to the human problem as inadequate. It is at this moment that the incompatibility of Shakespeare and Fletcher is fully brought home to us: what Fletcher saw in *The Knight's Tale* was a story with magnificent qualities of melodrama, pathos, and suspense; what Shakespeare saw in it we can only guess from Act I and his parts of Act V.

Clearly, as Muir has pointed out, the gods had some important function in Shakespeare's view of the story, but he did not write the central human action of the play which might have clarified just what that function was. What is lacking from the play is the central conflict of values which Shakespeare must have found in the relationship of Palamon and Arcite; what we have instead is Fletcher's accomplished presentation of conflicting passions and attitudes.

How did such a play come to be written? An attractive hypothesis has recently been put forward by P. Bertram, who suggests that the

66

haste after the Globe fire of 29 June, 1613, to
s Men with a new play with which to open their
Blackfriars the following winter, while they waited for
ng of the Globe. The quarto title-page says that the play
d at the Blackfriars and Bertram also finds strong support
Prologue and Epilogue, which, as he shows, must have been
tten for the first performance of a new play at a private theatre.
He accepts the familiar view that the reference in the Prologue to 'our
losses' is an allusion to the fire and sees the closing lines of the Epilogue,
with their promise of 'many a better' play 'ere long', as evidence of
haste in the writing and presentation of the play. His hypothesis about
the authorship is less persuasive: taking literally the Prologue's phrase
'such a writer', he supposes the play to be the work of a single playwright, namely Shakespeare. Accepting for the moment his account
of the occasion of the play, I would hazard an alternative suggestion
about its authorship. At the time of the Globe fire Shakespeare had
already completed the first Act of the play: after the fire the need for
a new play in a hurry for the opening of Blackfriars in the autumn
prompted the suggestion that this play be completed in collaboration
by Shakespeare himself, Fletcher, and possibly a third dramatist: Shakespeare wrote Act V, Fletcher wrote Acts II–IV, and the third man
wrote the subplot scenes of the Jailor's daughter and the morris dance.
There is nothing to prove that this is what really happened, but the
play's singular lack of coherence seems to demand some such hypothesis about the writing of it. This suggestion tries, in particular, to
account for the contrast, so often pointed out, between the assurance
and completeness of Act I and the inconsistencies and mixture of styles
in the later acts.

In Shakespeare's choice of *The Knight's Tale* as a subject for a play,
we can see that same return to earlier subjects which is apparent in the
choice of stories for *Pericles*, *Cymbeline*, and *The Winter's Tale*. The
use of Chaucer parallels that of Gower in *Pericles*, of the old romantic
play, *The Rare Triumphs of Love and Fortune*, in *Cymbeline*, and of
Greene's *Pandosto* in *The Winter's Tale*. The sense of return to earlier
interests is reinforced by the connection of Theseus and his wedding
with *A Midsummer Night's Dream*, and the resemblance between
Emilia's description of her friendship with Flavina and the friendship
of Helena and Hermia as Helena describes it (III. ii. 198–214). The
story of Palamon and Arcite requires dramatic handling of the theme

of love and friendship, which Shakespeare had not made central to any play since *The Two Gentlemen of Verona*, but as this part of the play was left to Fletcher we cannot tell whether he would have recalled his own early work here as he did *The Comedy of Errors* in *Pericles*.

But not everything is familiar and indeed it seems that in this play, as so often before, Shakespeare was calling in question some of the conclusions of earlier plays. The redemptive power of love which dominates the closing scenes of *Pericles, Cymbeline, The Winter's Tale,* and *The Tempest* is far from the dangerous passion that destroys Arcite, leaves Palamon a disconsolate bridegroom and is only mastered by Theseus. Even the emphasis on the restoring power of love in Palamon's prayer to Venus has a grotesque quality, first noted by Theodore Spencer, which has more in common with the irrepressible lust of Caliban than with the clear-eyed passion of Ferdinand and Miranda or Florizel and Perdita. The gods of the play are powerful and not clearly benevolent, although just, and temperance and chastity—the key virtues of Shakespeare's scenes in *The Two Noble Kinsmen* as they are of *The Tempest* and its immediate predecessors—are man's best protection in dealing with them. But *The Two Noble Kinsmen* is unlike these plays in that the winning of love and the death of Arcite are juxtaposed at the end so that the overwhelming impression is not so much of the value of love as of its appalling cost. Not since *All's Well that Ends Well* had Shakespeare written a play whose conclusion leaves such a sense of unease. It is almost as if he was beginning once more to call in question the positive power of love. If he had written the whole play we could be more confident that it represents a new direction, perhaps as far from the spirit of the late romances as *Measure for Measure* is from *Twelfth Night*.

Index

[*This index excludes the information, systematically arranged for reference purposes, given in the notes before each chapter.*]

262